ART IN UNEXPECTED PLACES II

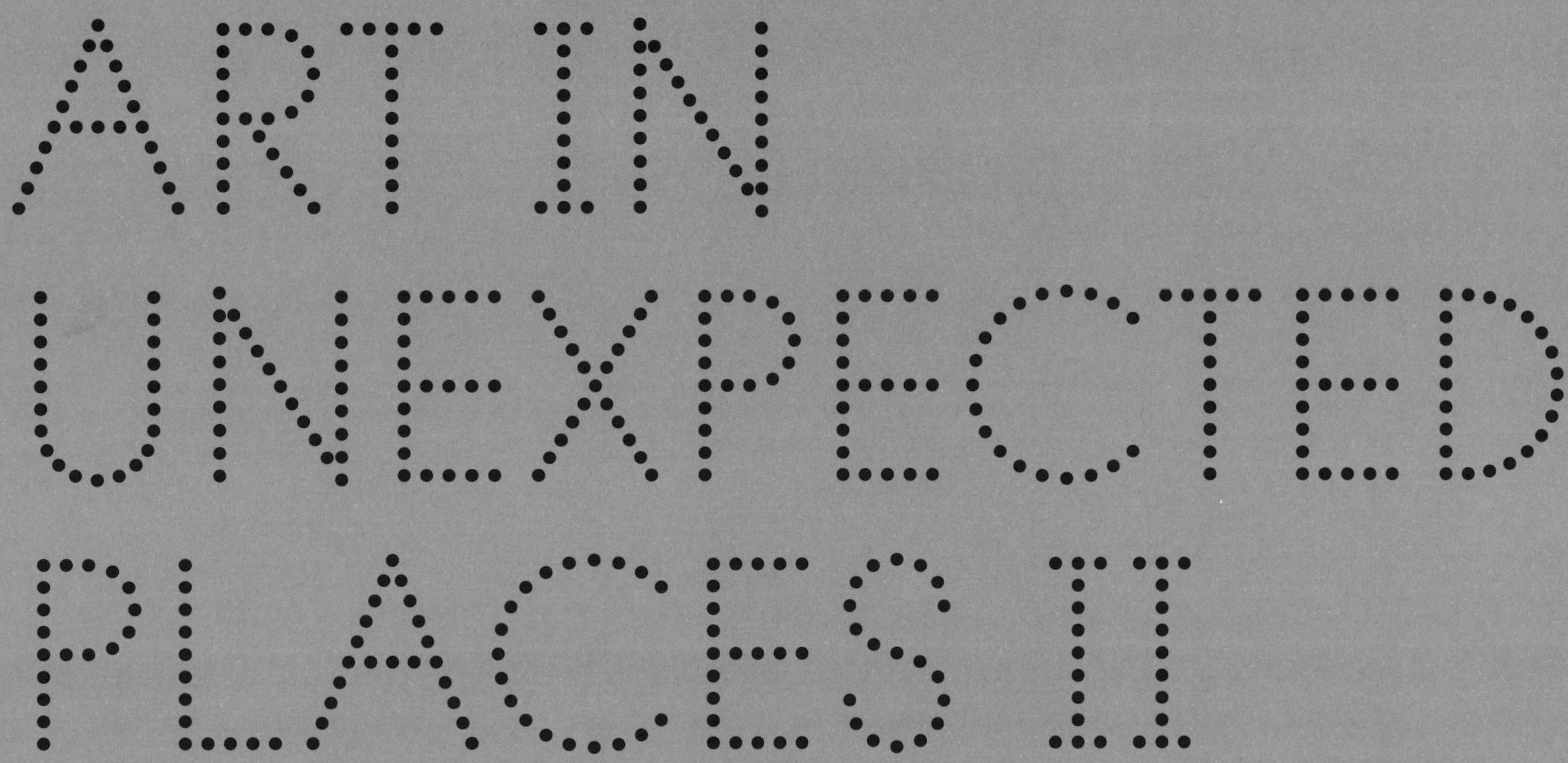

Aspen Art Museum   Aspen Skiing Company

Published by
Aspen Art Press & Aspen Skiing Company

Aspen Art Museum
637 East Hyman Avenue
Aspen, CO 81611
United States
aspenartmuseum.org

Aspen Skiing Company
Post Office Box 1248
Aspen, CO 81612
United States
aspensnowmass.com

The Crown Family
222 North Lasalle Street
Suite 2000
Chicago, IL 60601
United States

Available through
Artbook, LLC
Distributed Art Publishers
155 Sixth Avenue, 2nd Floor
New York, NY 10013
artbook.com

ISBN: 978-0-934324-73-1

Library of Congress
Cataloging-in-Publication Data

Title: Art in unexpected places / Aspen Art
Museum, Aspen Skiing Company.
Other titles: Art in unexpected places (2016)
Description: Aspen, CO : Aspen Art Press,
Aspen Art Museum, 2016.
Identifiers: LCCN 2015050495 | ISBN
9780934324731 (hardcover)
Subjects: LCSH: Art--Colorado--Aspen--21st
century--Catalogs. |
    Artists--Colorado--Aspen--Interviews. |
    Aspen Art Museum (Aspen, Colo.)--Art
    patronage. | Aspen Skiing Company--Art
    patronage.
Classification: LCC N6535.A67 A783 2016
| DDC 709.788/43--dc23
LC record available at
http://lccn.loc.gov/2015050495

Editor
Sarah Stephenson

Designer
Michael Aberman

Printer
die Keure, Bruges, Belgium

Aspen Art Museum
Aspen Art Museum
Aspen Art Museum
Aspen Art Museum

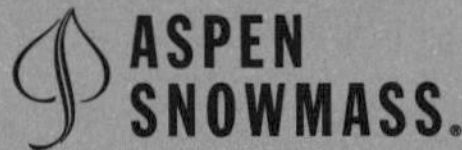

Introduction   8

Foreword   9

Paula Crown in   10
conversation
with Dave Muller

Mike Kaplan in   14
conversation
with David Shrigley

Heidi Zuckerman in   20
conversation
with Gretchen Bleiler

Alchemy of the Authentic   26
William Morrow

The Art of Surprise   30
Dan Cameron

Project Timeline   44

Mark Grotjahn   54

David Shrigley   76

Dave Muller   88

Mark Bradford   104

Teresita Fernández   120

Cai Guo-Qiang   134

Anne Collier   142

Takashi Murakami   150

Shinique Smith   156

Acknowledgments   166

Contributors   167

Contents   7

Introduction

The history of art is as old as any chronicle of human accomplishment. Everywhere mankind has existed, there is a record of artistic expression. The impulse to manifest ideas through mark-making and object creation is an essential feature of our humanity. Historical records underscore the fundamental importance of art to our survival.

It is a unique characteristic of our species that enables connection and communication through creativity and imagery. We turn to art when words fall short—in times of unfettered imagination, immense joy, or astonishing difficulty. In its myriad forms, art creates moments of spaciousness and focus. It encourages us to engage, to extend our capacity to see, to understand, and reflect. Like being in the mountains, it changes our point of focus from small-scale interruptions—like telephone screens and other distracting media—to, quite literally, a bigger picture.

In 2009, we concluded that we should capture the magic of the Art in Unexpected Places program and create a series of books. The ongoing collaboration between the Aspen Skiing Company and the Aspen Art Museum was resonating in important ways. The placement of art throughout the mountains and on our lift tickets connected the Aspen community, the artists, and our guests. Working with our friend and partner, Heidi Zuckerman, we created a series of illustrations and interviews to capture the narrative for each of the artists who had contributed to Art in Unexpected Places. We thought of this as a small social movement: instead of Stand UP, Look UP, or Man UP, we wanted people to ArtUP.

In 2011, we copublished the first volume of *Art in Unexpected Places*, celebrating five years of our creative partnership. We are now pleased to bring you *Art in Unexpected Places II*, which covers the most recent five years through the 2015–16 season; this year, we were thrilled to feature wonderful works by Takashi Murakami on our ski pass.

Mike Kaplan, our CEO, and all of us associated with the Aspen Skiing Company are proud to provide a canvas for artists and their creative interventions. Our mission articulates the importance of providing experiences to our guests that enhance the body, mind, and spirit.

This year, the Aspen Skiing Company turns seventy. Since its inception, the Company has celebrated the intersection of art and commerce; this was a guiding principle when the Paepckes founded modern Aspen at the end of World War II. They saw Aspen as an ideal venue to blend natural and human-created beauty. The ArtUP program is a logical extension of the aspirations of the founders. It is a unique collaboration that celebrates Aspen's special sense of place and is available for the whole community. It reflects a generosity of spirit among all participants that is so welcome in these turbulent times.

The two of us represent a multigenerational presence in the Roaring Fork Valley. We have been part of the Aspen Skiing Company since 1985. We are so fortunate to be part of a company and a community that is blessed with awesome natural surroundings, a vibrant and engaged citizenry, and such a special history. We encourage everyone to engage in the larger conversation of art in unexpected places, and hope you enjoy your chance to ArtUP while in Aspen.

Paula and Jim Crown
March 2016

Foreword

In this publication of *Art in Unexpected Places II*, the Aspen Art Museum (AAM) and Aspen Skiing Company (ASC) celebrate the second five years in a decade of continuing collaboration. As a way to think about the connectivity of art and skiing as well as to introduce this book in the series, Heidi Zuckerman, AAM Nancy and Bob Magoon CEO and Director, and Mike Kaplan, ASC President and CEO, respond to the following question: Being in the "zone"—where we are so focused on what we are doing, we lose our sense of place—is something that is frequently referenced within the context of skiing. How can art also help us be in the zone?

Mike Kaplan

The zone is an elusive place, and for me, is a state that feels like the subconscious melding with the conscious. The result is one of hyper-focus and an ability to anticipate external forces that allow me to stay totally centered—physically and mentally. Some days on skis, the zone is just there on every run without fail. Other days, it's virtually impossible to find. One of my mentors, Dadou Mayer of Taos, once told me that anyone can ski well when they've got it, but real skiers are the ones who can get into that zone of high performance on days when it's not coming easy. I believe these experiences can apply to the way that we work too and definitely apply to artists as well. When a talented artist is in the zone and producing a work representing that state, it's apparent and contagious. Whether it's the grace of a brushstroke or the power of provocative imagery, the artist's state is transferred to the viewer in ways that can be subtle, enough to make you smile, or to truly move you closer to humanity and our shared reality. On those days, in those moments, when I'm out of sync, engaging with great art—whether in a museum, or better yet, an unexpected place—is often just enough to bring me back to center.

Heidi Zuckerman

For me, the zone describes a place of immediacy and presentness. Being there occurs when nothing else seems to matter, where everything else has fallen away. Small things, like the phone call that needs to be returned or the bill that needs to be paid, as well as big things, like what to do with the rest of my life, who matters most, and what I should do about it, all of them vanish. If I *try* to get in the zone, it's not possible; it only occurs when I'm doing something that I know can put me there, but when I'm not trying. I am interested in Buddhist thought, and the idea of non-attachment is linked with the notion of freedom. For me, the zone is about freedom. I have been in the zone while skiing, but it's much harder for me because only infrequently can I lose myself in what I'm doing there. More often, I find it through hiking or yoga. I have found the zone in art enough times to know that it's the place that I go to seek solace, understanding, and connection. That's why I feel so profoundly grateful that sharing art with others is my life's work. ✳

Paula Crown in conversation with Dave Muller

Paula Crown and Dave Muller, in the following conversation that took place in September 2015, discuss the role that music has played in Muller's work and what it was like working on his Art in Unexpected Places project.

Paula Crown
Dave, you are a visual artist that incorporates image and text into your work. You are also a DJ. How do music and art connect in your creative endeavors?

Dave Muller
I started listening to my parents' records in my bedroom when I was six. At nine, I began playing the trumpet. At twelve, the French horn. At thirteen, the baritone horn and the sousaphone. Bass guitar at nineteen. I started doing radio shows at nineteen as well. And started playing in rock bands at twenty-one. I also learned how to silkscreen at twenty-one so I could make T-shirts of my favorite bands. At twenty-two, when I was about to graduate with a degree in chemistry, I took a drawing class as an elective. In retrospect, playing music (and records) was my gateway to making art. I've never given up any of these practices; they all feed each other.

PC
How do making music, a playlist, and a painting intertwine?

DM
They're all such different acts in a material sense, yet the way I approach each of them might suggest a similar path in their creation. I'm a fan of complexity. I like to focus intensely on very small parts that I eventually compile to create a complicated whole.

PC
I understand you have quite a large collection of vinyl records. How many do you own?

DM
Between 8000 and 9000.

PC
Do you also have CDs and tapes?

DM
Yes.

PC
Is it important to have the vinyl to play once the music has been digitally transferred?

DM
About twelve years ago, I decided to

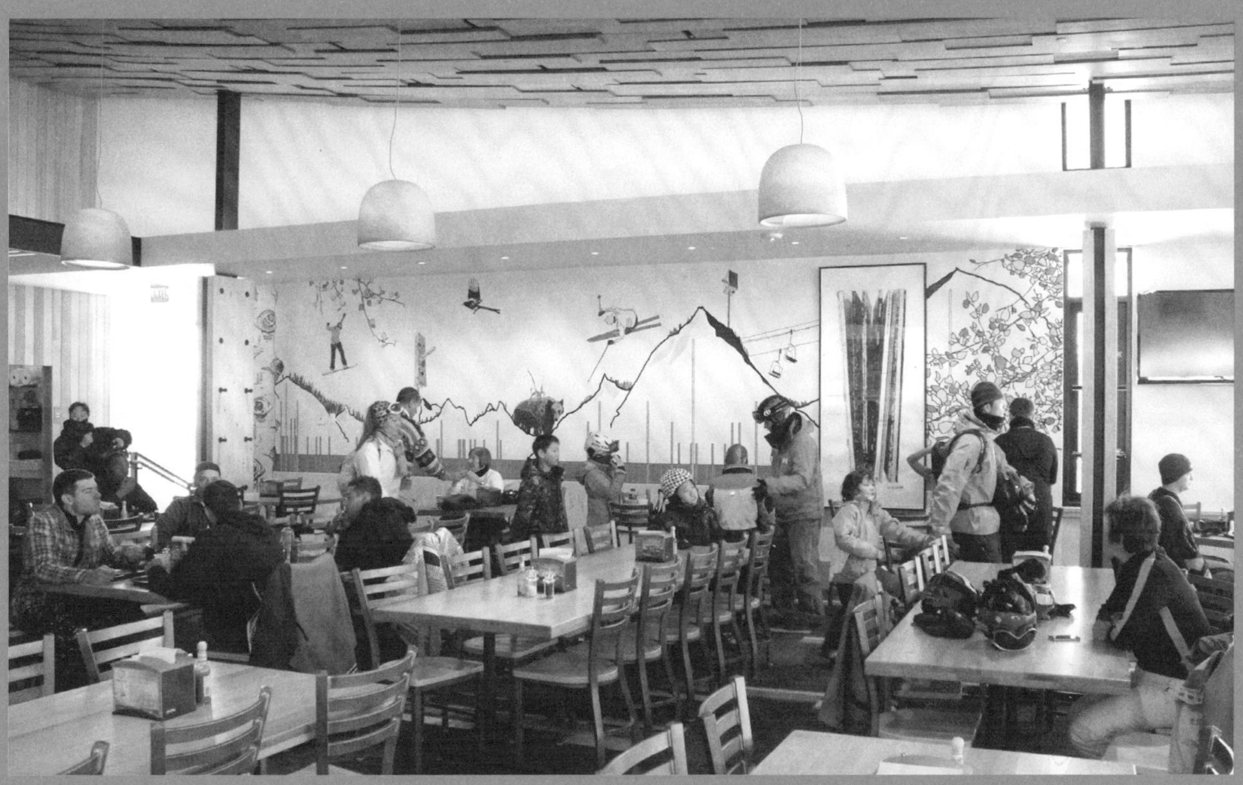

PC

What was unexpected about doing this Art in Unexpected Places project?

DM

I had to think about the site in a different way than I might if it had been in a gallery or a museum. My initial thoughts involved piping music into the site that people listened to at various lodges and ski lifts. But I had to reckon with the function of the site as a restaurant. Adding more sound seemed confusing and unfeasible in a space that would already have a bit of ambient chatter. So I stuck with visual renditions of sound artifacts [Fig. 1].

PC

Would you do it the same way again?

DM

Probably. Although always wanting "more," I might try to reach a larger number of subjects to answer the "favorite album questionnaire" [Fig. 2]. And since then, I've figured out how to paint a "blue sky" without spilling paint all over the place, so I might have added that. Aspen 2.0.

simplify and only DJ with vinyl. It's how I learned to DJ in the first place. Things were getting too complicated with CDs and MP3s. Too much equipment. I tried DJing on the computer, but found it boring. I pretty much only buy vinyl now, but I will buy downloads or CDs if that's the only way to get something. I listen to MP3s a lot as I move around and travel, vinyl and radio at home.

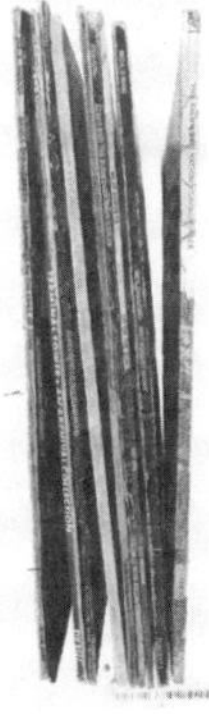

Hello,

My name is Dave Muller. I'm an artist working with the Aspen Skiing Company and the Aspen Art Museum on a project for next fall, and I'm hoping that you can help me.

One of my interests is music. I'm conducting a survey to see what the top ten albums are amongst the employees at Aspen Skiing Company. I'll use this information to make a drawing, which will be displayed along with a mural in the Elk Camp Restaurant.

Here's a previous example:

Dave Muller, Tim's Top Ten, 2004 Acrylic on paper, 86 1/2 x 38 1/2 in (219.7 x 97.8 cm)

And here's what I need from you:

A list of your favorite albums: any performer/group, any year, any number of albums.

Your height: I draw the records as tall as the person who chooses them. In this case, I'll make the records as tall as the average of all the heights I gather.

Thank You,

Dave

Fig. 2
Dave Muller, Survey created for Aspen Skiing Company Top Ten, 2012

PC

Did it inspire new work or subject matter?

DM

It always does. Sometimes in ways I can easily see. It further encouraged my interest in asking a community what their preferences are.

PC

In what way did the temporary nature of the installation (two seasons) affect the choices you made about the work?

DM

Well, to me, the installation was up for a long time. I'm used to wall drawings being up for five weeks in a gallery, maybe two to three months in a museum, so ten or eleven months seemed like an eternity. I wanted to think of how the work might look as the scenery outside changed with the seasons.

PC

There is an indexical nature to your work—you often graph and measure. Is that why you separately record the colors that you use in your paintings?

DM

When I started painting on paper, I found that sometimes the colors I mixed looked different when they dried on paper. So I started applying "swatches" to margins on the same piece I was working. Initially, the margins were trimmed, but I came to like these swatches and figured out how to integrate them into the final work—sort of like a list of ingredients.

PC

You have done a series of "portraits" based on various subjects' selections of their top ten albums [Figs. 3–5]. What do music selections reveal about a person's identity?

DM

Nothing scientific, as far as I can tell. I used to think that the top tens were a sidestep around the various masks we put up when we present ourselves to the world. Now, I think they function more as a Rorschach test for the viewer.

PC

What did you learn about the employees of the Aspen Skiing Company based on their music preferences?

DM

Hard to say. It reminded me of my own upbringing as a white male growing up in the seventies, eighties, and nineties. There are always surprises though. ❋

Fig. 3
Dave Muller, <u>Tim's Top Ten</u>, 2004. Acrylic on paper, 86 1/2 x 38 1/2 in (219.7 x 97.7 cm). Courtesy the artist and Blum & Poe, Los Angeles

Fig. 4
Dave Muller, <u>Larry's Top Ten</u>, 2006. Acrylic on paper, 86 1/2 x 38 1/2 in (219.7 x 97.7 cm). Courtesy the artist and Blum & Poe, Los Angeles

Fig. 5
Dave Muller, <u>Dave's Top Ten (Week of October 16th, 2006)</u>, 2006. Acrylic on paper, 86 1/2 x 38 1/2 in (219.7 x 97.7 cm). Courtesy the artist and Blum & Poe, Los Angeles

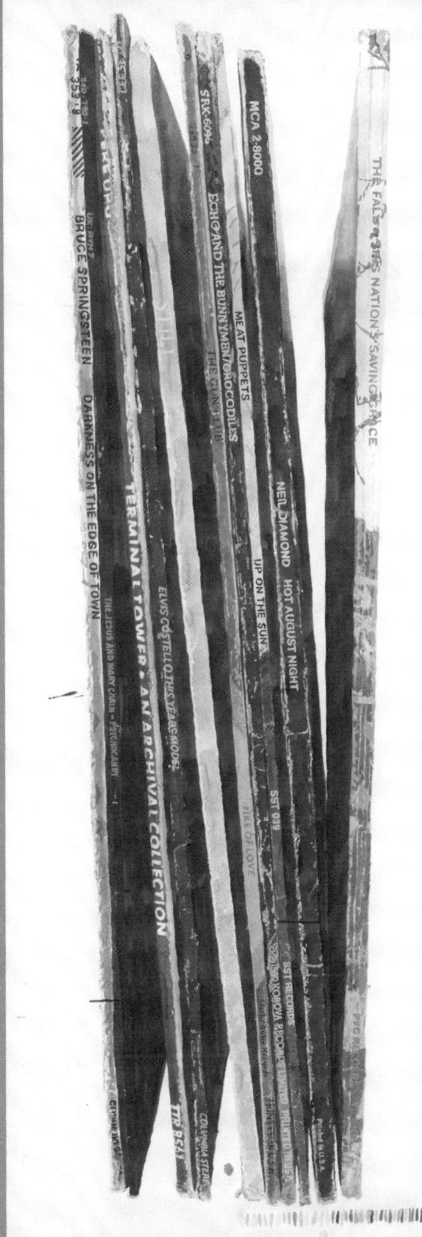
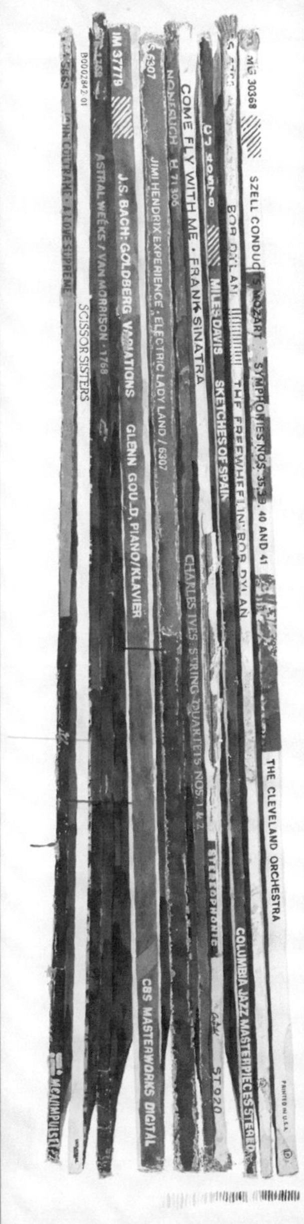
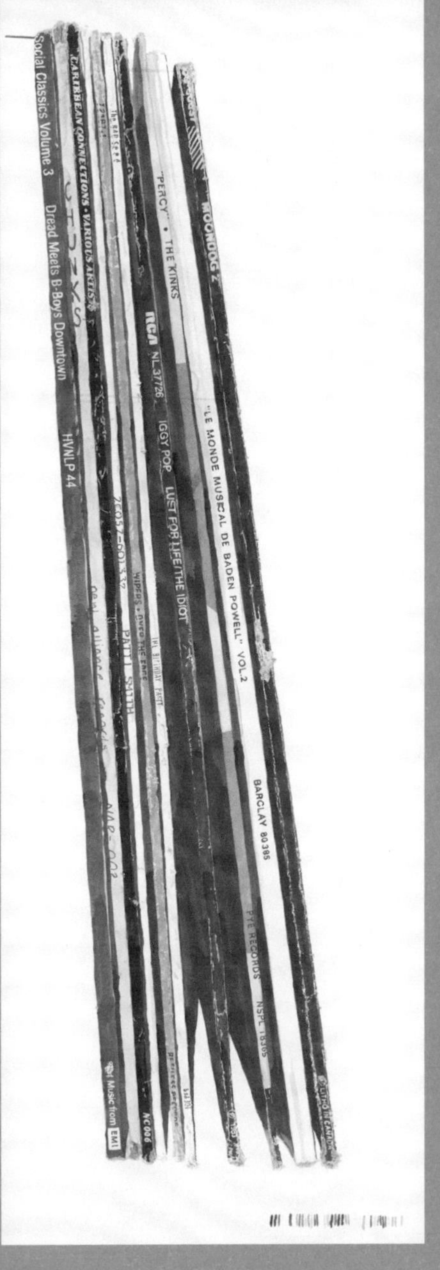

Mike Kaplan in conversation with David Shrigley

In the following conversation, which took place in August 2015, Mike Kaplan and David Shrigley discuss the artist's lift ticket project in Aspen and the business of art.

Mike Kaplan

My favorite work from the series you made for the 2012–13 ski season lift ticket read *PLEASE DO NOT SHOW THIS TO ANYONE* [Fig. 1]. The simple, surface-level irony made you smile the moment you saw it. The more you thought about it, the more irony you could derive from it. You could think of it as something so special it's only for you, as something so sinful that you don't want others to know about it (in the context of Aspen), or even as a simple way of suggesting that the ticket's radio frequency chip means it doesn't need to be presented to get on the chairlift. There's also the societal standpoint in terms of it relating to the lack of privacy in this age of technology. Maybe I'm reading way too much into those seven words. Is there any significance to the word "please"? Also, which was your favorite of the series?

David Shrigley

I'm glad that you like that work. I don't think there is much more I could add. My favorite pieces among what I make tend to change depending on what mood I'm in. When I make an artwork, I tell myself that the goal is to make something that's "good enough," rather than something that is amazing. It's not that my aspirations are modest; it's just that you never realize the resonance of a work until long after you have made it. And my opinion of the work also changes depending on what mood I'm in. If you ask artists what their favorite piece of theirs is, it would often be the work that they are currently making or even the work that they haven't started yet. I get bored of my own work. The stuff I still like from the past is often the stuff I have forgotten about.

MK

I like hearing about how your mood affects your perception of your own work. From a skiing standpoint, just getting up on the mountain can change my mood almost instantly. But my style of skiing and what line I choose down the mountain are also definitely influenced by mood. Another piece that was included in the lift tickets, *I DIDN'T NOTICE THE MOUNTAINS* [Fig. 2], implies being in the "zone," where you are so focused on whatever you are doing, you lose your sense of place. How does your mood affect a piece while you are creating it?

"

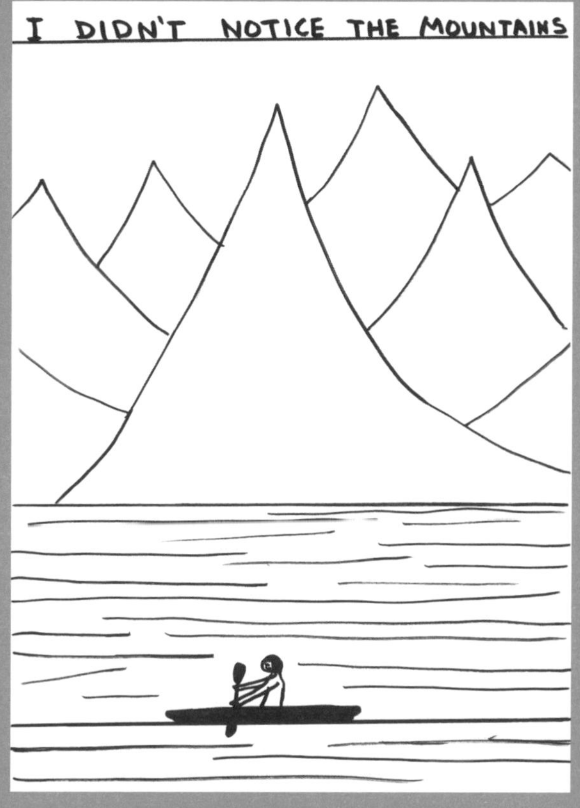

Fig. 1
David Shrigley, Untitled (Please do not show this to anyone), 2009. Ink on paper, 16 1/2 x 12 in (42 x 30 cm). Courtesy the artist and Stephen Friedman Gallery

Fig. 2
David Shrigley, Untitled (I didn't notice the mountains), 2011. Ink on paper, 16 1/2 x 12 in (42 x 30 cm). Courtesy the artist and Galleri Nicolai Wallner. Photo: Anders Sune Berg

whether a work is "good enough" and that decision cannot be unmade—such are the rules I have set myself. I might feel more or less disposed to a work that I have made in the past, but it's still "good enough"—I am not allowed to destroy it. I make art regardless of what mood I'm in. I'm asked sometimes whether I get "artist's block." I do, but I still make the work. I focus on the process rather than the outcome. I make a certain number of drawings in a day, whether I feel like it or not. In that way, the work somehow makes itself.

MK

I just went to California to get "next to the sea" for a few days—I definitely needed an electrochemical reset, or maybe the ability to see over the mountain. I'm curious how you perceived Aspen before you visited and how you see it now?

DS

I can imagine how going up a mountain can make you feel better. I go to the beach every morning and that makes me feel good. I think it's to do with the electrochemical effect on your body being next to the sea. In a way, I try to ignore my mood when I'm thinking about work. I make a decision at some point as to

DS

Aspen is an interesting place for lots of reasons. However, the most memorable thing over the couple of times I've visited has been the temperature. The last time I visited was in January and the temperature the night before I left was

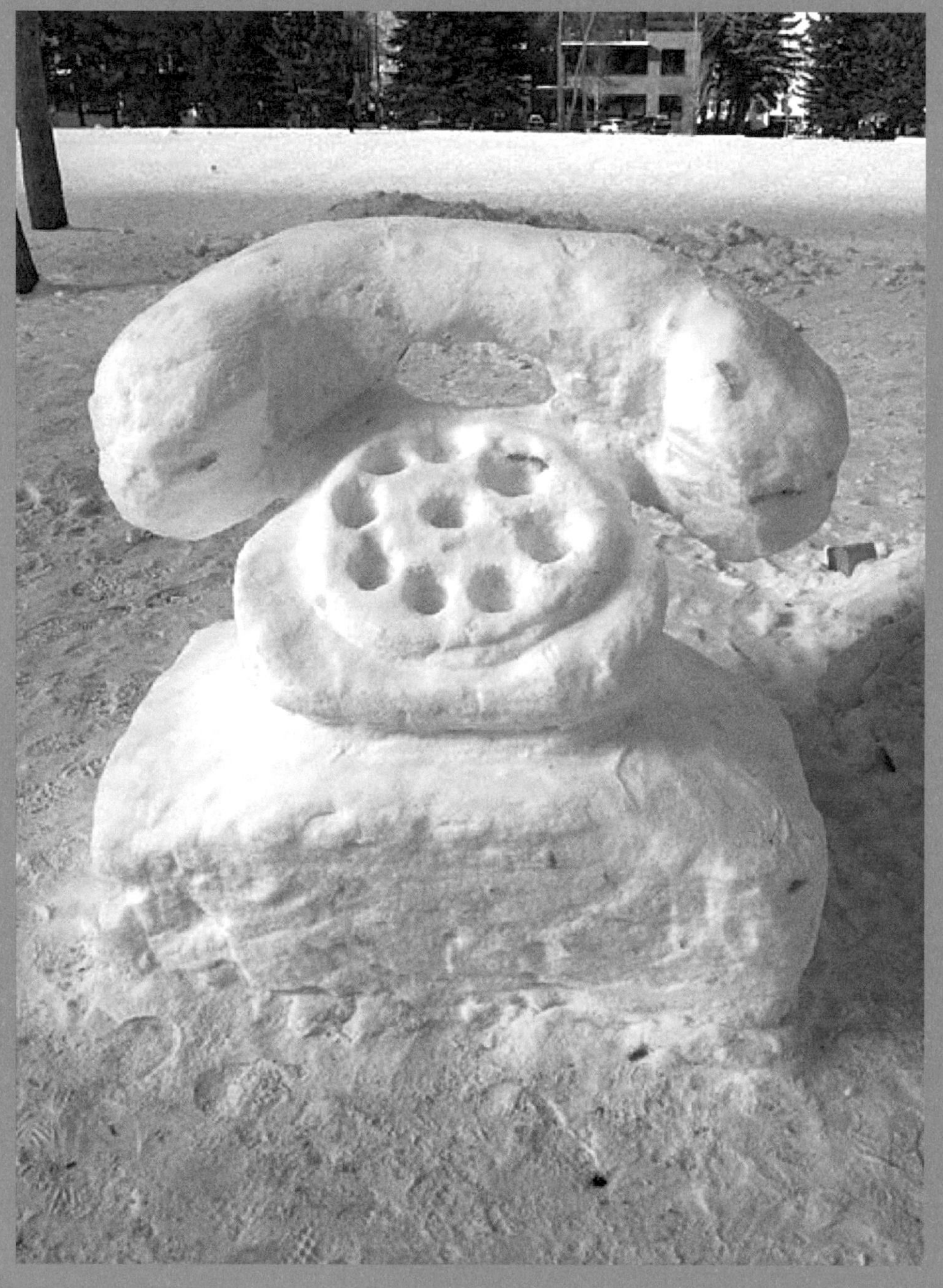

Mike Kaplan in conversation
with David Shrigley

Fig. 3
Photo: David Shrigley

-20 F (-29 C)—colder than the coldest ever recorded temperature in the UK. One other thing I remember was the snow sculpture that the kids had made. That was pretty great [Fig. 3].

MK

I love it, thanks for sharing the image. Interesting impression about Aspen and the cold, -20 F is probably close to a record for Aspen. Last year was just the opposite—but each day and each year are different.

At Skico, we view art as an opportunity to expose our customers to a deeper level of engagement with our product and nature. Hopefully, it also helps our employees and guests see the world through a different lens. It appears that you apply your art in commercial applications via the note cards and playing cards, so I wonder how you feel about the relationship between art and business as both an entrepreneur and as an artist?

DS

I've made a lot of work that exists outside the world of fine art—illustration, advertising, pop promos, merchandise, etc. There is a misconception that if you do commercial art such as advertising then you get paid a lot of money. This might have been true at some point in the eighties, but it certainly isn't now. I embarked on these projects because they were interesting more than anything else: I learned something from doing them. It was also an opportunity to speak to a different audience. Generally speaking, fine art pays better and you can do whatever you like, but sometimes you feel like you are just making work for the same small audience every time.

I didn't really see the work I did for the Aspen Skiing Company as a commercial project, though I suppose that's what it was. Aspen is an "art" town in my eyes, so everything I might do there is art. The corporate world is a very conservative place, so it's unlikely I'd be allowed to do anything as interventional as I did in Aspen anywhere else. When you work with ad agencies, they are all really interesting and creatively dynamic, but by the time your idea gets put before a client, it has been compromised to the point of being unrecognizable and then usually gets rejected. Not many companies are prepared to take risks. Some are, but they are hard to find. Businesses are always focused on making money. I guess that's the problem.

MK

Interesting thoughts. From my standpoint as a CEO, I don't view art as something for a business to monetize, but really as a way to deepen our relationship with our employees, our customers, and even society, such that people will get more out of their time with nature, with friends and family, and being part of Aspen. In doing so, I'm hoping employees will be more productive, our guests will be more loyal, and we will subsequently make more money, but that should be a natural outcome of doing right by all these stakeholders. To me, the problem doesn't lie in making money, but how the money is made. It's the responsibility of a business to make money in a way that is sustainable and is appropriate to the impacts and benefits that the profit endeavor has on society. I believe art can play a pivotal role in balancing a business's profit motive with its social responsibilities.

One of the issues we struggle with is analogous to the "Fine Art" dilemma, as we run the risk of appealing to a very small audience. One of the brilliant aspects of your work is that it resonates with the sophisticated collector who happens to ski as well as the hardcore ski bum who doesn't typically get it when it comes to art. I really enjoy seeing customers out and enjoying our mountains, do you do much of that around your exhibits? If so, I bet you see some interesting reactions and interpretations of your work?

DS

I think you're in a minority with your ideas about art and business. But BRAVO anyway.

After I've made an exhibition, I usually can't wait to get out of there. The installation of a show is usually the end of a long working process that can be quite emotionally draining. So I tend not to stick around and hear people's reactions. But after some time has elapsed, it's always entertaining to hear peoples' interpretations of the work (qualitative judgments aside), especially kids. I sometimes think my target audience should be the eight to twelve age group. They tend to be well represented whenever I do book signings.

I suspect it's probably a bad thing to harvest too many responses to the work, as it can be a distraction. I think the only way I can effectively make art is to ignore most of other peoples' opinions and just listen to myself. I try to ask myself the same questions that I would ask a student in a tutorial situation, like:

What's the point of this artwork?
Could it be made differently?
Why do I like it?

That's not to say that I never ask for advice. I often ask friends their opinions, such as: what do you think this is? I don't ask people to make qualitative judgments though. I have to make those calls myself and stick by them even if other people say the work is rubbish. Curiously, I never ask myself the question, "What does it mean?" I guess it's not a question I'm interested in answering in any definitive way.

MK

It's interesting to hear how you balance listening to yourself against when and how much you listen to others. Again, another parallel in business: customer

feedback is critical to ongoing success, but sometimes you have to ignore what the data says and just go with your instincts.

Not seeking to definitively answer what your work means to you reminds me of your comment about how your work makes itself. I'm reminded again of skiing: how no two runs are the same and the mountain makes the turn or determines the skier's line as much as the skier. It's what makes this way of life so compelling and captivating.

DS

I've only ever been skiing once in my life (on the nursery slope). The last time I was in Aspen, I went up the mountain on the ski lift just for the view [Fig. 4]. People found it curious that I was going up to look around and not to ski. I was the only one in the lift on the way down, watching everyone else having fun on the slope. Next time I'll ski…※

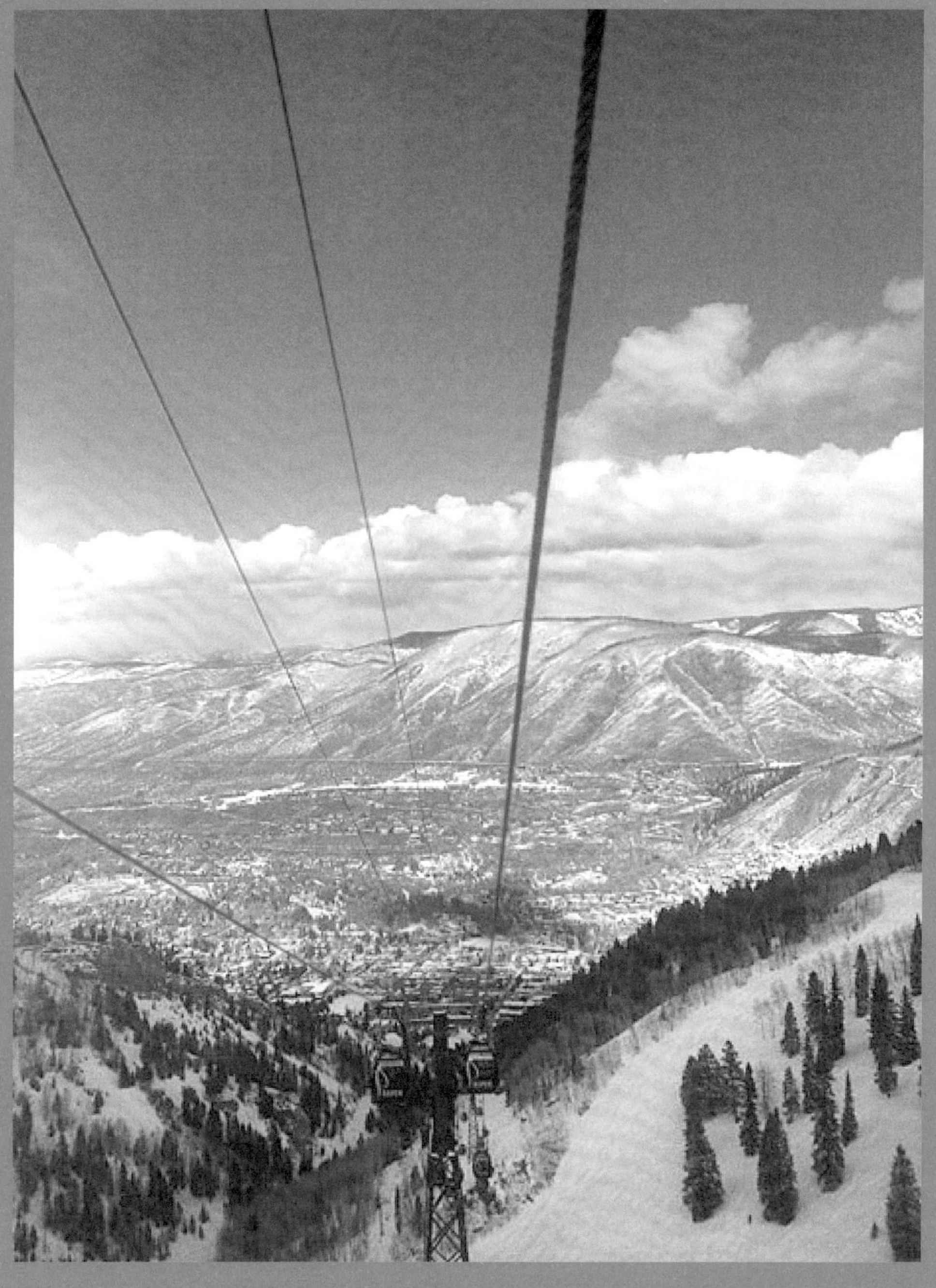

Fig. 4
Photo: David Shrigley

Heidi Zuckerman in conversation with Gretchen Bleiler

The following conversation took place in September 2015. In it, Heidi Zuckerman and professional snowboarder Gretchen Bleiler discuss the roles that art and snowboarding have played in their lives.

Heidi Zuckerman
You have said that you come to the museum a lot and my first question is: what is your experience with art both here in the museum and out in our community?

Gretchen Bleiler
I love that question, it's a good one. To be honest with you, my experience with art has always felt distant. I don't have a knowledge of art and it doesn't relate to me and my life or lifestyle. But what I'm finding more and more, and maybe this is something that you develop as you get older and worldlier, is that art is available to everyone and what's meaningful to you is what art is.

I love having the art museum here to make art so much more accessible to everyone. I love being able to come here, go through all the new installations, and pick out meaning from my perspective—without necessarily relying on someone else's interpretation, but finding what's meaningful to me.

HZ
When you talk about the relevancy of art for you and your lifestyle, one of the things that's interesting to me about the partnership between the art museum and the Aspen Skiing Company is this idea of reaching across traditional groupings, interests, or lifestyles.

When I do conversations with artists, the first thing I always ask is: "Why don't you tell me about your work?" When you think about your lifestyle and what it's been and what it represents, how do you explain that to people?

GB
I feel as though snowboarding has really been a vehicle for me to push past my own boundaries and limitations and really be able to explore who I am and what's possible. And not just for myself, but also to be a spark and an inspiration for others, to light them up in terms of what's possible in their own lives and living their own dreams.

HZ
That's really interesting. One of the things I love about art is the inherent possibility of it, not just in terms of taking something that used to be something else and giving it new meaning through the intention of the artist, but also through the opportunity

of someone else seeing it and thinking or feeling differently about it.

That really connects to what you're saying, too, and in watching you do something that seems impossible, like a number of rotations or a height or even this idea of flying. Thinking about it logically, it seems impossible, but then actually participating in it or watching it is so impactful because it distorts your whole notion of truth.

GB

Yeah, exactly. I love that and I think this is why I really wanted to come and have this conversation. I feel like art and snowboarding and sports are all sort of the same thing—this idea of opening yourself up to what's possible in your own life.

We are all different and unique; we all have individual talents, gifts, skills, and different expressions of them. Also, our willingness to explore them is always evolving; it's this constant allowance of what's inside of us to be let out into the world.

I feel that way with art and I feel that way with sports. It touches you in a way that it changes your perception and helps you see more and have more awareness in general. I feel like that's what life is all about.

HZ

I did this executive seminar at the Aspen Institute some years ago. They asked us to plot where we were on a moral compass and they had four standard points on a grid. I felt that they didn't really relate to me and I wanted to come up with my own terms.

For my vertical, the top was transcendence and the bottom was fear. The closer you are to fear, the further you are from transcendence, and vice versa. It strikes me that fear must be something that you've had to address in your life, in your work, and I wonder how you feel about that?

GB

Yeah, absolutely. It's funny, people always come up to me and say, "You must be fearless for what you've done on a snowboard your whole life." My response is actually the opposite. I feel it's been my job and my mission to scare myself every single day, not in a radical way, but in a conscious way, where I'm walking the line of being outside of my comfort zone. When you're outside of your comfort zone, that's when you are opening yourself up to something new and something that you don't necessarily know. It's uncertain—you're not sure what's going to happen—you're aware of what you're doing, but you're also stepping outside of that place. I feel fear is one of our greatest teachers because it's something that's there for every single one of us in everyday life. That's why I've loved snowboarding so much. It's been such a great teacher for everyday life—realizing that when there is fear or there's something to acknowledge and feel, you then choose from there. You don't let fear take control of you and your actions and decisions. You feel it and you acknowledge it and then you choose from your highest place.

HZ

I think that same notion is something that I deal with all the time. How much do you want to put yourself out there? How do you convince other people to put themselves out there and share?

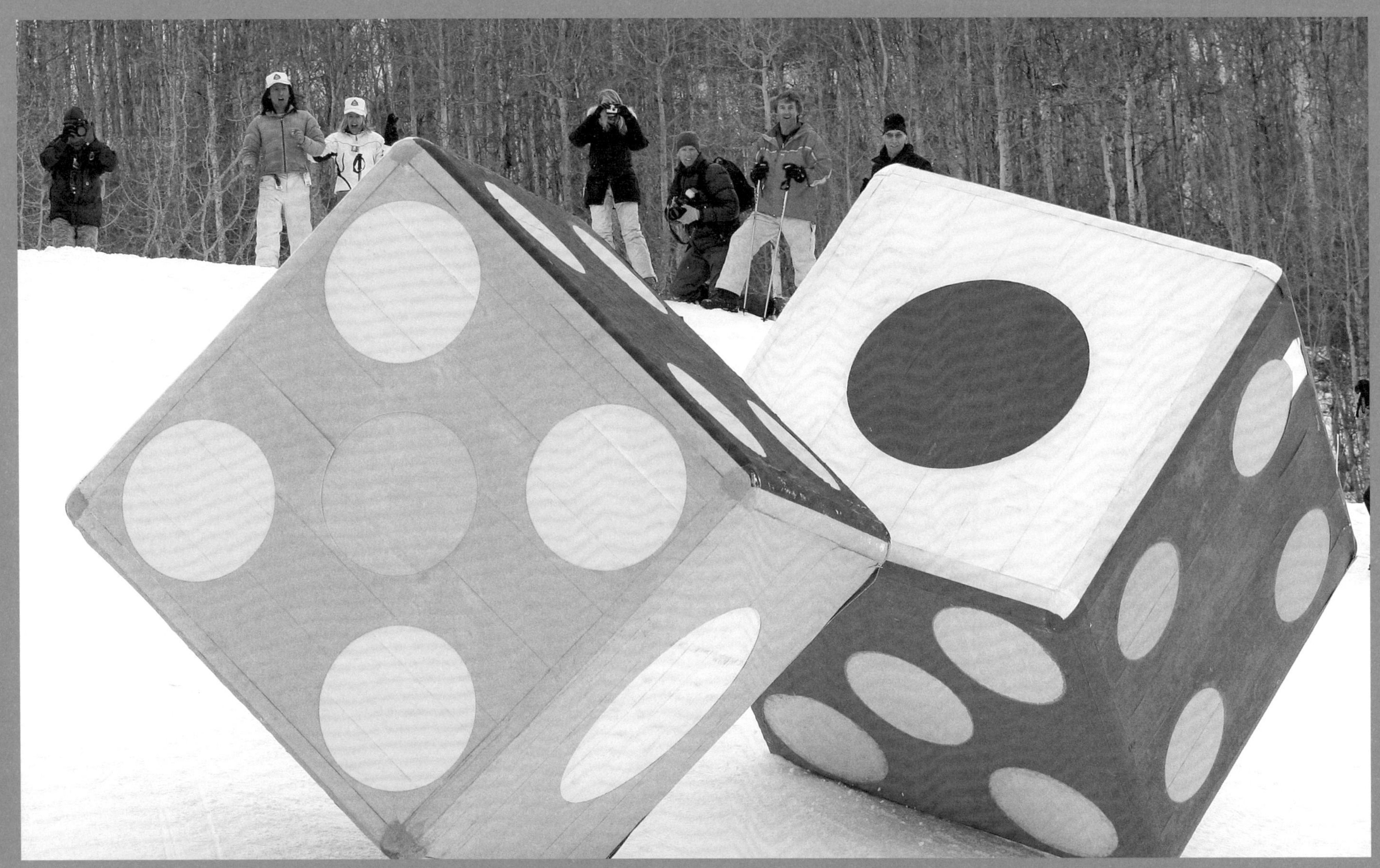

Fig. 1
Yutaka Sone, _Mt. 66_, 2006. Performance at Buttermilk Mountain, Aspen.
Photo: Daniel Bayer

Heidi Zuckerman in conversation
with Gretchen Bleiler

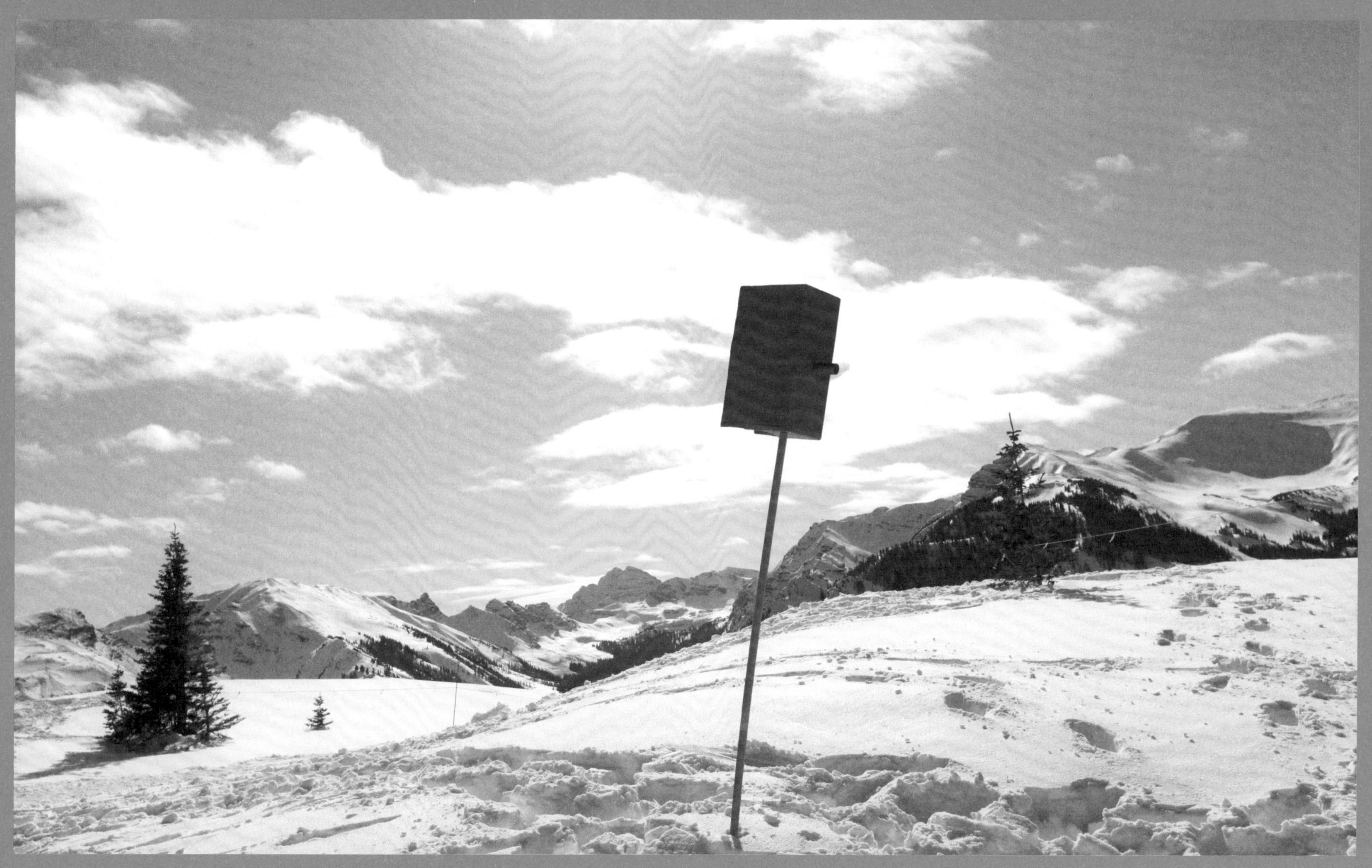

Fig. 2
Installation view: Mark Grotjahn, <u>Untitled (Rose Dore Madder Lake Antique Extra and
Schevenigen Red Deep Mask M17.a)</u>, 2011. Painted bronze, 14 1/2 x 8 x 10 3/4 in (36.8 x 20.3 x 25.4 cm).
Courtesy the artist and Blum & Poe, Los Angeles. Photo: Jeremy Swanson

Whether it's sharing an artwork or an idea or building a new museum or doing something that's counter to an expectation. Not taking the easy way, always stepping up. For someone to be fearless, they would have to be not smart.

GB
Right. Not seeing the whole picture.

HZ
Exactly. If you don't acknowledge the possibilities of what could go wrong, then you can't make good decisions.

GB
I agree. How have you used that in your own life—in building a museum that might have been controversial in the town, but staying true to the vision of Aspen in you and the vision for the town?

HZ
It's an interesting question. I do a lot of yoga and I know that you do, too. There were so many days as we were going through the approval process, and then going through construction, and dealing with all the perspectives that were being expressed.

I would always love it when we did Warrior II Pose. I would look down my arm and out my middle finger and just feel the energy and that power. A lot of life is a fight. If you're in a fight, you have to fight to win. Otherwise, you're going down no matter what. You may go down anyway, but you have to fight. There has always been clarity in the fact that I think art makes the world better. It's essential for the good society and the more people that are exposed to it, the better. Art is for anyone even if it's not for everyone. And it's never been about me, it's always been about the artist or the artwork or the institution.

GB
Right. I don't think you would have done what you have done if it was just about you. Obviously, it was for a greater cause and that is so evident when you come here and spend time going through the different galleries. Thanks for having the courage to stand up. I know that feeling. I think it's huge. When you have something within you that's moving you, no one else can really understand the depth that is within you, and in that place, you have to stand alone and keep fighting.

That's the lifestyle that I want to promote in my whole life. It's the path less traveled, it's uncertain and it's scary, and it takes a lot of courage. But I also think at the end of the day, it's the only life worth living because it's a life of meaning and fulfillment and purpose, not just safety and security.

HZ
I agree with you. First of all, thank you for saying that. I joke with people sometimes that the only thing I wanted when the museum opened was for people to say thank you. When they do, it's so gratifying because that's really the only thing I wanted. I really believe that everyone is seeking a life of meaning. I feel like that's why people come to the museum, why they look at art, and why they support what we do. People want to be a part of something that matters.

There are so many distractions in our lives and it takes a lot of effort to focus on what matters, to find meaning, and to not be distracted by who people think you are or what people want from you or their expectations or societal perspectives. It's hard to do things differently, but I think that's where those opportunities for being of service come into place.

GB

I totally agree. Thank you, really. Like I said, I've really enjoyed being able to come here and create a new relationship with art because of everything that you've done.

HZ

That's awesome. That's the whole idea. That's the idea of Art in Unexpected Places, too. If you can put it in front of people who are coming for that experience—whether they know exactly what it is or not, they're open to it.

The idea of rolling the Yutake Sone dice down the SuperPipe or putting the Mark Grotjahn masks on the top of the mountain—giving someone a moment of pause and wonder—is important [Figs. 1–2]. It's enabling that curiosity and getting people to open up to different questions. What does it mean? What is this? How do I do that? Why doesn't this work? Everyone always wants to know the answer.

But let's be a little uncomfortable. Let's not necessarily give this thing a name, or let's be OK with it evolving or figuring it out. Allowing ourselves to sit in places of uncertainty or discomfort is a good thing.

GB

I totally agree, especially for Aspen. We happen to be this very linear, masculine town where we climb mountains and there's an end and there's a race. It's awesome. That's what makes us so amazing; we have warriors who live here. It's really important for all of the warriors to also have exactly what you're talking about—the endless curiosity and constant evolution. It's so important to have that balance. ✳

Alchemy of the Authentic

William Morrow

"The public is diverse, variable, volatile, controversial; and it has its origins in the private lives of all citizens. The encounter of public art is ultimately a private experience; perception outlasts actual experience. It is these rich ambiguities that should provide the subject matter for public art…"

Patricia Philips, "Temporality and Public Art," *Critical Issues in Public Art: Content, Context, and Controversy* (1993)

Critics and writers of art history have been examining public and private partnerships/patronage for centuries. Yet, the partnership between the Aspen Art Museum and Aspen Skiing Company presents a relatively new twenty-first-century model in contemporary art production. It coincides with the advent of the hyphenated artist [1] and a bond of trust established between an entrepreneurial, informed curator and a socially engaged patron open to building bridges. Outside of major art centers in the US, when curatorial and patron objectives are aligned, it can pave the way for pioneering opportunities to support the creation of original artwork, has the ability to introduce a high level of art to a community, and can develop new audiences and appreciation for art in unexpected places—beyond the museum walls.

In 2005, I was fortunate enough to be on the ground floor of a unique private art venture: the 21c Museum Hotel in Louisville, Kentucky. 21c played a significant role in the evolution of contemporary art within the city's public realm and has been the catalyst for institutions across the city to engage with contemporary art in new ways. One of the most pivotal projects I commissioned as the Director, along with the vision of 21c's founders, was the first US public sculpture by the Austrian artist Werner Reiterer [Fig. 1]. In 2006, I was also on the City of Louisville Mayor's Advisory Committee for Public Art, and although I had to recuse myself from committee discussions and approvals for this particular project, Reiterer's chandelier was unanimously approved—marking the first commissioned installation of an internationally recognized artist in the city in over twenty-five years.

Reiterer's sculpture is in direct opposition to the trend of nostalgic, monumental art that dominates Main Street America. The Baroque-style brass chandelier, suspended from its white, powder-coated, gallows-shaped pole, is as much a commentary on the lynching history of the South, as it is about the

"

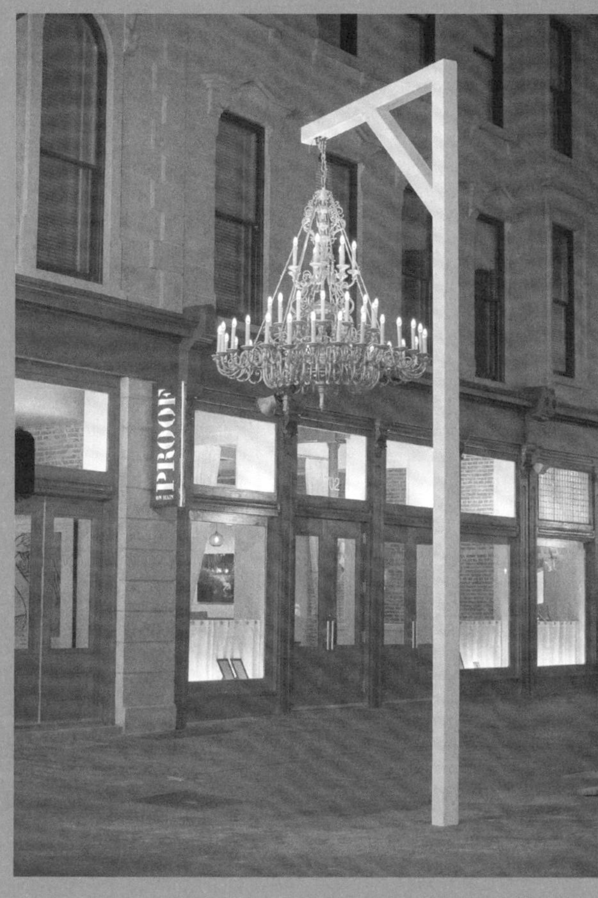

Fig. 1
Installation view: Werner Reiterer, *Untitled*, 2006.
Brass chandelier, gallows pole, fifty custom LED
lights, electronics, megaphone, sound. 21c Museum
Hotel, Louisville, KY. Photo: Kenneth Hayden

demise of the class systems in Europe and North America. Passersby are unexpectedly invited to engage and question their relationship with the work. The quasi-participatory element of pulsating lights and the synchronized sound of a man breathing (activated by a faux bellman's bell inside the museum restaurant) additionally challenge the formal characteristics of public art as static objects. Although the artist's intent is layered and not immediately defined, the piece's elegant and seemingly simplistic components make it user-friendly, not in a reductive way, but through its accessibility and openness to discovery.

Along with the outdoor installations, for the first time in the city, there was a commitment to exhibit international artists alongside regional and local artists. Within a year of opening, 21c would become a hub of cultural programming for the city. And while the country was going into one of the largest financial recessions since the Great Depression and the threat of drastic funding cuts in the arts was looming, the promise of private funding attracted collaborations with many of the key arts organizations in the state, including the Actors Theatre, Louisville Ballet, Kentucky Center for the Arts, and regional universities.

The public installation *Going Home* (2009; Fig. 2) was one of the earliest collaborations between 21c and a regional institution. Led by Mary Carothers, University of Louisville (UofL) Associate Professor of Art (perhaps best known for her ambitious outdoor installation addressing climate change, *The Frozen Car* [2008]), a team of UofL 2-D design students created ten thousand hand-cut monarch butterfly–shaped designs and fourteen sets of plaster-cast hands for the façade of 21c. Inspired by Luis Alberto Urrea's novel *The Devil's Highway*—a story about the Yuma 14, a group of Mexican immigrants who died attempting to cross the Arizona desert—the installation was successful on many levels. It not only brought together a diverse community of artists and students, but also became a meeting place for groups and activities focused on immigration issues. Coinciding with Day of the Dead celebrations, *Going Home* ultimately attracted a responsive public that might not usually have engaged with contemporary art.

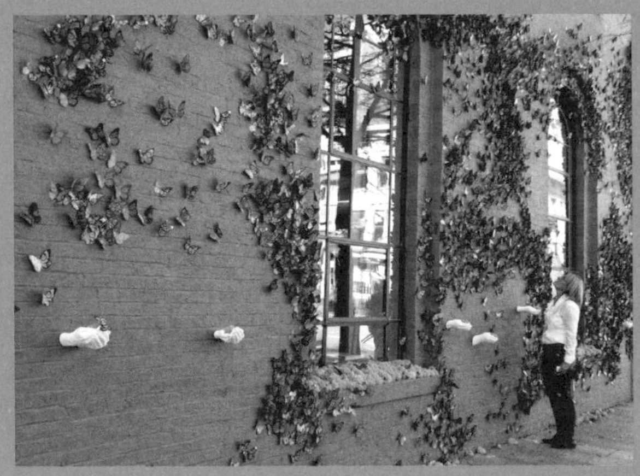

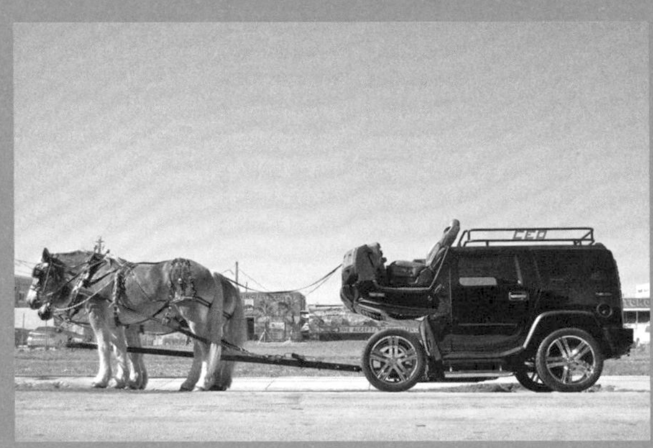

Being in direct conversation with the founders and owners of 21c, and operating without the typical board structure of public institutions, opened up the opportunity to curate exhibitions in a staggeringly short period of time. Adding to the fluidity of projects at 21c—as a privately funded, collecting institution—we had the ability to be nimble and responsive in our acquisition of recently created art.

Another artist that has been on my curatorial radar over the past few years is Jeremy Dean. When we first met in New York City in 2010, he had just completed *CEO Stagecoach* (2010; Fig. 3). The piece was quickly acquired by 21c and became the focus of the exhibition *Back to Futurama* later that year. For *CEO Stagecoach*, Dean took a working early model Hummer H2 truck and transformed it into a functioning horse-drawn carriage. At face value, the work can be perceived as a pimped-out Hummer with twenty-four-inch rims and five onboard TVs looping Dean's video art. Alternatively, as Dean suggests, the Hummer can be considered "a rolling indictment of the American psyche on wheels,"[2] and its layered meanings allude to energy consumption and issues of sustainability.

CEO Stagecoach was first exhibited as a performative piece navigating through Central Park earlier in 2010. Pulled by a stagecoach driver and a team of draft horses, the work garnered an enormous amount of attention in the press, from NBC News to the *Village Voice*. However, it was particularly insightful seeing its impact firsthand in the streets of Louisville and then the public reactions when 21c funded its performance in Miami to coincide with the December 2011 art fairs. When I think of art in unexpected places, I will always recall sitting atop *CEO Stagecoach* with the artist as we navigated the streets of Little Haiti in Miami. The visceral reactions of locals were a stark contrast to the perceived spectacle of art world attendees in Wynwood and South Beach.

The hybridity of context within each of these examples was heightened by the ability of the works to operate outside the normal environs of the institution. Much like the excitement I experienced when I unexpectedly encountered my Mark Bradford–designed lift ticket [see pages 116–17] on the slopes of Snowmass or witnessing a throng of skiers reflected in the polished surface of Teresita Fernández's wall installation in the Elk Camp restaurant [see pages 130–32], it is the openness to discovery, or as Heidi Zuckerman puts it, "The possibility of transcendence," that lends to their success. It is the emotional response from the viewer that each of the artists seeks in their work, and by taking the art outside of the museum walls, the artist is able to achieve a more authentic reaction. The suspension of disbelief is more likely to occur when art is not confined by a prescribed set of values or defined within a museum context. As each of the artists in the Art in Unexpected Places program illustrates, when we are confronted with the unexpected, we can begin to see the world through a different lens.

Despite the artists in the program being diverse in their formal approaches to art and coming from very different backgrounds, they each share in their pursuit of an authentic experience. Bradford's ability to combine his interests in the ubiquitous nature of advertising with the mass distribution of a ski lift ticket opens up new potential for engagement into the layers of the urban-sourced materials that inspire his larger body of work. The use of ephemera in his lift tickets is at odds with the pristine mountain landscape. Yet, the fragmentation of the familiar style of information speaks to a more universal questioning of ritual and truth that the audience can explore in the five lift ticket designs. Similarly, Shinique Smith's sculpture and mural work is steeped in layers of fragmented personal history along with her interest in street art, calligraphy, fashion, and childhood memories. While viewers may not be familiar with the depths of Smith's cultural references, it is her willingness to be vulnerable that empowers others to be open to embracing the unknown and finding beauty in their individual expression [see pages 160–64].

Fernández likens the artistic challenge of finding meaning beyond the sum of an object's parts to alchemy. For Fernández, her work is as much about place as it is about materiality. Inspired by an aerial view of Snowmass, the reflective qualities of *Golden Panorama (Snowmass Mountain)* (2013) render the familiar in an unfamiliar way, creating an opportunity for the viewer to reexamine their relationship to the landscape. Fernández's alchemist approach lends itself to moments of realization and the transformative power of art.

It is the notion of the authentic that according to Philippe de Montebello, after three decades at the helm of "The Metropolitan Art Museum, is one of the greatest challenges for museums in the twenty-first century. He credits his generation of museum leaders for inventing the quagmire facing large collecting institutions—stuck in the vicious cycle of large, expensive banner exhibitions that are more focused on visitor numbers than audience engagement. There is little room for embracing the unknown in this model, and therefore, the AAM's Art in Unexpected Places is as important as ever in creating a paradigm shift in the way that museums are able to celebrate the artist's voice, trust the curatorial vision, seek alternative partnerships, and perhaps most importantly, engage the authentic experience. ✳

Notes

1   The term "hyphenated artist" refers to the twenty-first-century artist who is no longer bound by a specific medium.

2   Interview with William Morrow and Jeremy Dean, "21c Museum presents Jeremy Dean's CEO Stagecoach, part of Back to Futurama" YouTube, 2:23 min, https://www.youtube.com/watch?v=jsXn5zVW-CA (accessed September 1, 2015).

The Art of Surprise
Dan Cameron

Ambitious art projects realized in public spaces have become such a fixture of contemporary urban existence that, at times, it helps to be reminded that they are also a relatively recent phenomenon. Granted that, in the US, the roots of public art can be traced to the Federal Art Project (FAP) during the New Deal and the scores of hand-painted post office murals commissioned throughout the country in the 1930s. The FAP's spinoff agency, the Art in Architecture Program, transferred much of its attention during the 1960s to the exteriors of large public projects. In addition, the program's famous 1 percent formula for proportioning building funds toward the commissioning of public artworks became synonymous with the often-unspoken civic agreement that such pieces are a boon to the citizenry and a cultural investment in the future.

Even so, when we try to envision the kinds of artistic interventions within zones and locales that are designated for public use today, it often seems their first manifestations took place in the 1970s. Examples include semi-clandestine sculptural reconfigurations of derelict buildings (Gordon Matta-Clark; Fig. 1) or vacant lots (Agnes Denes; Fig. 2), or at a much grander scale, in locations from skyscrapers to city lights (Robert Smithson, Walter De Maria; Figs. 3–4). Smithson's principle of the non-site discursively tied the contained space of the art gallery to remote locations at the edge of civilization. It provided the exhibition model with the opportunity to include artworks that might be located thousands of miles away, but whose essence could be conveyed through the hand-made artifact displayed in the gallery or museum space (Christo, James Turrell; Fig. 5).

For the sake of contrast with our apparently enlightened perspective relative to public art, consider the situation in 1989, when Richard Serra lost the legal appeal to prevent the dismantling of his *Tilted Arc* (a twelve-foot-high, 120-foot-long Corten steel sculpture shaped like a curved wall; Fig. 6) from Foley Federal Plaza in Lower Manhattan. *Tilted Arc* had been erected in 1981 as a permanent *in situ* sculpture by the General Services Administration based on a recommendation by the National Endowment for the Arts (NEA), but residents and workers had petitioned for its removal.

Although the surrounding controversy never reached the public level of acrimony linked to the figurative works of the so-called

"

Fig. 1
Gordon Matta-Clark, Documentation of Conical Intersect (1975) in Paris. Courtesy The Estate of Gordon Matta-Clark and David Zwirner New York/London

Fig. 2
Agnes Denes, Wheatfield – A Confrontation: Battery Park Landfill, Downtown Manhattan – The Harvest, 1982. © Agnes Denes. Courtesy Leslie Tonkonow Artworks + Projects, New York

Fig. 3
Robert Smithson, Spiral Jetty, 1970. Great Salt Lake, Utah mud, salt crystals, rocks, water, 1500 x 15 ft (457.2 x 4.57 m). Dia Center for the Arts Collection, New York. © Holt-Smithson Foundation/Licensed by VAGA, New York, NY. Courtesy James Cohan Gallery, New York and Shanghai. Photo: Gianfranco Gorgoni

Fig. 4
Walter De Maria, The Lightning Field, 1977. Long-term installation, western New Mexico. © The Estate of Walter De Maria. Courtesy Dia Art Foundation, New York. Photo: John Cliett

Fig. 5
Christo, Over the River, Project for the Arkansas River, State of Colorado, 2011. Pencil, fabric, twine, pastel, wax crayon, charcoal, enamel paint, aerial photograph with topographic elevations, and fabric samples; collage in two parts: 20 1/2 x 12 in (77.5 x 30.5 cm); 30 1/2 x 26 1/4 in (77.5 x 66.7 cm). © Christo 2011, Ref. #136. Photo: André Grossmann

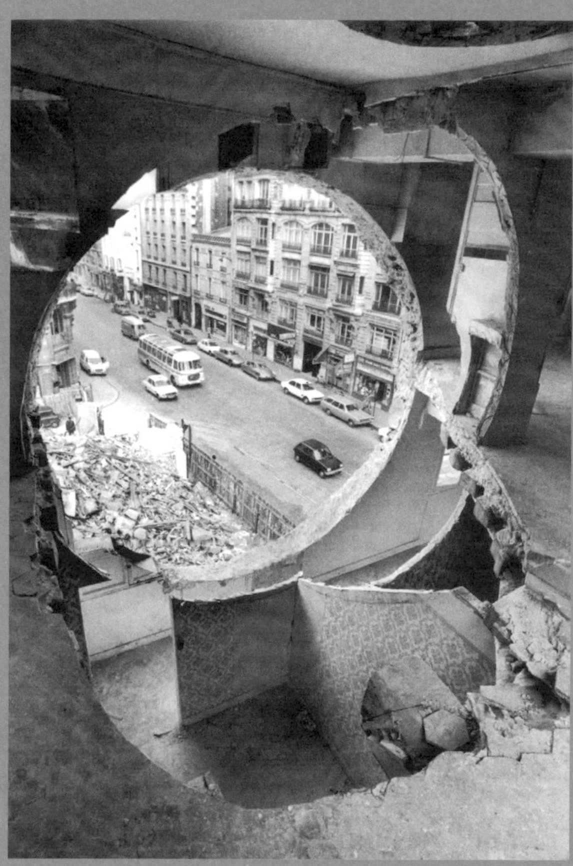

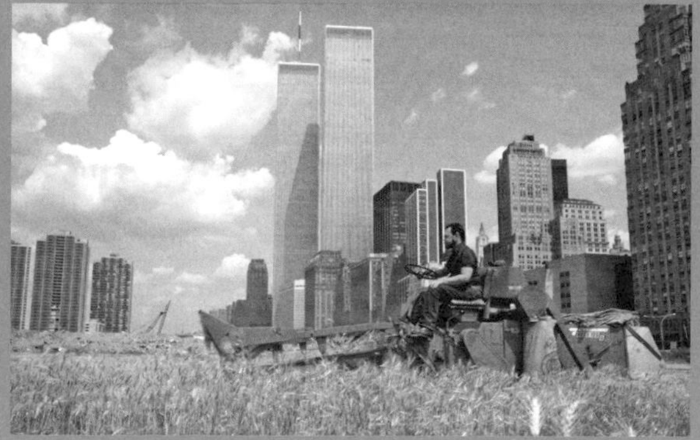

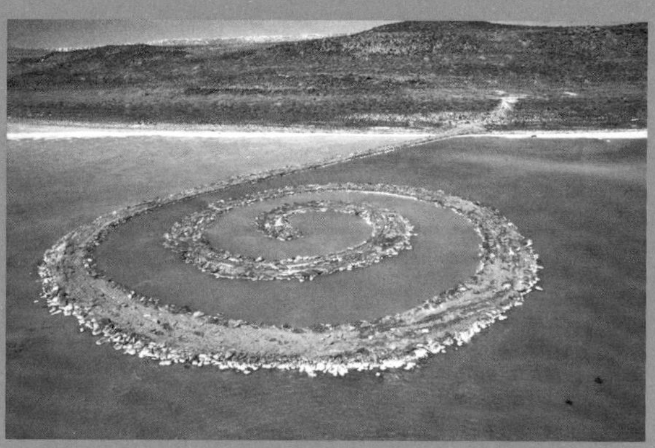

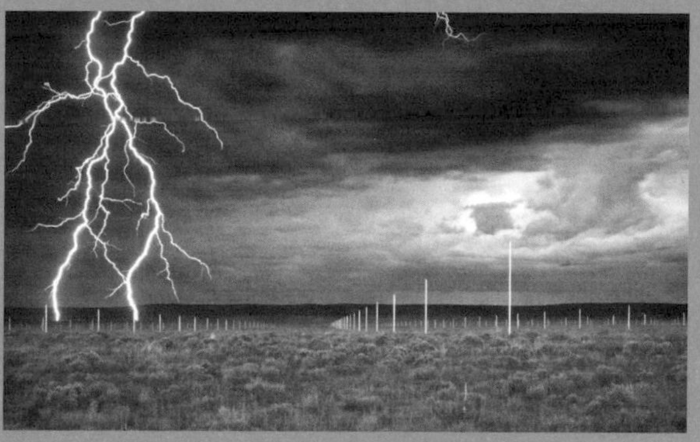

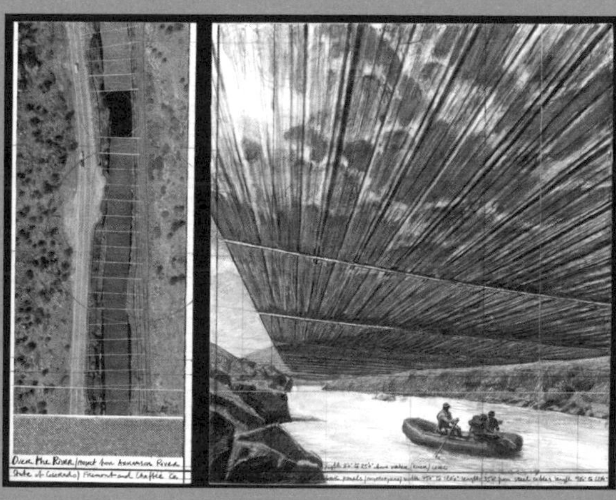

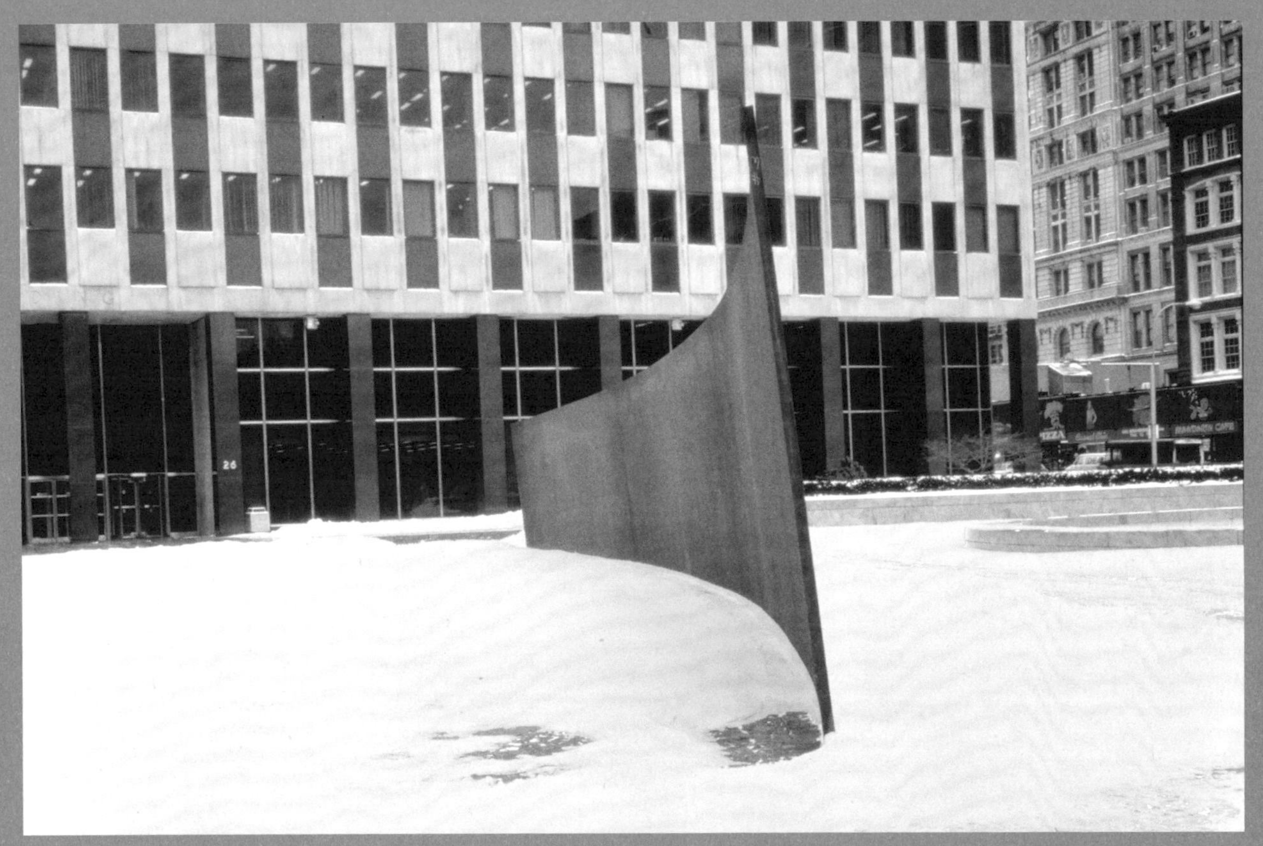

Fig. 6
Richard Serra, Tilted Arc, 1981. Weatherproof steel;
12 ft x 119 ft 3 in x 2 1/2 in (3.7 x 36.3 m x 6.4 cm).
Collection US General Services Administration,
Washington, DC. Destroyed by the United States
Government, March 15, 1989

such large undertakings with suspicion or downright hostility.

One important change of direction in the nature of public artworks during the post–*Tilted Arc* era has been away from permanent or even long-term structures, and toward works that last a single season or less. This formula was already coming into existence in New York by the late 1970s, with the formation of the Public Art Fund and Creative Time. The evolution of these two organizations as independent curatorial agencies—which navigate the halls of urban power and skillfully lead contemporary debates over the meanings and uses of public art—has drastically altered the rules for how artists engage with complex social environments.

In contrast to the more combative 1980s, works of art that would have been almost unimaginable thirty years ago—*A Subtlety*, Kara Walker's massive sugar nude from early 2014 [Fig. 7] being one particular example—come into being in part because they dispense with any requirement that they be maintained in perpetuity. In cases where the artist's intervention is intended to be permanent, a growing vitality in projects requiring

"NEA Four," certain features of contemporary public art seem to have come into existence as a result of the highly public battle over the work's ultimate fate. For a brief unhappy moment, it even appeared that the long-established civic accord that had greeted new public artworks, even those that at first seemed baffling or disruptive, had collapsed and the general public increasingly viewed

The Art of Surprise
Dan Cameron

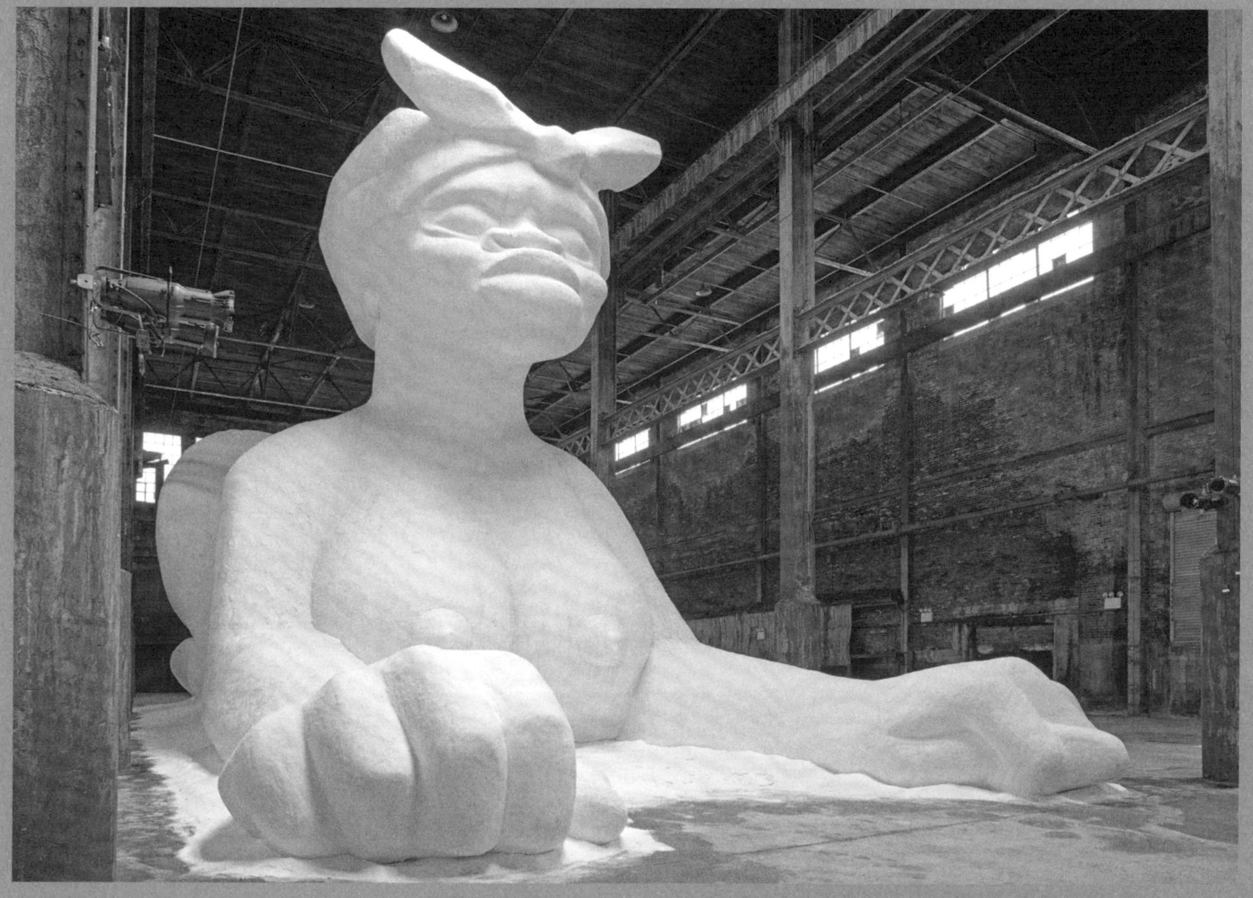

the confines of museums and designated cultural spaces altogether, and is often hard to distinguish as art at all.

Another major development in the field has been an increased artistic sensitivity toward the social fabric of the specific communities for which public art is being developed. If a single antithesis to *Tilted Arc* can be said to have played a decisive role in this change, it would probably be 2002's *Tribute in Light* [Fig. 8]. The unexpectedly successful time-based memorial work by Julian LaVerdiere and Paul Myoda mirrored the positioning of the Twin Towers—literally envisioning their ascension into the cosmos. Coming on the heels of such a collectively traumatic event as the 9/11 attacks, *Tribute in Light* demonstrated that projects that employ recognizable conventions of gallery-based practice can nonetheless, at a certain scale, touch the lives of millions of individuals.

Within my personal curatorial experience, the biggest testing ground for such a possibility came after the flooding of New Orleans in the wake of Hurricane Katrina in 2005. The feelings

intense long-term interactions with at-risk neighborhoods and communities—Theaster Gates in Chicago and Rick Lowe in Houston are the most recognized pioneers in this area—has given shape to an entirely new category of artistic practice based on social engagement. This frequently manifests itself outside

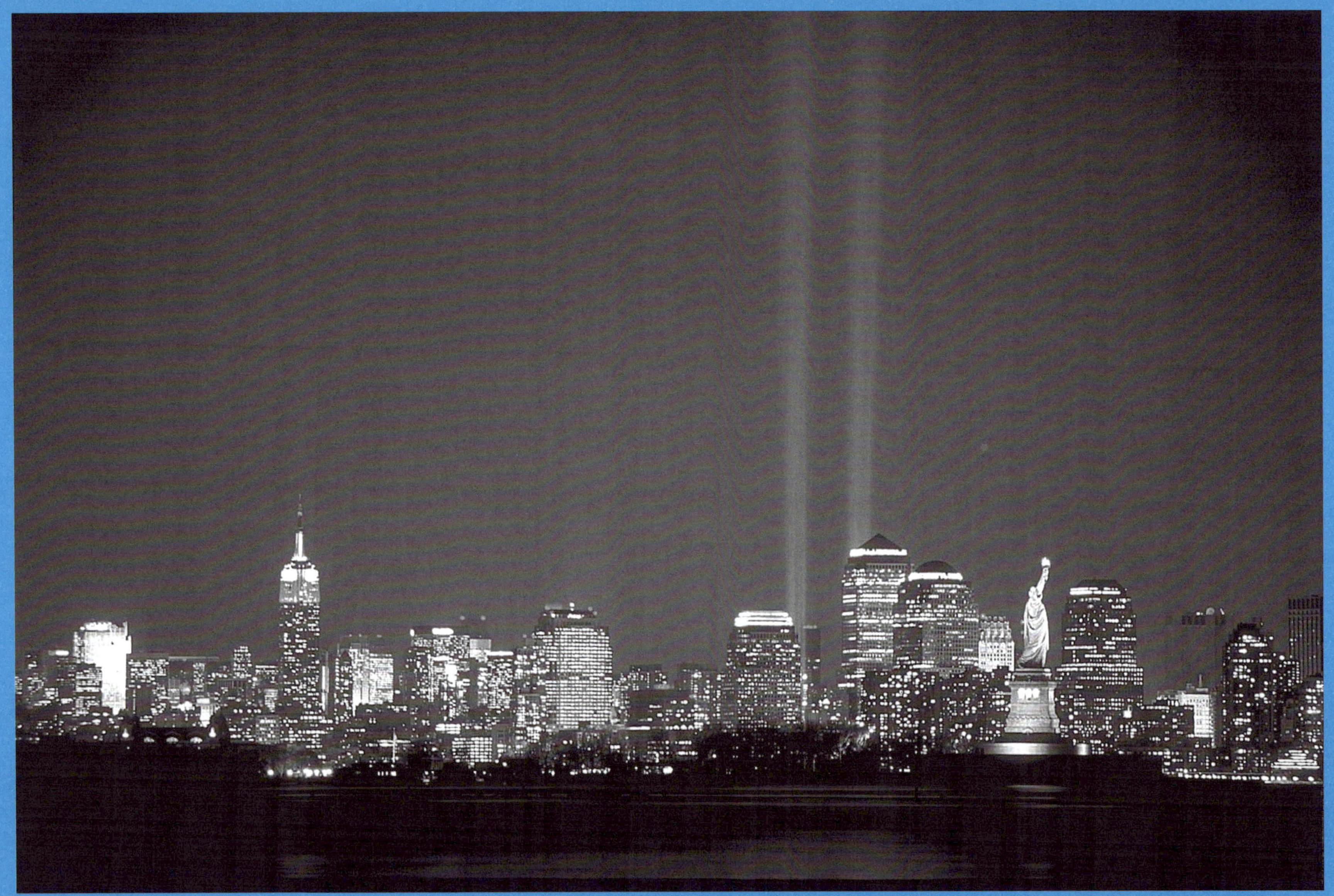

Fig. 8
Julian LaVerdiere and Paul Myoda, Tribute in Light, 2002.
Courtesy Creative Time. Photo: Charlie Samuels

The Art of Surprise
Dan Cameron

of invisibility that friends in the city's art community complained of in the months afterward were prevalent. High-profile national efforts by musicians, writers, and filmmakers to support their friends and colleagues in southern Louisiana did not trigger parallel manifestations within the US art world. Finding myself in the unexpectedly useful position of an established New York–based curator with serious inroads into New Orleans's small, but robust art community, I was inspired to develop a structure for bringing the larger art world to New Orleans. This took the form of Prospect New Orleans, now an international triennial exhibition approaching its fourth edition in 2017.

The two-year process of organizing Prospect.1 (2006 to 2008) unfolded parallel to the city's efforts to rebuild those parts of the infrastructure that the storm and flooding had decimated, and signs of hardship were ubiquitous. Bringing artists from far-flung parts of the world to New Orleans to develop new projects in a city that hadn't fully recovered from an epic disaster meant walking a narrow line between contributing to an overall community effort, while remaining

committed to the artists' capacities to communicate about their work and ideas. Empathy toward the often-bereft residents of neighborhoods like the Lower Ninth Ward—where thirteen artists eventually developed individual proposals at nine locations—was key to maintain.

During this period, I seem to have undergone a fundamental shift in how I understood the ways that artists invite us to use our senses to explore the social and cultural realities of our surrounding environments, and how we respond to that invitation. Before Prospect, it had seemed that nearly all public artworks functioned with an implicit understanding between artist and viewer that the work would not aspire to challenge the status quo and a galaxy of often-unspoken laws governing how the world operates would never be directly challenged by the artist. But in New Orleans, and in particular the Lower Ninth Ward, artists were inviting both visitors and local residents to make the same leaps of faith regarding what art was expected to accomplish and the extent to which reality itself could be upended.

Mark Bradford's *Mithra* (2008; Fig. 9) was a case in point. The three-story wooden

arc built out of construction-grade plywood was shipped from Los Angeles inside the same containers that provided ballast for the final work as it towered over windswept lots, which in pre-Katrina days were dense with single-family homes. It best embodied art's potential to reimagine not simply the state of the world in the present moment, but in the past and future as well. The question hanging over this neighborhood, where far too many people were trapped on their roofs for several days—"Why weren't there enough boats to rescue people?"— is transformed in Bradford's work to a wry forecast: "This is the boat we'll need."

For Wangechi Mutu, the moral offense embodied by the badly poured foundation where Sarah Lastie's home had stood pre-Katrina—she'd unknowingly hired fake contractors who then absconded with her money—could only be responded to with a process that ended in Lastie getting her house back. Using available wood and the existing foundation for a floor, the first phase of Mutu's contribution to the exhibition consisted of a quick-and-easy framing of the house on-site, strung with small lights that went on when darkness fell, making a ghostly outline of the

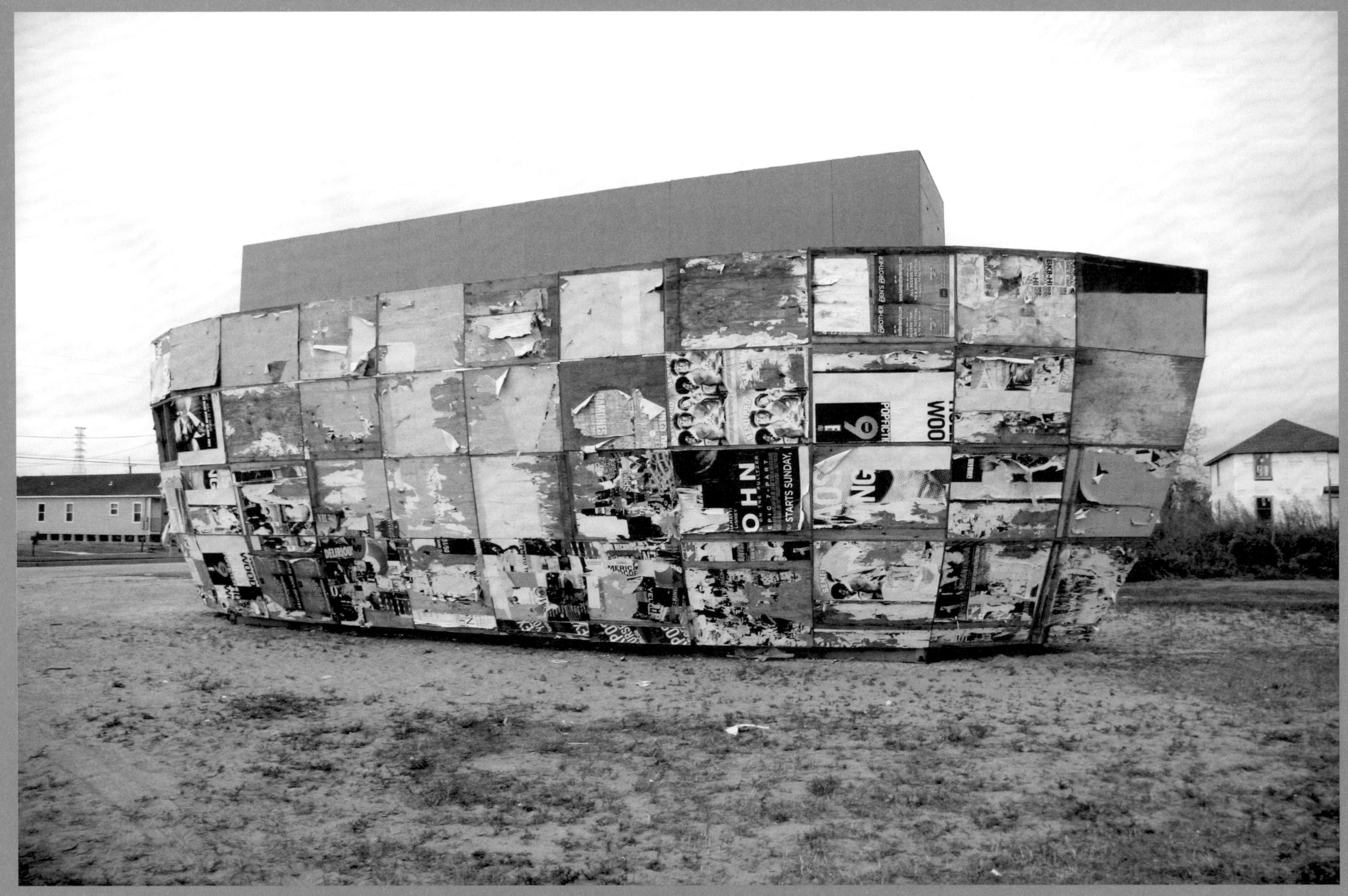

The Art of Surprise
Dan Cameron

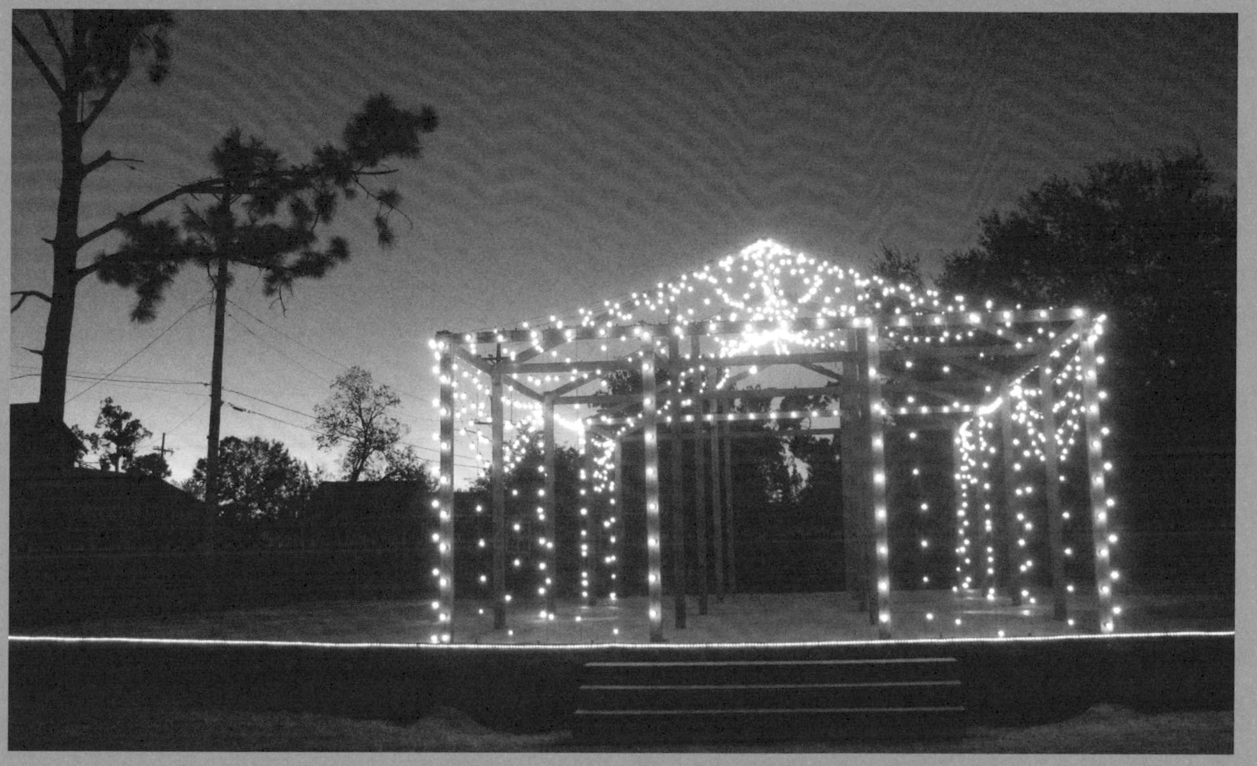

It isn't easy to categorize works like *Ms. Sarah's House* (2008; Fig. 10), in part because it occurs in stages, with each autonomous chapter revolving around a particular mode of artistic expression and targeted to a distinct group of receptors: collectors who acquired Mutu's etchings, say, along with Lastie's neighbors. But the process of developing the work began with a fundamental insight that artists are just like the rest of us, subject to the same whims of fate, injustice, and good fortune. Even if neither Bradford nor Mutu had lived through the experience of seeing their own neighborhoods washed away, they possessed both the empathy and the imagination to be able to reverse-engineer some small part of the post-Katrina aftermath. This resulted in a narrative centering on a few of the multiplicity of creative ways we can make our fellow humans' lives a bit easier. This is where the second insight into artists applies, namely that they aren't like the rest of us at all, if only because, regardless of how complex and multilayered the rationale or process for their works, the results that are generated are, in fact, artworks. The scale, shape, and surface of Bradford's

original house. The second phase consisted of producing two colored etchings based on this image and directing proceeds from the sale of both editions toward a fund set up in Lastie's name, making it possible for Mutu's participation in Prospect.1 to be followed, barely a year later, by the third phase: a housewarming for Lastie's permanent new home, back in her old neighborhood at last.

Mithra were all remarkably satisfying from an aesthetic perspective, just as Mutu's vision of an illuminated scarecrow of a house lingers in our visual memory long after the piece has been replaced by the more solid and comfortable home. In strictly vocational terms, both Bradford and Mutu are primarily recognized for their paintings, and it is their shared status as painters that, somewhat paradoxically, has provided them with the visual and conceptual tools to transform a knotty moral conundrum into a work of both visual and intellectual elegance.

Of the many public artworks over the past ten years that explore how art ultimately finds its audience, one of the most effective is Elmgreen and Dragset's permanent installation, *Prada Marfa* (2005; Fig. 11). Named both for the high-end Italian fashion empire and the small West Texas town where the late Donald Judd created some of his most important sculptures, the work stands alongside US Highway 90 about twenty-five miles from Marfa proper. Designed and built at the scale of a roadside farm stand, *Prada Marfa* conflates the values of exclusivity and remoteness by presenting what appears to be a miniaturized boutique along a stretch of road that is, if anything, even more remote than the town after which it's named. In fact, a typical encounter with the artwork consists of a blur glimpsed from one's car window (or rear-view mirror) while speeding by. It is at once a tribute to the pioneering artists of the 1960s and 1970s, who first developed the possibilities for art in rural areas of the US, and a parody of efforts on the part of certain local residents to appear rustic and unworldly.

Prada Marfa's impact derives not so much from seeing it in person as simply knowing it's there. Although it sells no actual merchandise, the roadside "boutique" seems to bask in its atmosphere of exclusivity, since even the act of decoding its tangled message requires a familiarity with luxury brands and art world behavior that qualifies it as the ultimate insider joke. And yet, by placing their work at such a dramatic remove from the art world's center of attention, the artists invite us to experience their creation either in passing, or in one's own imagination. By envisioning the art world as a safe place for artists to metaphorically bite the hand that feeds them, Elmgreen and Dragset's work also suggests that the confrontational spirit of Richard Serra's *Tilted Arc* has not vanished entirely. Instead, it has merely taken the form of an artwork that is irritating to some, amusing to others, and for the vast majority of viewers, seems to be a figment of the imagination, barely glimpsed out of the corner of the eye. ✳

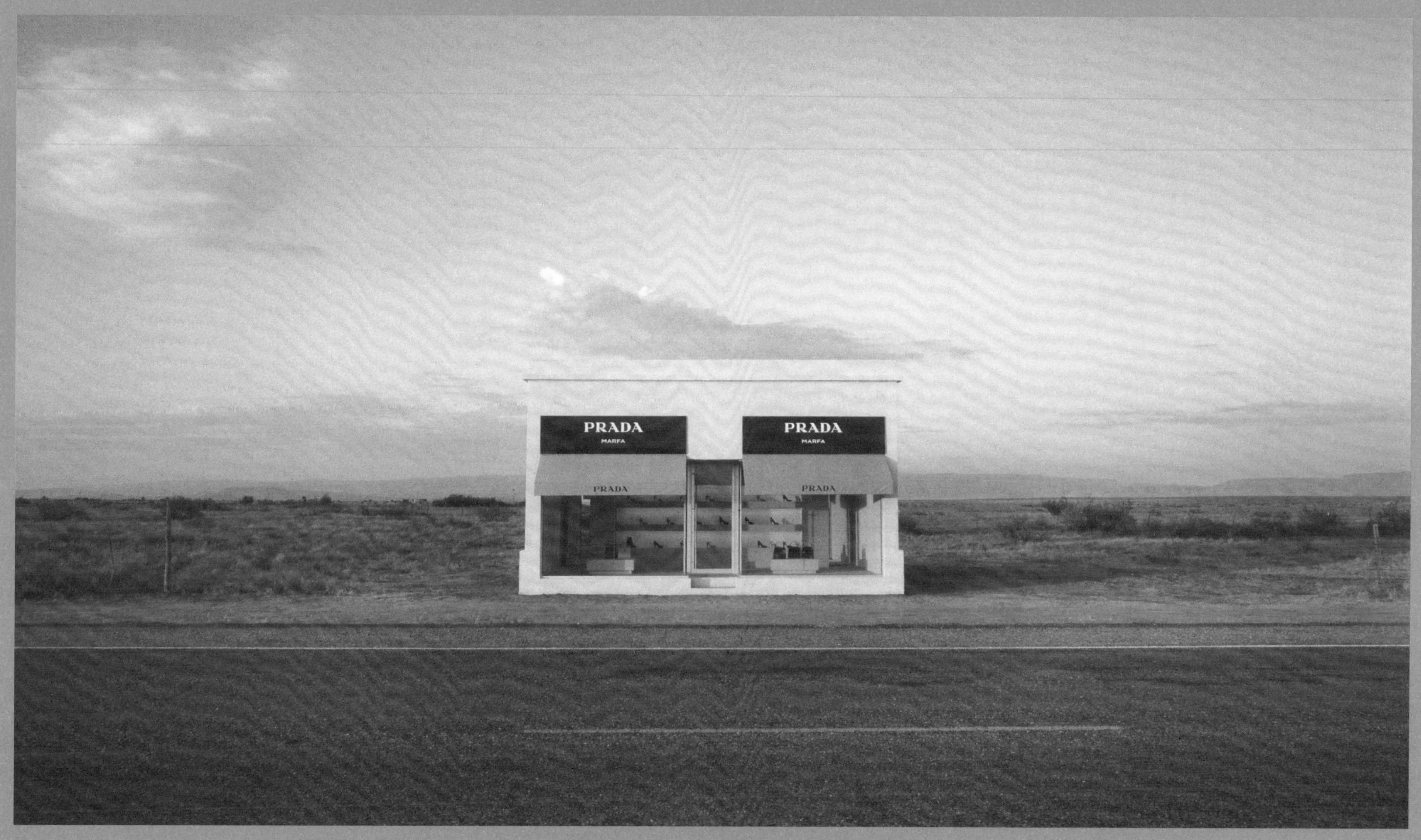

Fig. 11
Elmgreen & Dragset, _Prada Marfa_, 2005. Adobe bricks, plaster, aluminum frames, glass panes, MDF, paint, Prada shoes and bags, 299 1/5 x 185 x 188 9/10 in (760 x 470 x 480 cm). Courtesy Art Production Fund, New York, and Ballroom Marfa, Texas. Image: courtesy the artists and Galerie Perrotin, New York, Paris, and Hong Kong. Photo: James Evans

Aerial view of Aspen, Aspen Mountain, and Aspen
Highlands. Photo: Dan Bayer

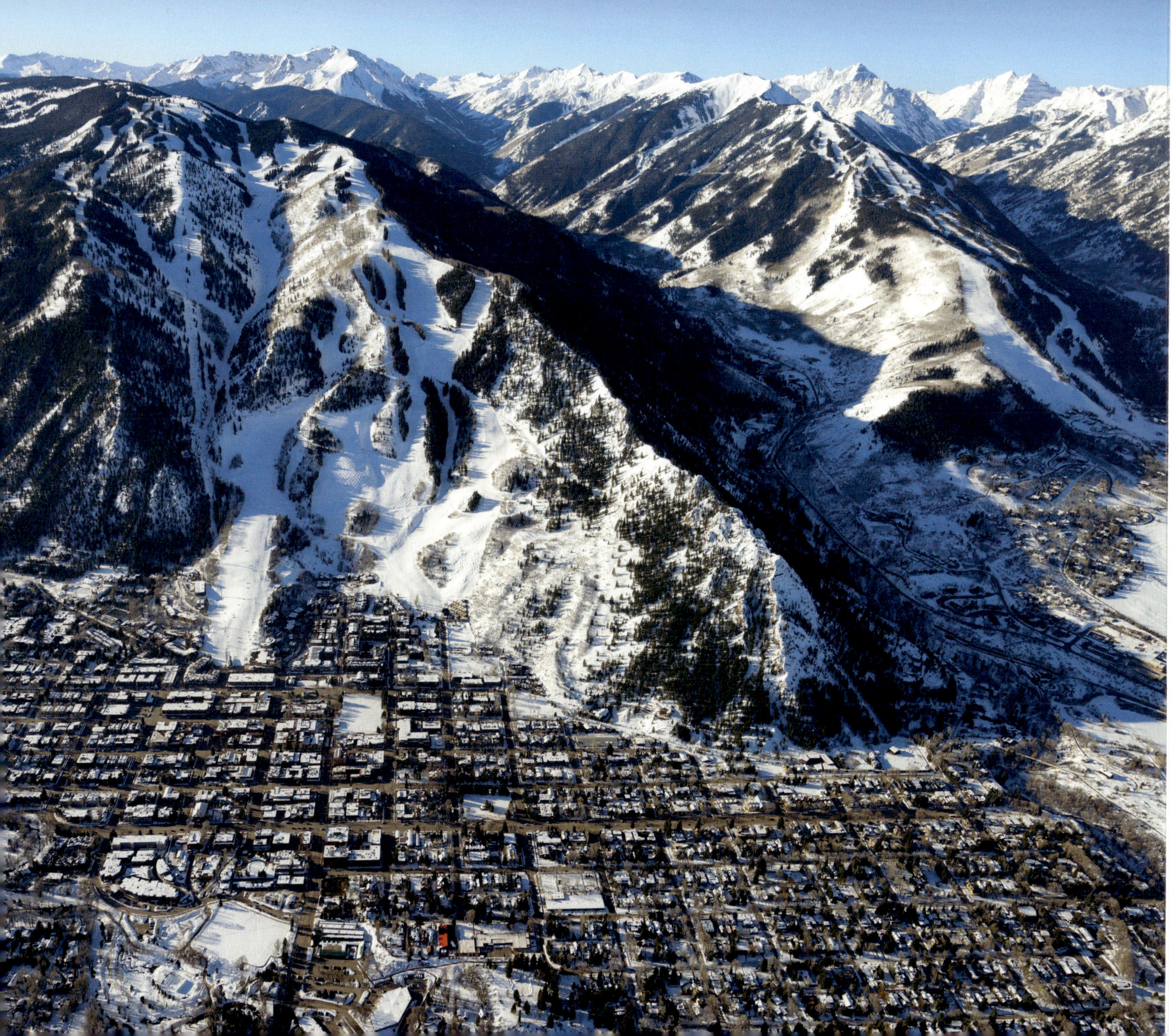

Project Timeline
2011–16

Lift Tickets

Mark Grotjahn

ASPEN SNOWMASS.

November 2011
April 2012

David Shrigley

ASPEN SNOWMASS.

PLEASE
DO NOT
SHOW
THIS TO
ANYONE

November 2012
April 2013

Elk Camp Installation

Dave Muller

November 2012
September 2013

Special Projects

Mark Grotjahn

November 2011
April 2012

Dave Muller

February 16–18, 2013

2011

2012

March 2012: ASC wins
Colorado Business Committee
for the Arts Award

2013

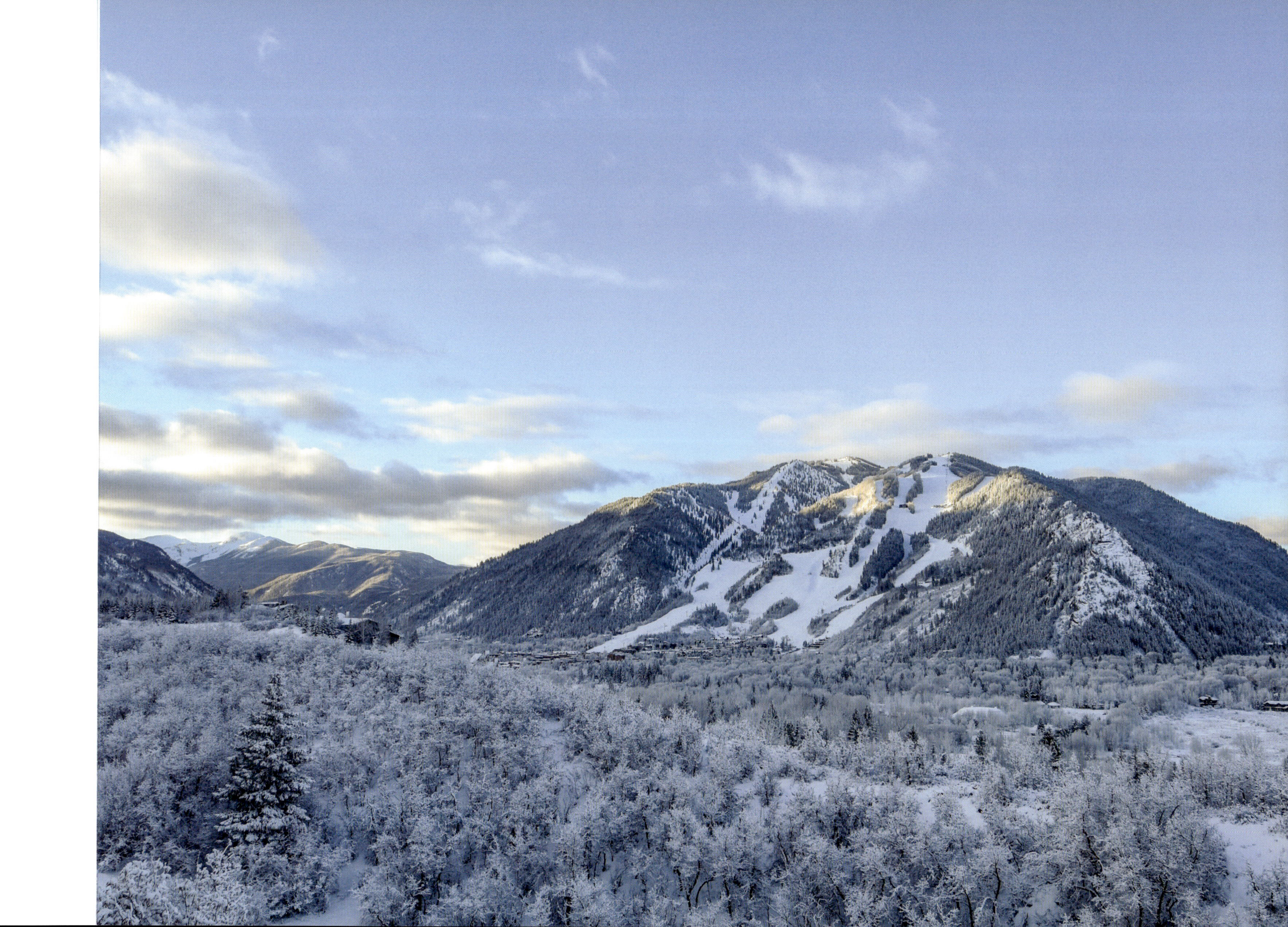

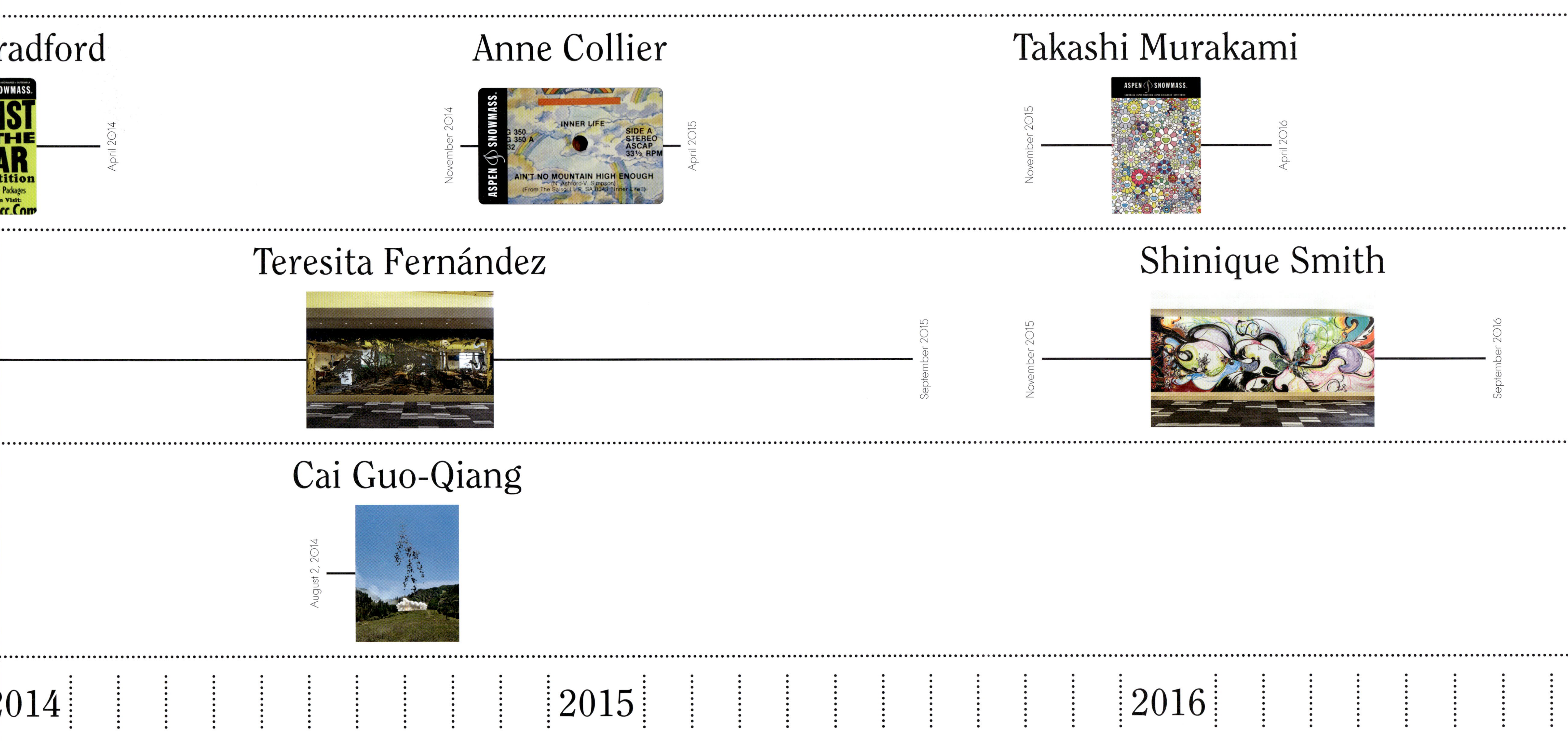
radford
Anne Collier
Takashi Murakami
April 2014
November 2014
April 2015
November 2015
April 2016
Teresita Fernández
Shinique Smith
September 2015
November 2015
September 2016
Cai Guo-Qiang
August 2, 2014
2014
2015
2016

Looking east toward Aspen Mountain and
Independence Pass. Photo: Tony Prikryl

Mark Grotjahn

2011–12 Lift Tickets & Installation on all Four Mountains and AAM Grounds

The following interview took place in February 2012 between Heidi Zuckerman and Mark Grotjahn on the occasion of his exhibition at the Aspen Art Museum.

Heidi Zuckerman

We had a conversation at one point where you explained that you have been a skier for a long time and that you always knew that part of your job would relate to skiing. I was hoping you could talk about your perspective on the lift tickets and the sculptures on the mountain.

Mark Grotjahn

When I heard that you guys were doing artist-designed tickets, I knew I had to do that. Somehow, I had to do a season—I always kept that in the back of my mind as something that needed to be accomplished.

When you came to my studio, I liked the way that you talked about my work, but we didn't talk about the tickets. It was only later that you brought up the possibility of doing the ticket, which of course, I was looking forward to doing.

HZ

It's nice when things work out that way!

Let's talk about your exhibition for a few minutes. I really wanted to have the opportunity to bring a curatorial perspective to the work that you've been making over the last eleven years. Although you make sculptures and drawings, we decided that the show would focus on paintings.

The exhibition is really focused on two distinct bodies of work and it draws some parallels between them. What were some of your first impressions on coming into the space and seeing your show here for the first time?

MG

The different colors, sizes, and bodies of work looked great together. I hadn't seen them in a long time. And I've never seen them that close together with the various sizes right next to each other. That really opened my eyes.

HZ

You have figured out how to balance color, composition, and texture in your paintings. When you were talking about the earliest work in the show, *Untitled (Three Tiered Perspective)* from 1998 [Fig. 1], you said that when you painted this,

you remembered the paint being really thick in its application.

The show also includes some of your most recent work that also has a really thick application of paint. Maybe you could talk a little bit about how you work with the paint.

MG

Right. *Three Tiered Perspective* starts out with primed linen over board—I was making my canvases in those days and that was the way I could get the best rectangle.

I would draw out the horizontal lines and the triangles in pencil and then I would pick colors. I would mix colors and do one triangle at a time and then go through and see what might work next. Occasionally, I would change the color of a triangle, but very rarely.

I was definitely thinking about color. I was thinking about Gauguin and the tropics, even though I'm not sure I see that anymore. I didn't see these as representational. I saw them as completely nonrepresentational, even though everybody else saw either the sun or the road. Of course, this is a traditional way of doing the sun or the road, like you see on the raisin packaging. But when I put them out there, I thought I was doing something really sophisticated with color, but the reviews and reactions I got were that I was deliberately trying to make bad paintings. But I was definitely trying to make good paintings, successful or not.

HZ

I find your work to be really sincere, so the implication that you would intentionally try and do something that wasn't your best seems off the mark.

MG

That's often the case with the work that I do. At first, it's seen as a "fuck you" and then that disappears.

HZ

When you were applying the color, you did each triangle, but you didn't necessarily know what color was going to come next?

MG

As I remember it, that was the case. Maybe I knew that the next three triangles were going to be browns or greens, or I was going to do blue-orange-blue, but I certainly didn't know five triangles on.

They took significantly longer than the butterfly paintings.

The butterfly series was more monochromatic, for the most part. I made my first butterfly piece in 2001. Technically, it happened because I wanted to do some horizontal paintings. But when I finished my first one, I couldn't handle it being horizontal so I decided to hang it vertically. For whatever reason, I'm drawn more to vertical painting.

The next one I decided to paint like a butterfly—where both perspectives face each other. It really felt like it became nonobjective painting. In some ways, I felt like I was even better able to indulge myself in painting when what had been seen as roads disappeared.

HZ

When any references were gone?

MG

Right. Also, because the critics had claimed that I didn't know what I was doing with color and that I wasn't good at color, part of me decided that I would show them what I could do. I would use the colors that are considered to be the sophisticated ones,

because of course, bright colors aren't sophisticated, so I would use blacks and whites. It was the first time I decided that I cared what people thought—after ten bad reviews, I finally cared.

HZ

Untitled (Yellow White Butterfly Mark 02) (2002; Fig. 2) is a gradient of white, but it has greens, grays, and yellows, as well as a vertical element, which appears as though it's a reference to Barnett Newman's zip paintings. And then there are the vertical strips on the sides. I'm curious about that, because not all the butterflies have these. Is it about containing the work and giving it a framing device?

MG

In terms of the butterfly paintings, there are only a few that don't have it, and they are really small. It comes out of the *Three Tiered Perspective*. I did the lines like that because it just didn't look good to have the triangles on top of the triangles. Although I did end up losing the bands on the sides with the drawings.

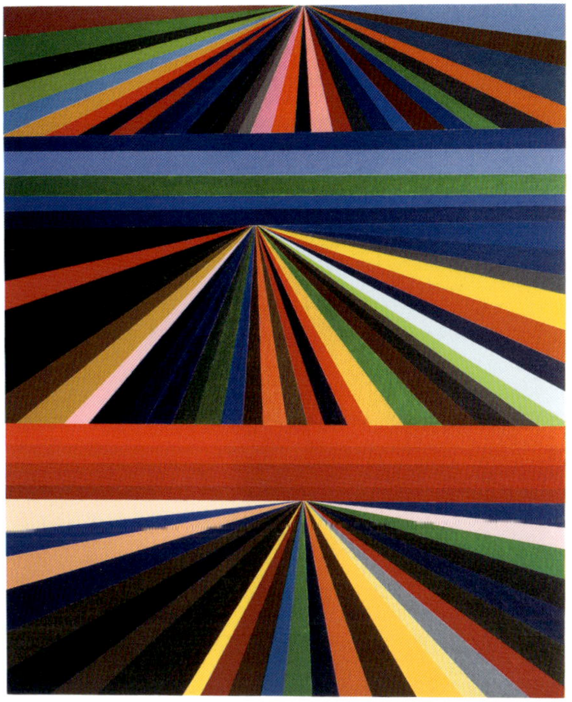

HZ

It seems as though you pay attention to the sides of the canvases, particularly in some of the more recent works where there's a painterly quality along with your fingerprints or some kind of palette references. We were looking at one of the works that has text along the side and you were talking about not wanting the text to extend all the way to the edge of the frame. And *Yellow White Butterfly Mark 02* has

your name in the four corners. Why did you decide to do that?

MG

To put my name in was specific to LA. The conceptual work that was being done there was very anti the artist's ego and anti the name of the artist, but every conceptual artist that started to get something going had a very specific style.

I don't know if this is to justify it, but I talked to Allan Kaprow about taking pictures of the Happenings and he explained how he gave the cameras to his friends. They would take pictures and pretend like they didn't know what they were doing, so they would have a specific aesthetic. It was really nice to hear that there were aesthetic choices— aesthetic choices are conceptual choices. To do something like that, to put your ideas out there and have it look like that, means something.

Visually, I think it's satisfying because of the color, but also because of the difference in the surface and the reveal; and it's satisfying because it draws you in and you look at the way that it's painted. It's one of my favorite things

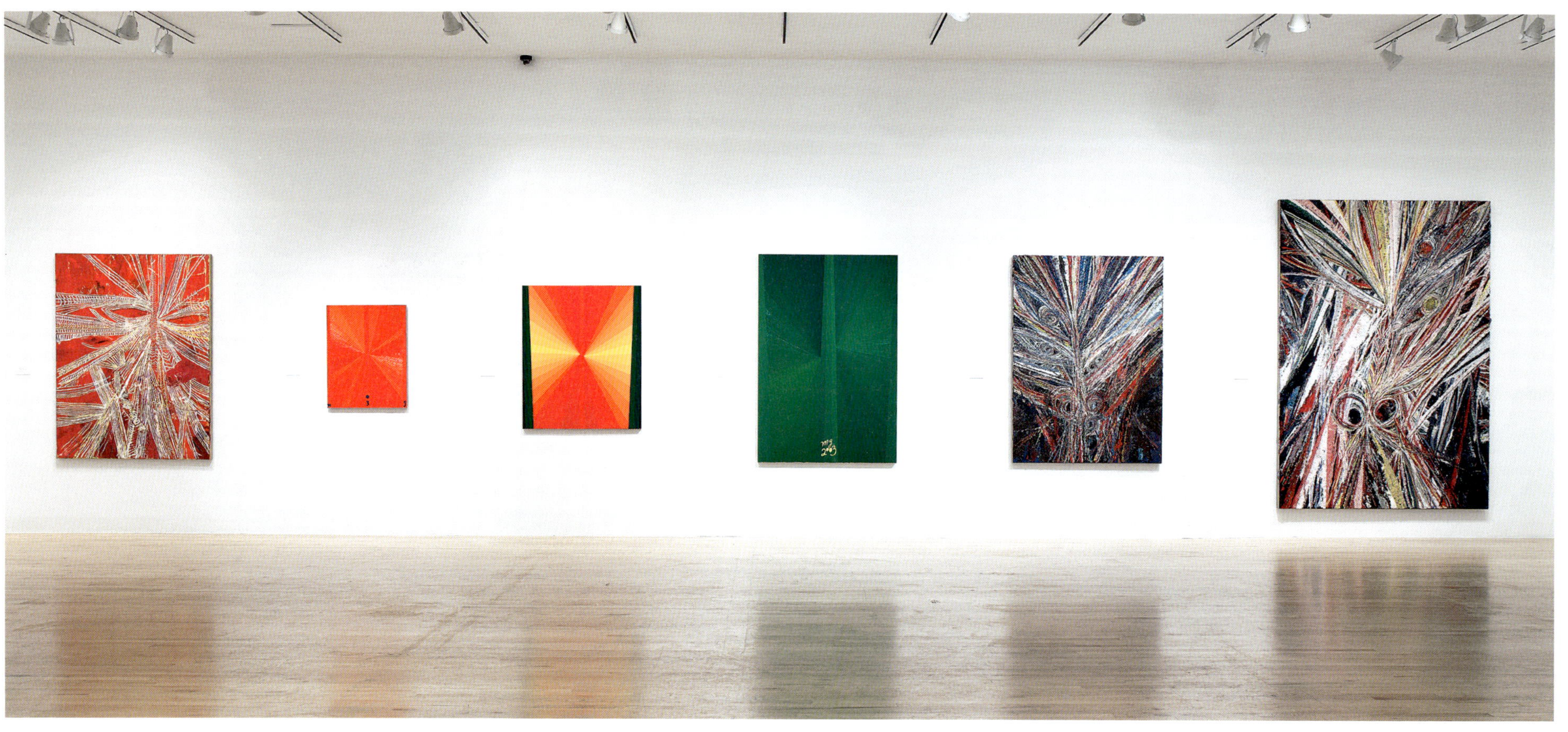

to paint. I get out maybe nine different sized brushes and I just dab it in there. It's really like being a dentist, and I paint around the letters that I've drawn and smooth around it.

HZ
Sometimes your initials are block letters, sometimes they're bubble letters, and sometimes they're script. And the date, referencing the year of the work, also becomes an element of the composition. It's also an indication of what the paintings were before they were finished, because they're different colors.

Mark Grotjahn
2011–12

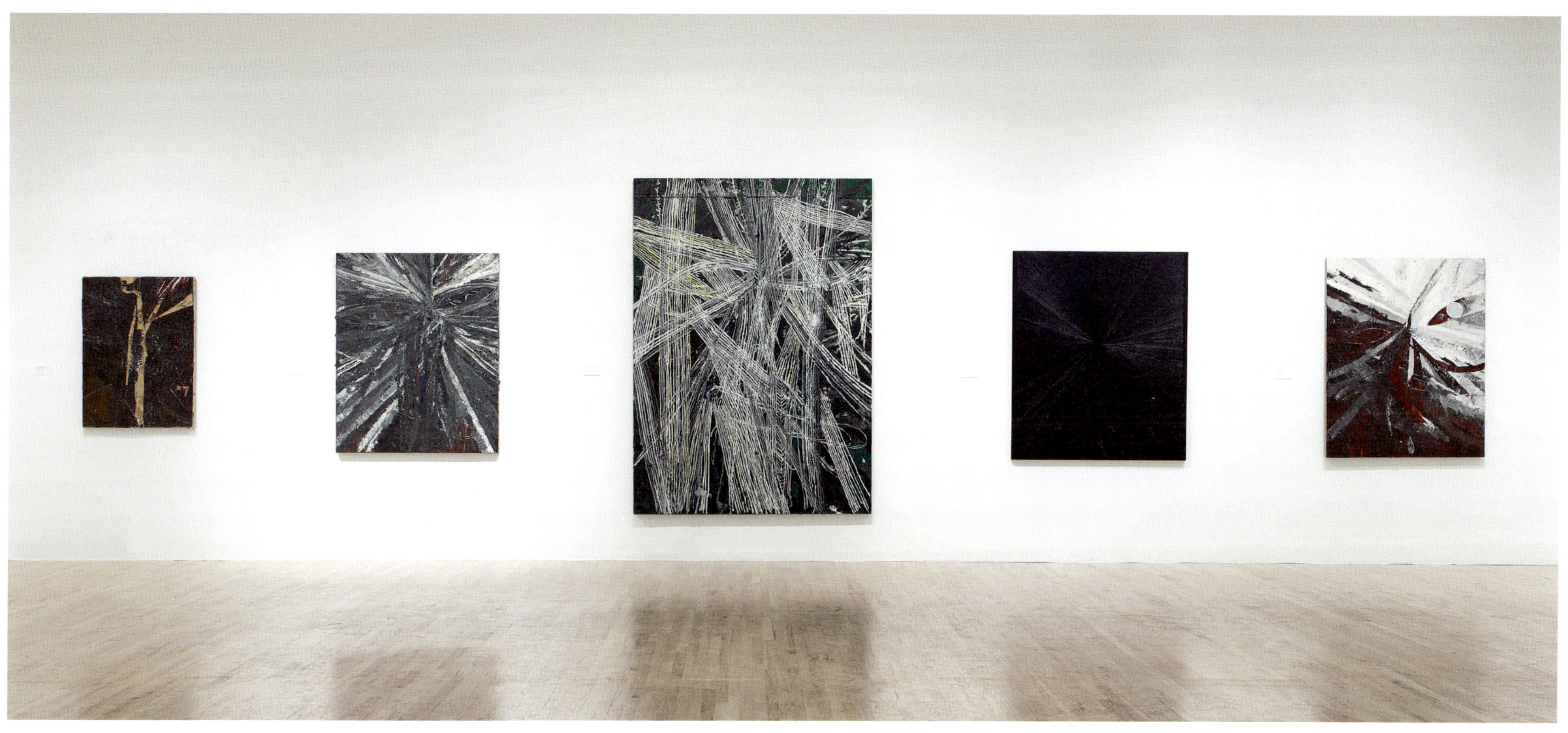

MG

It reveals the first layer of paint. All of the butterflies have just two layers of paint. There's an under-painting, and then I draw the triangles out and fill each triangle in just once with one thick layer. I paint around the letters and I always paint the triangles counterclockwise,

to see the painting disappear. Some of them have backgrounds that are like Ed Ruscha landscapes. With the black paintings, it was like I was bringing them into night—it was very satisfying. Where all the triangles meet at the center looks really nice when there's a color behind it, as opposed to it just being white.

HZ

Right. There's often a residue. I had always assumed that the first layer of paint was monochromatic, but sometimes it's not?

MG

I did the landscape so it would have a yellow base, and there's a small one in the show that is yellow at the top and then it goes to orange, like a Ruscha sunset. I always wanted to be a Neo-Expressionist, so sometimes I paint these big faces on them and then cover them up. Sometimes, you can see traces of them, like the glimmer of an eye. I've got all these little secrets in my work that I say aren't important, but then I talk about them.

HZ
I think they are important.

In *Untitled (Green Butterfly Yellow MG)* (2003; Fig. 3), the vertical element has some of its own perspective. The line is thinner at the top and thicker at the bottom, or goes from dark to light, which gives an illusion of it being circular. When you paint them counterclockwise and one triangle at a time, do you know what the color variations will be when you start?

MG
A lot of times, I would let them get lighter and then slowly bring them back to a darker color—systematically, but intuitively. I might reach a point where I decide that it's time to make it darker.

HZ
And you can tell the slight variations in tonality because you mix the paint yourself?

MG
Right, I have a recipe. I don't know if I always did, but I know with these, I would write down how much I had put in. *Untitled (Tequila Sunrise)* (2003; Fig. 4) is the only butterfly painting where I started in the middle—on both sides—and then I worked out. It was based on a bug I stepped on in Mexico. I don't know if I stepped on a green bug that had red legs that then went to little yellow feet, but it gave me permission to indulge in colors the way you see them in nature.

HZ
Tequila Sunrise has a really different title compared to all of your other paintings.

MG
It goes back to being in Mexico, but also to the movie.

HZ
I was thinking about the drink…

MG
I think it looks like the drink too.

HZ
I've also talked about how important *Untitled (Grey Face 778)* (2009; Fig. 5) is, in my perspective, to your work. I wonder what your perspective is on this painting?

MG
It's hugely important to me, too. At the time, all the faces had been made with paintbrushes. There is still some paintbrush action in it, but basically, this was one that had gone through a number of layers. I worked on it for a few years and would carve the cardboard off until I got down to the last piece of paper in the cardboard, except for the top part. Then, somehow, I managed to make a painting in two days and feel good about it, and that was really amazing. The way I was doing it with the palette knife and taking my hand out of it was very freeing.

I started with the butterfly pattern just to put paint onto the cardboard and begin with something—not knowing that it would be retained in the way that it was. It's one of my favorite paintings, because it came easy and just felt right.

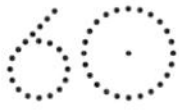

Mark Grotjahn
2011–12

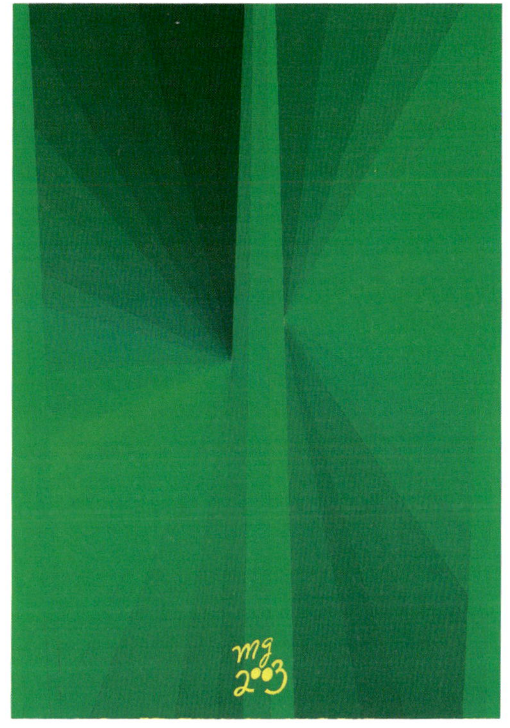

Fig. 3
Mark Grotjahn, Untitled <u>(Green Butterfly Yellow MG)</u>, 2003. Oil on linen, 73 x 49 in (185.4 x 124.5 cm). Courtesy the artist and Anton Kern Gallery, NY. Collection of David Teiger. Photo: Thomas Müller

Fig. 4
Mark Grotjahn, <u>Untitled (Tequila Sunrise)</u>, 2003. Oil on linen, 50 x 40 in (127 x 101.6 cm). Courtesy the artist and Anton Kern Gallery, NY. Collection of Milton and Sheila Fine. Photo: Adam Reich

Fig. 5
Mark Grotjahn, <u>Untitled (Grey Face 778)</u>, 2009. Oil on cardboard mounted in linen, 60 x 48 in (152.4 x 121.9 cm). Courtesy the artist. Photo: Douglas M. Parker

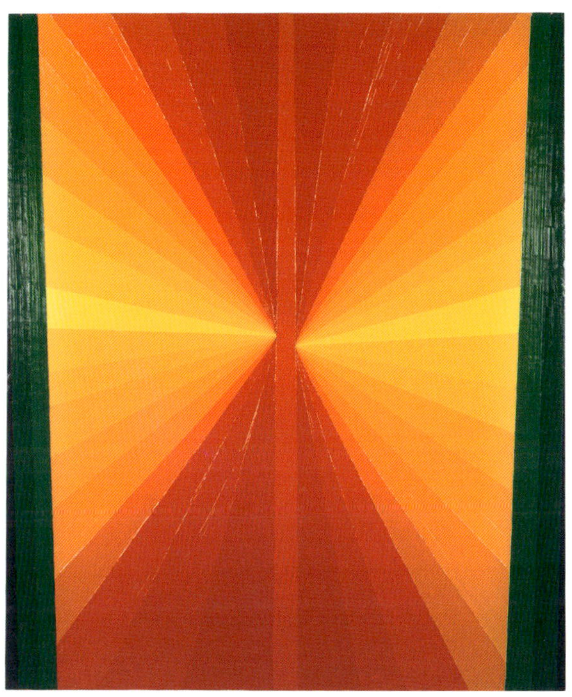

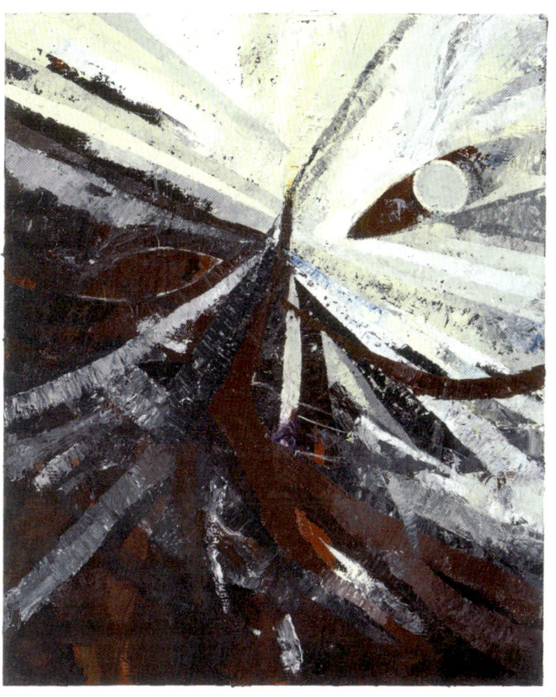

HZ
For me, it's a combination of these two iconic styles and painting practices that you have.

MG
That was definitely the jump.

HZ
That's what I think too. Then there are a couple of more idiosyncratic and eccentric works in the show. *Untitled (Face on Palette)* (2007; Fig. 6) retains the masking

tape on the edges—you said it served as a palette—and there's text in it too.

MG
Right. I would cover the tables with paper or museum board, and then tape it down so I could put linseed oil or whatever on it. I always save the paper or board, and then I decided to paint on this one. I took notes on it, too.

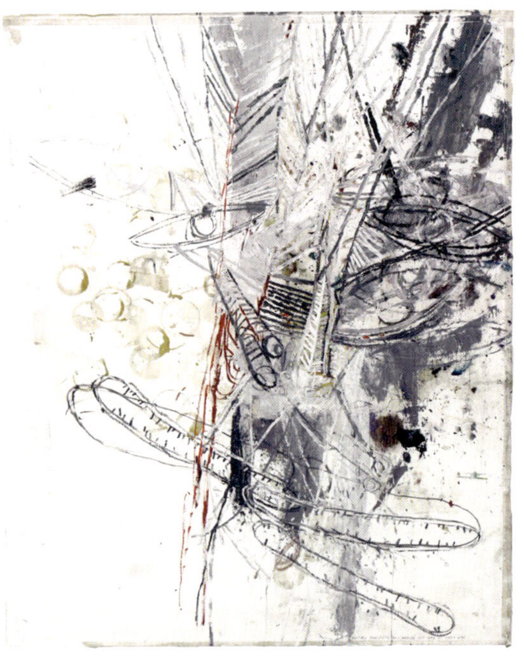

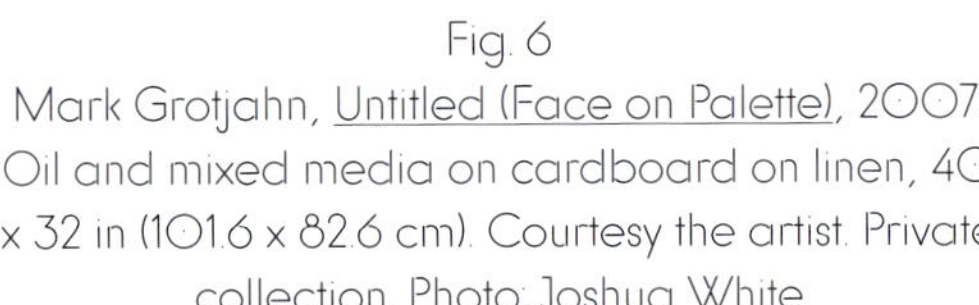

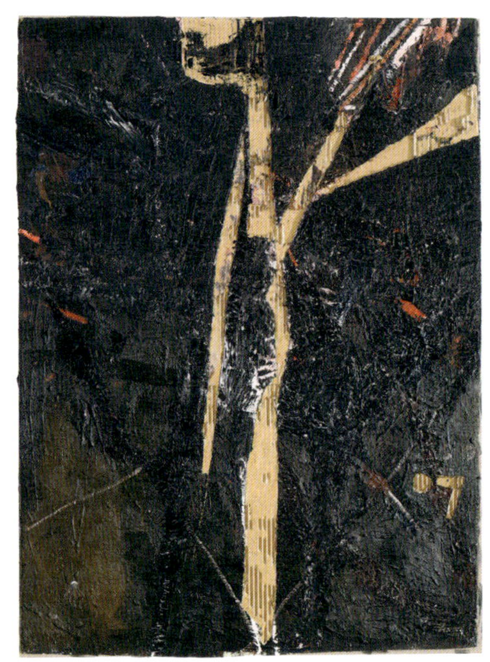

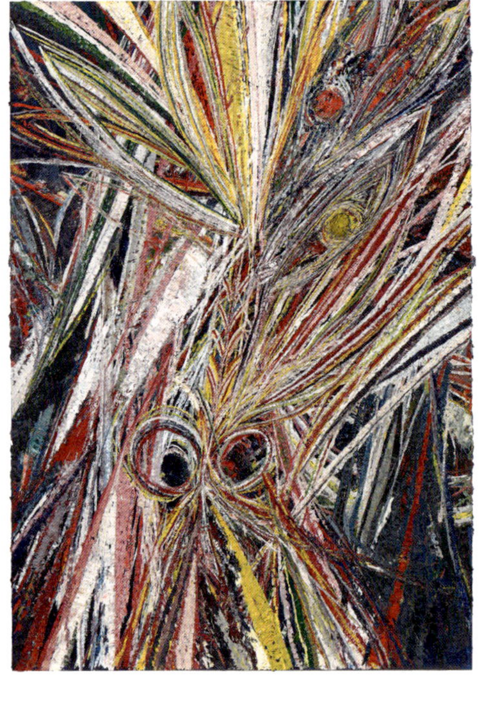

Fig. 6
Mark Grotjahn, Untitled (Face on Palette), 2007.
Oil and mixed media on cardboard on linen, 40
x 32 in (101.6 x 82.6 cm). Courtesy the artist. Private
collection. Photo: Joshua White

Fig. 7
Mark Grotjahn, Untitled (Carve Room 702 Memories
of the Nile 737), 2007. Oil on cardboard on linen
mounted on panel, 45 1/2 x 33 in (115.6 x 83.8 cm).
Courtesy the artist. Photo: Robert McKeever

Fig. 8
Mark Grotjahn, Untitled (Geo Abstract Reveal Face
41.61), 2011. Oil on cardboard mounted on linen,
108 1/4 x 73 1/8 in (275 x 186.1 cm). Courtesy the artist.
Photo: Douglas M. Parker

HZ
There are appointments, song titles, and things like that.

MG
Like "Psychiatrist, 3 O'Clock."

HZ
Right. The multiple eyes are a key signifier of your work—they are something that is more easily readable—but there's a mouth element in this piece that also shows up in later works as a disassembled part of the elements. These mouths play a subtler role—there's always a reference to them, but they're not always as apparent as the eyes—however, they are significant as well.

MG
That's true.

HZ
I have this theory that all artworks are actually self-portraits.

MG

Self-portraits and latent sexuality.

HZ

Right, you've got both of them.

Untitled (Carve Room 702 Memories of the Nile 737) (2007; Fig. 7) is another very unusual work that's in the show.

MG

I could see myself doing more work like this, and seeing it in the show reminds me that my work can get a lot better and more aggressive in different ways. I think there was supposed to be a face in it at one point, and then I carved the date in and it just felt good. I planned on going back and making a whole series, but I never have.

The title comes from when I had a gallery in the late nineties with a friend of mine, and we saw some really nice cement floor under the tile so we chipped it all away. After a day and a half of revealing this beautiful terrazzo, we hit dirt and then we hit more dirt, and it was probably from a busted sewer line. It went the whole length of the gallery, so we called it "The Nile."

HZ

The most recent work in the show, *Untitled (Geo Abstract Reveal Face 41.61)* (2011; Fig. 8), has lots of very thick paint.

MG

Surprisingly thick. I didn't remember it as being that thick. I feel like it resembles the Post-Impressionist painters that I like, who made small paintings that could really hold a room. This is a bigger painting, but with beautiful colors. It's not painted like they painted, but it has a relationship to it. I like the colors. I like Monet. It's as close as I get to Monet at this point. ✳

Born in Pasadena, California, in 1968, Mark Grotjahn studied at Skowhegan School of Painting and Sculpture, Maine, the University of California, Berkeley, and the University of Colorado, Boulder. Grotjahn currently lives and works in Los Angeles. He has had one-person exhibitions at distinguished institutions such as the Kunstverein Freiburg, Germany; Nasher Sculpture Center, Dallas, Texas (both 2014); Aspen Art Museum (2012); Portland Art Museum, Oregon (2010); Kunstmuseum Thun, Switzerland (2007); and the Whitney Museum of American Art, New York (2006). His work has been included in major group exhibitions including The Forever Now: Contemporary Painting in an Atemporal World, Museum of Modern Art, New York (2014); Variations: Conversations in and Around Abstract Painting, Los Angeles County Museum of Art (2014); Contemporary Painting, 1960 to the Present, San Francisco Museum of Modern Art (2012); The Artist's Museum, Museum of Contemporary Art, Los Angeles (2010); Benches and Binoculars, Walker Art Center, Minneapolis (2010); Saints and Sinners, Rose Art Museum, Brandeis University, Massachusetts (2009); and Eyes Wide Open, Stedelijk Museum, Amsterdam, Netherlands (2008); amongst many others.

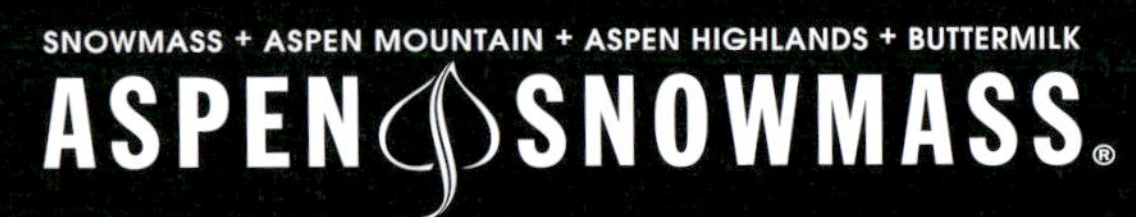
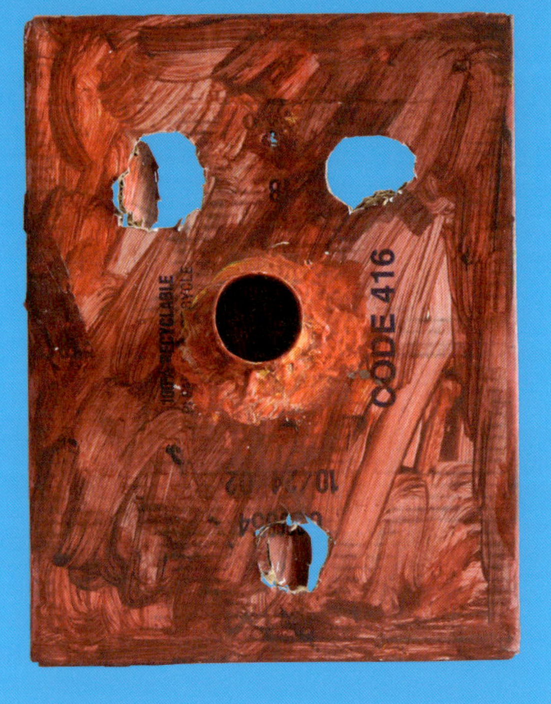

Lift Ticket: Mark Grotjahn, <u>Untitled (Red Mask 41.92)</u>, 2004–5

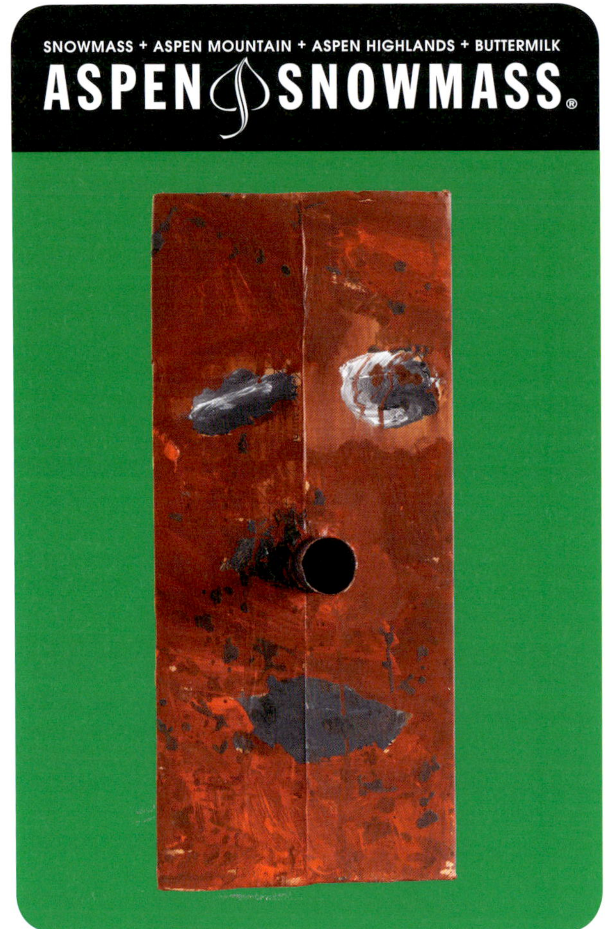

Lift Ticket: Mark Grotjahn, <u>Untitled (Red with Grey Freckle Mask 43.11)</u>, 2011

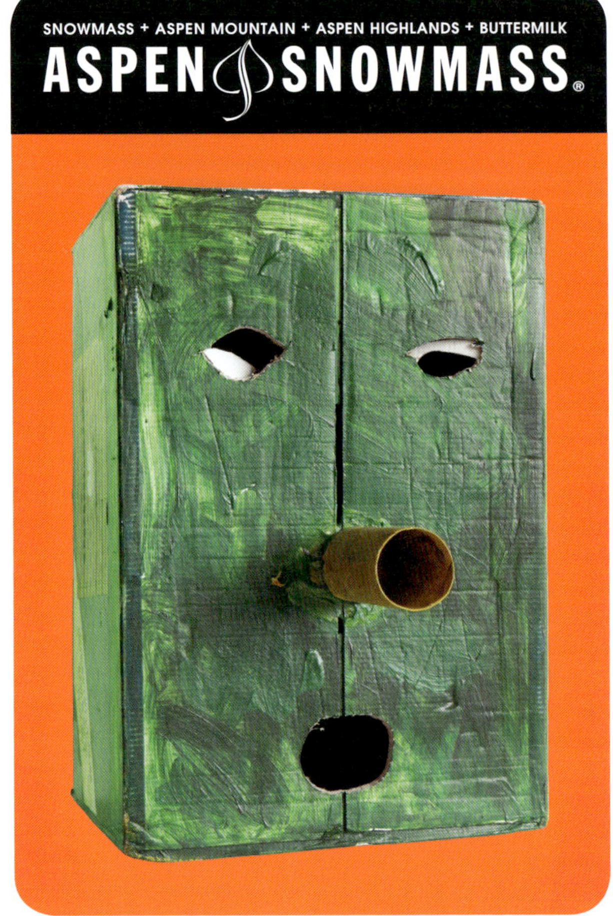

Lift Ticket: Mark Grotjahn, <u>Untitled (Green with Yellow Nose Mask 43.10)</u>, 2004

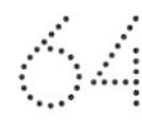

Mark Grotjahn
2011–12

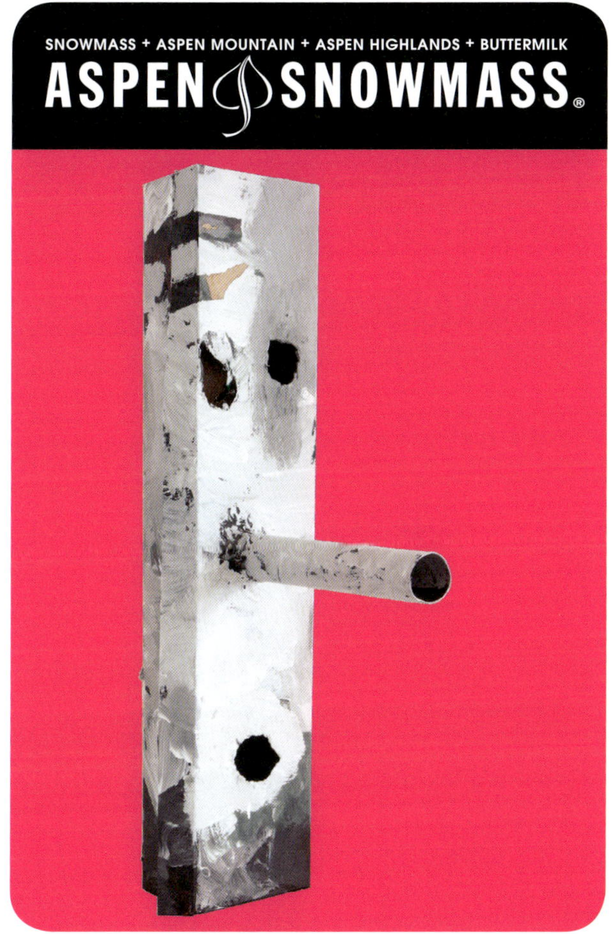

Lift Ticket: Mark Grotjahn, <u>Untitled (Skinny Big Nose Mask 43.12)</u>, 2011

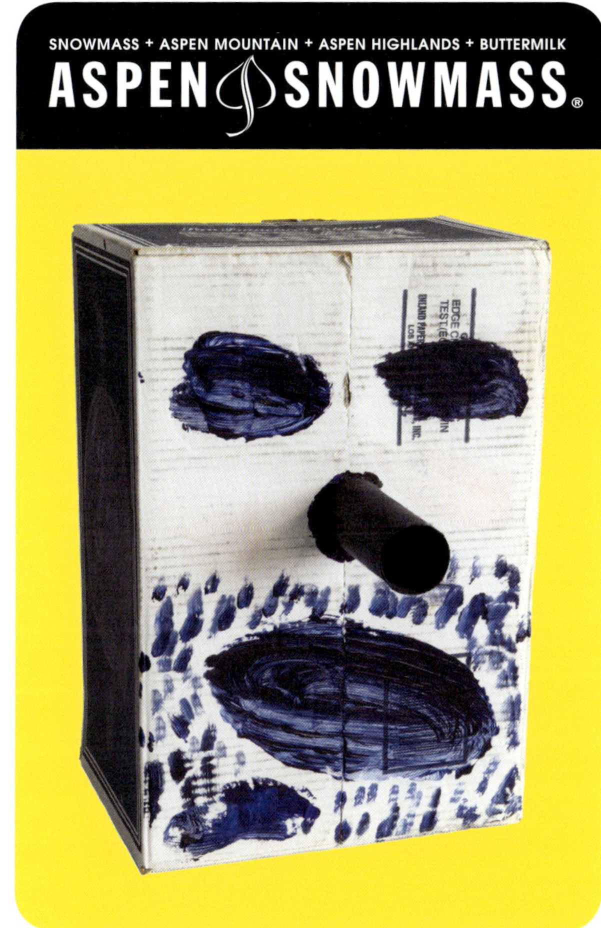

Lift Ticket: Mark Grotjahn, <u>Untitled (Blue Anchor Steam Wedding Mask 4194)</u>, 2004

For the 2011–12 ski season in Aspen, Grotjahn designed five limited-edition lift tickets that feature his animated mask sculptures. Extending the artist's focus on the ritual of painting into three dimensions, the five mask sculptures were also on view around Aspen—one on the grounds of the museum and one on each of the peaks of the Aspen Skiing Company's four ski mountains.

All works acrylic and collage on cardboard.
Courtesy the artist

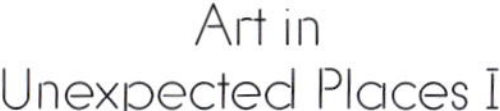

Art in
Unexpected Places II

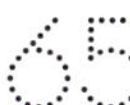

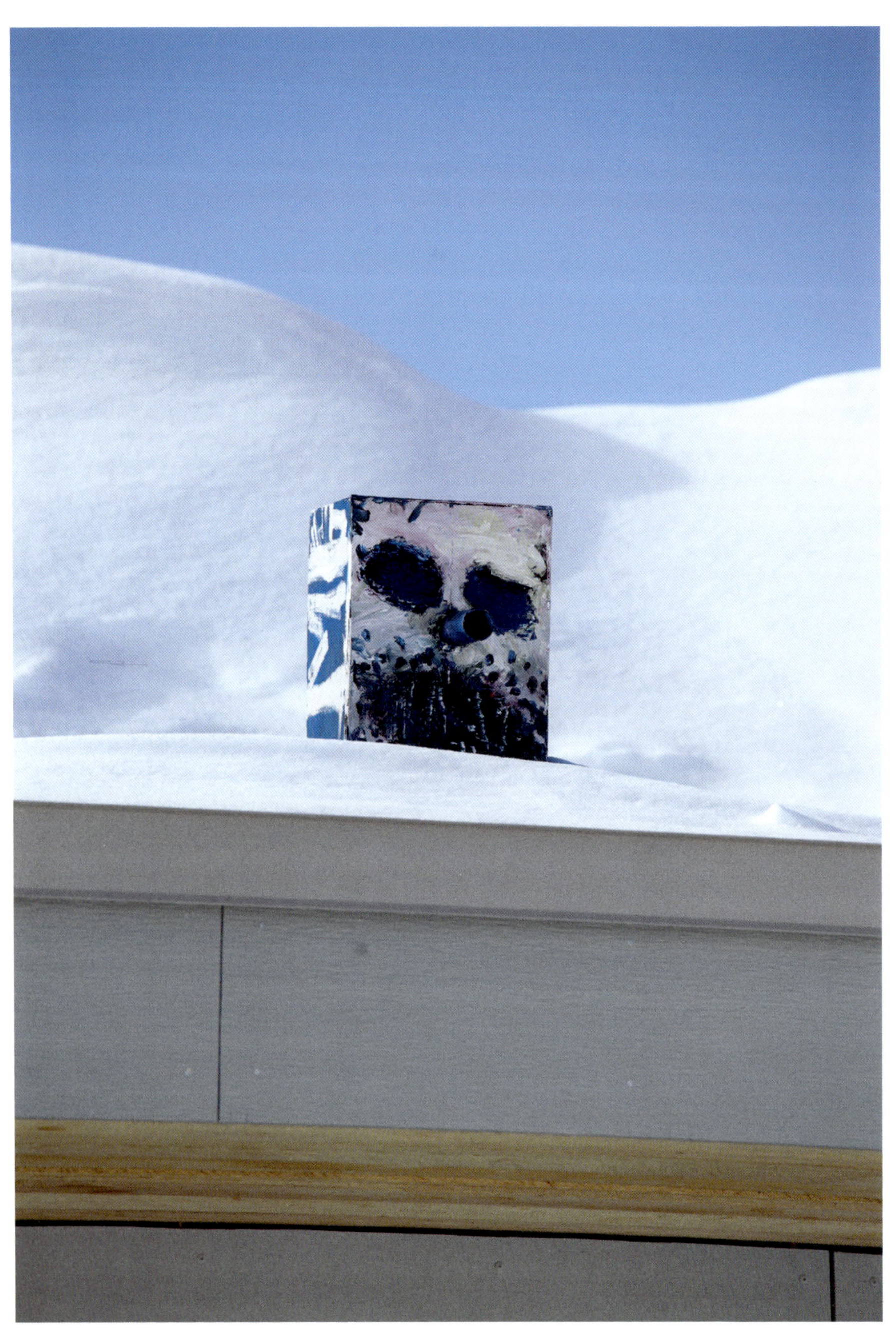

Installation views: Mark Grotjahn, <u>Untitled (Blue and White Wedding Mask M19.a)</u>, 2011. Painted bronze, 16 1/2 x 8 x 11 in (41.9 x 20.3 x 28.6 cm). Buttermilk Mountain. Photos: Jeremy Swanson

Mark Grotjahn
2011–12

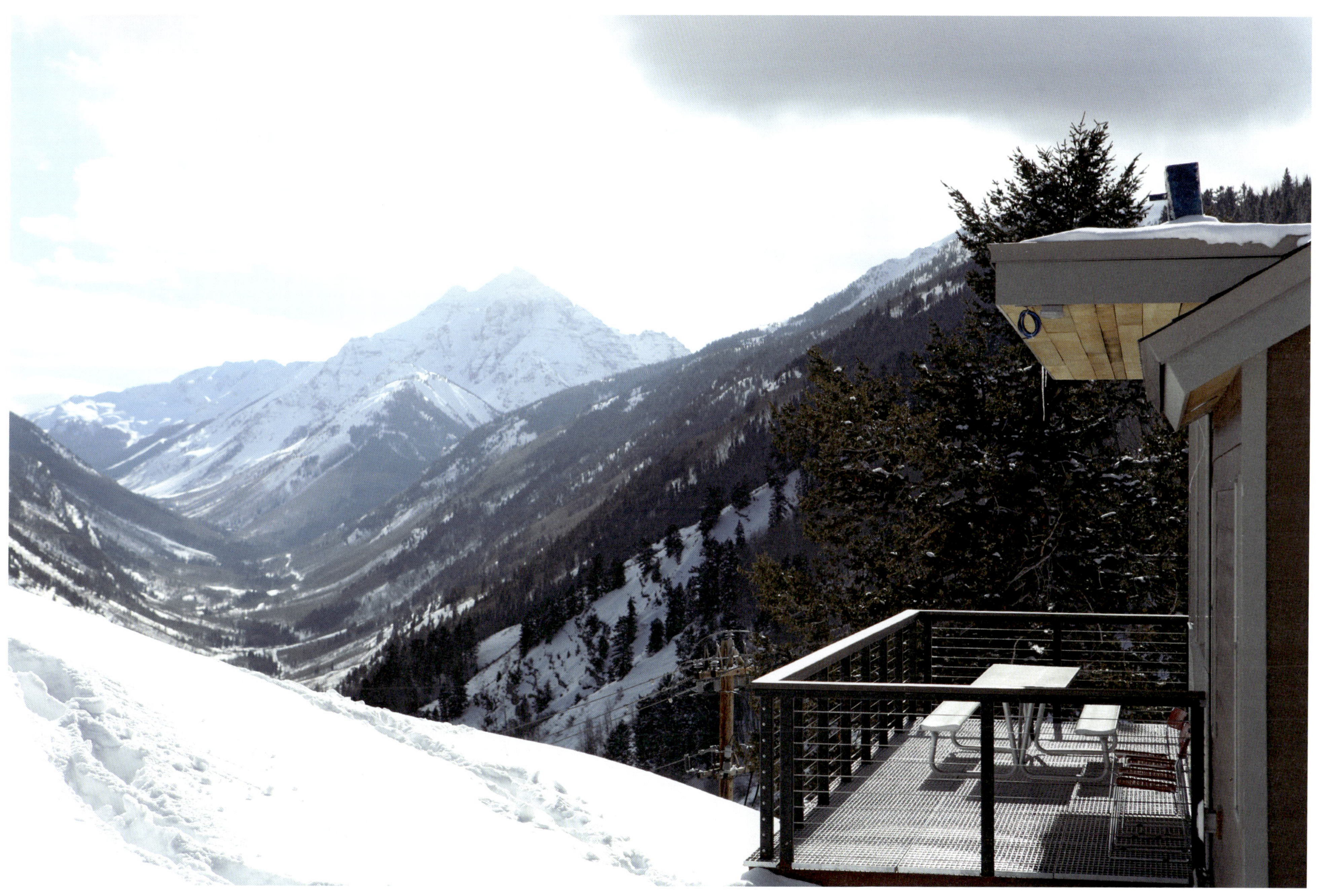

Art in
Unexpected Places II

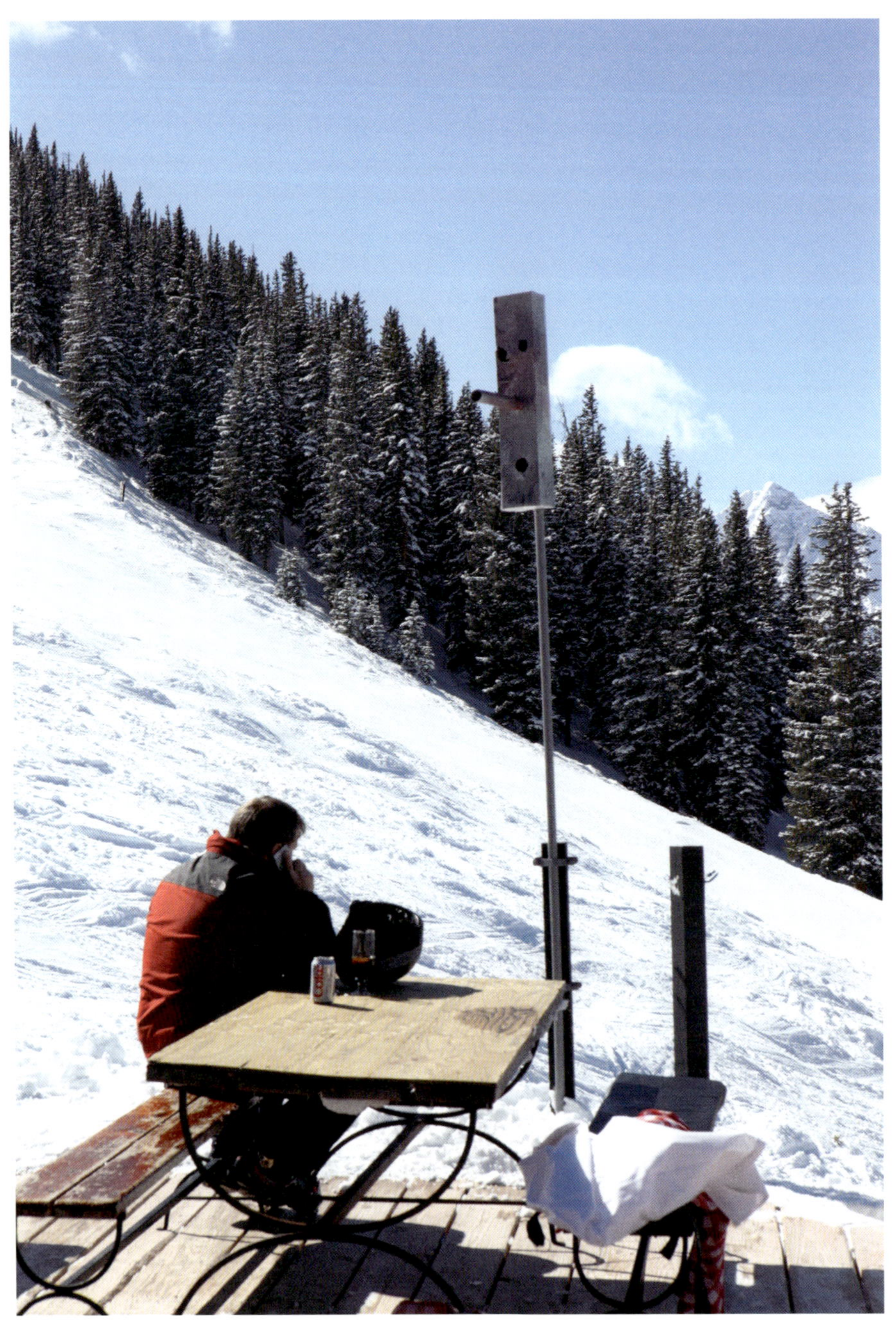

Installation views: Mark Grotjahn, <u>Untitled (Tall Skinny Big Nose Mask M12.a)</u>, 2011. Painted bronze, 29 1/2 x 6 1/2 in (74.9 x 16.5 cm). Highlands Mountain. Photos: Jeremy Swanson

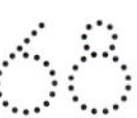

Mark Grotjahn
2011–12

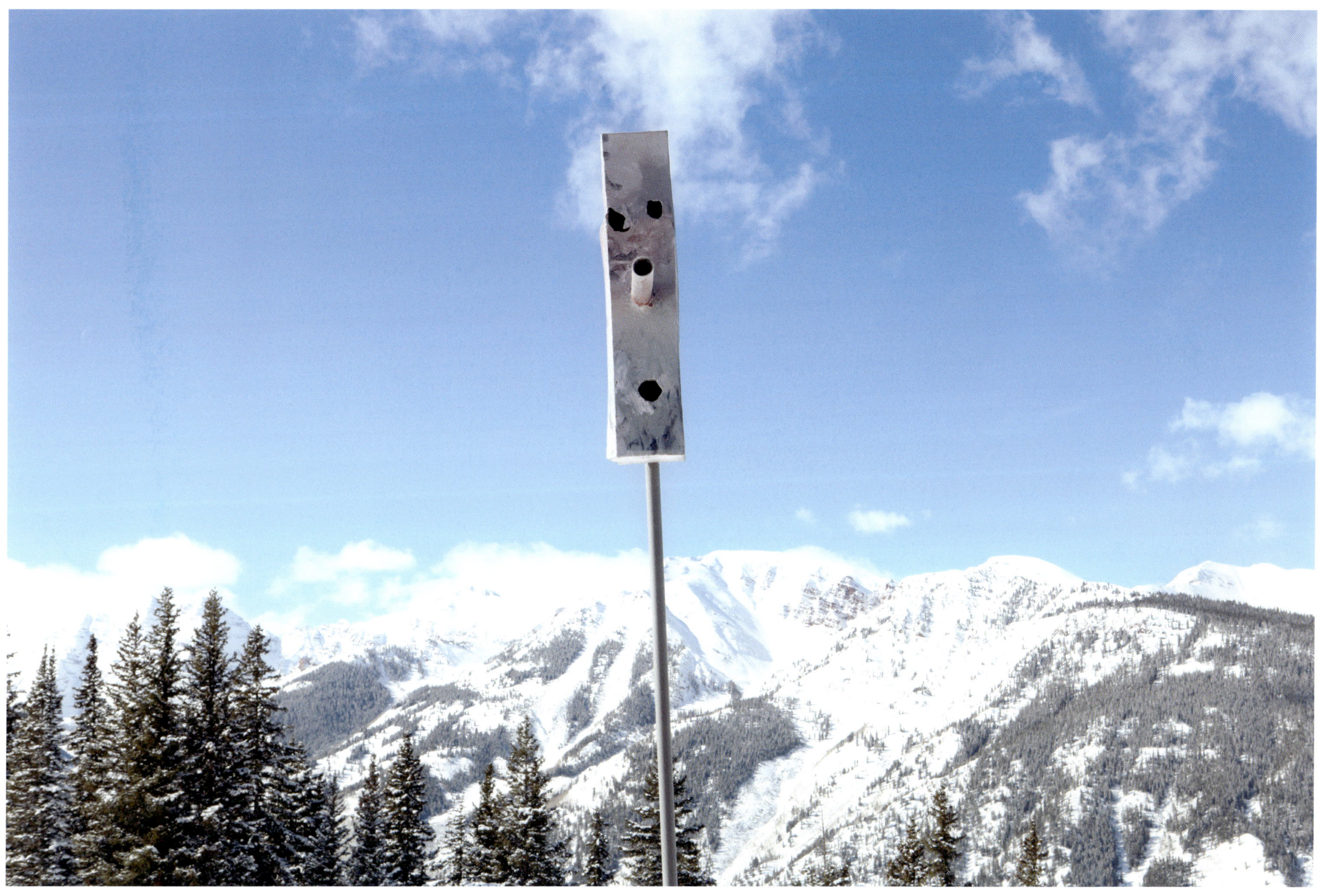

Art in
Unexpected Places II

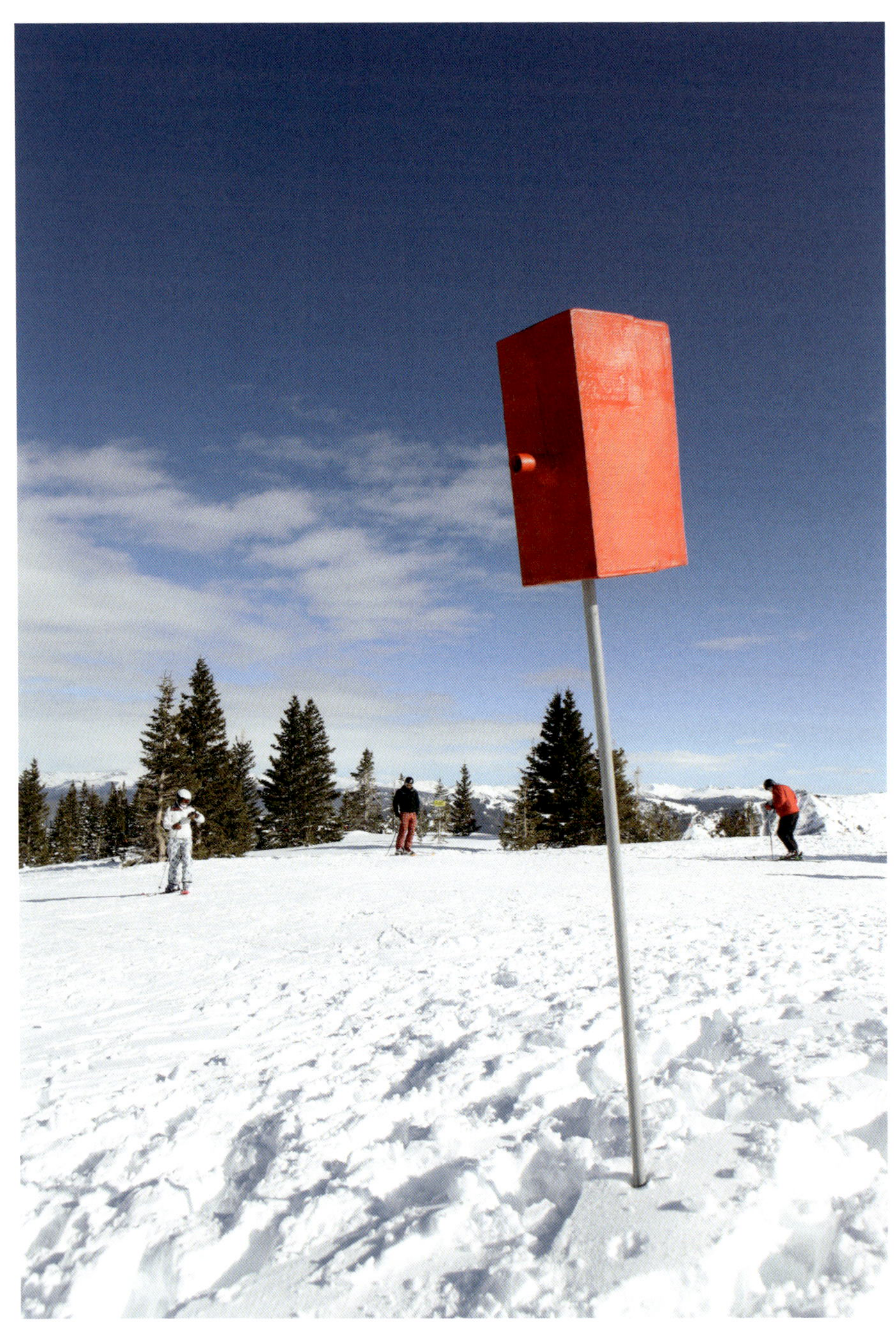

Installation views: Mark Grotjahn, <u>Untitled (Cad Red Light and Dark Mask M14a)</u>, 2011. Painted bronze, 23 1/2 x 10 x 17 in (59.7 x 25.4 x 44.5 cm). Snowmass Mountain. Photos: Jeremy Swanson

Mark Grotjahn
2011–12

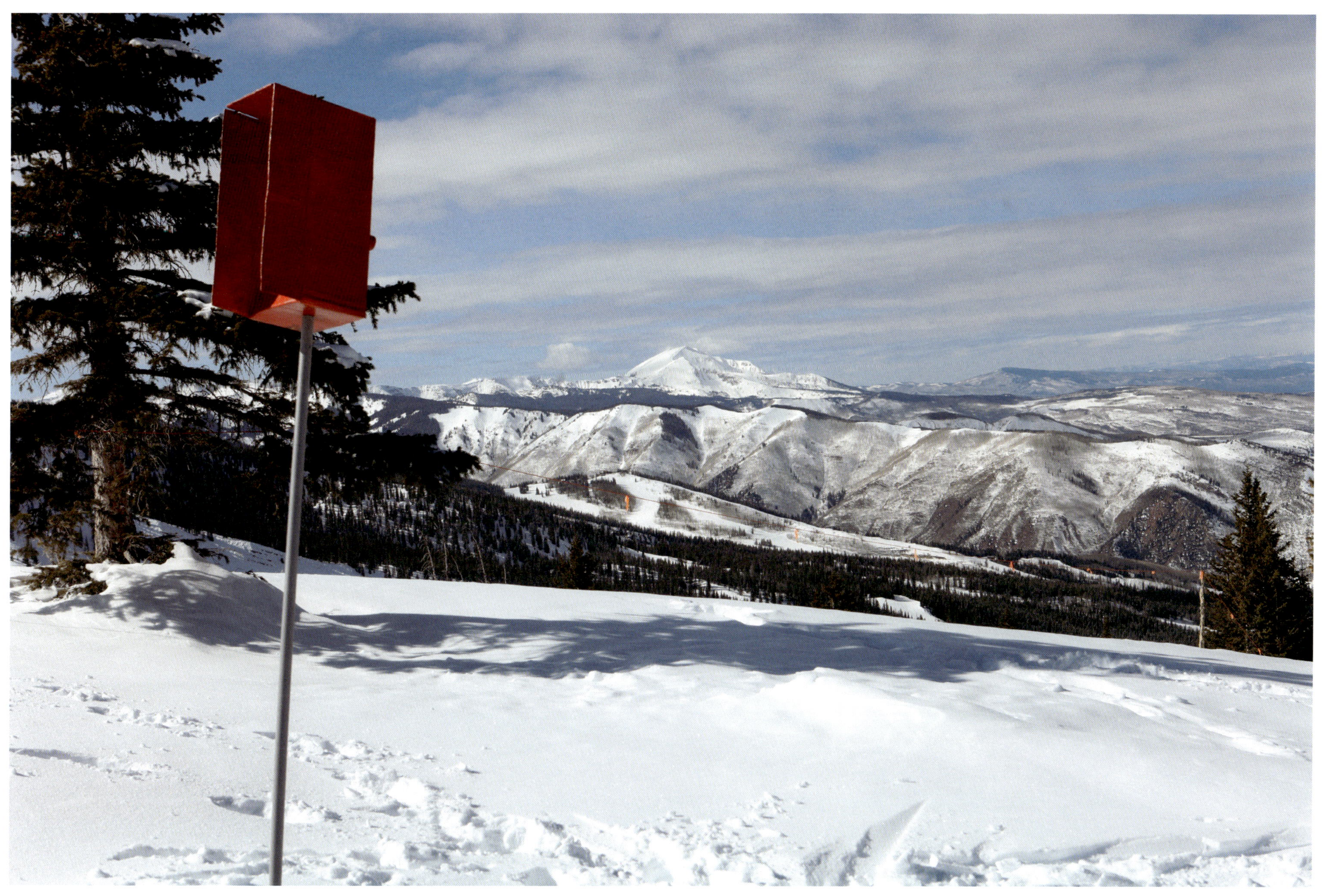

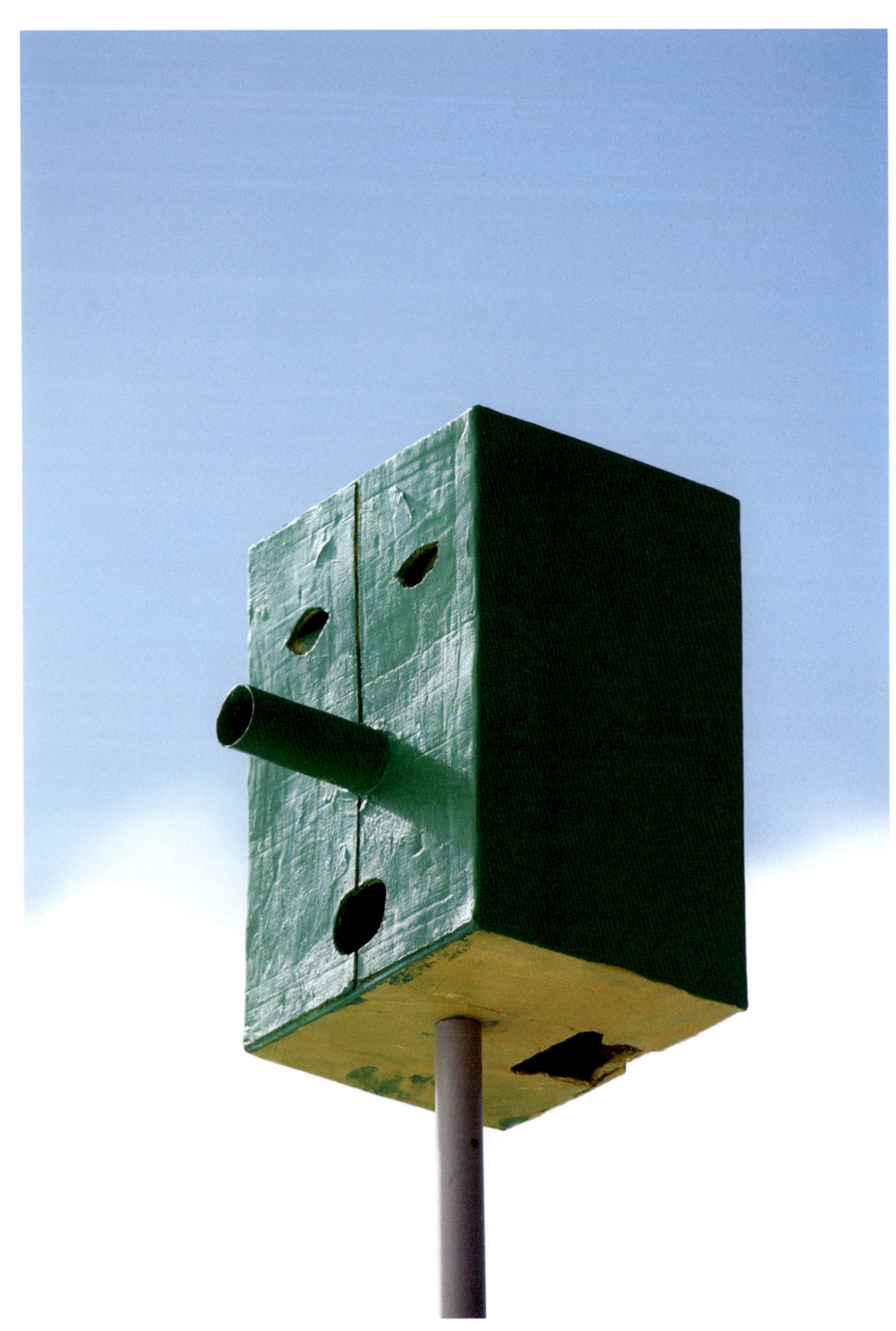

Mark Grotjahn
2011–12

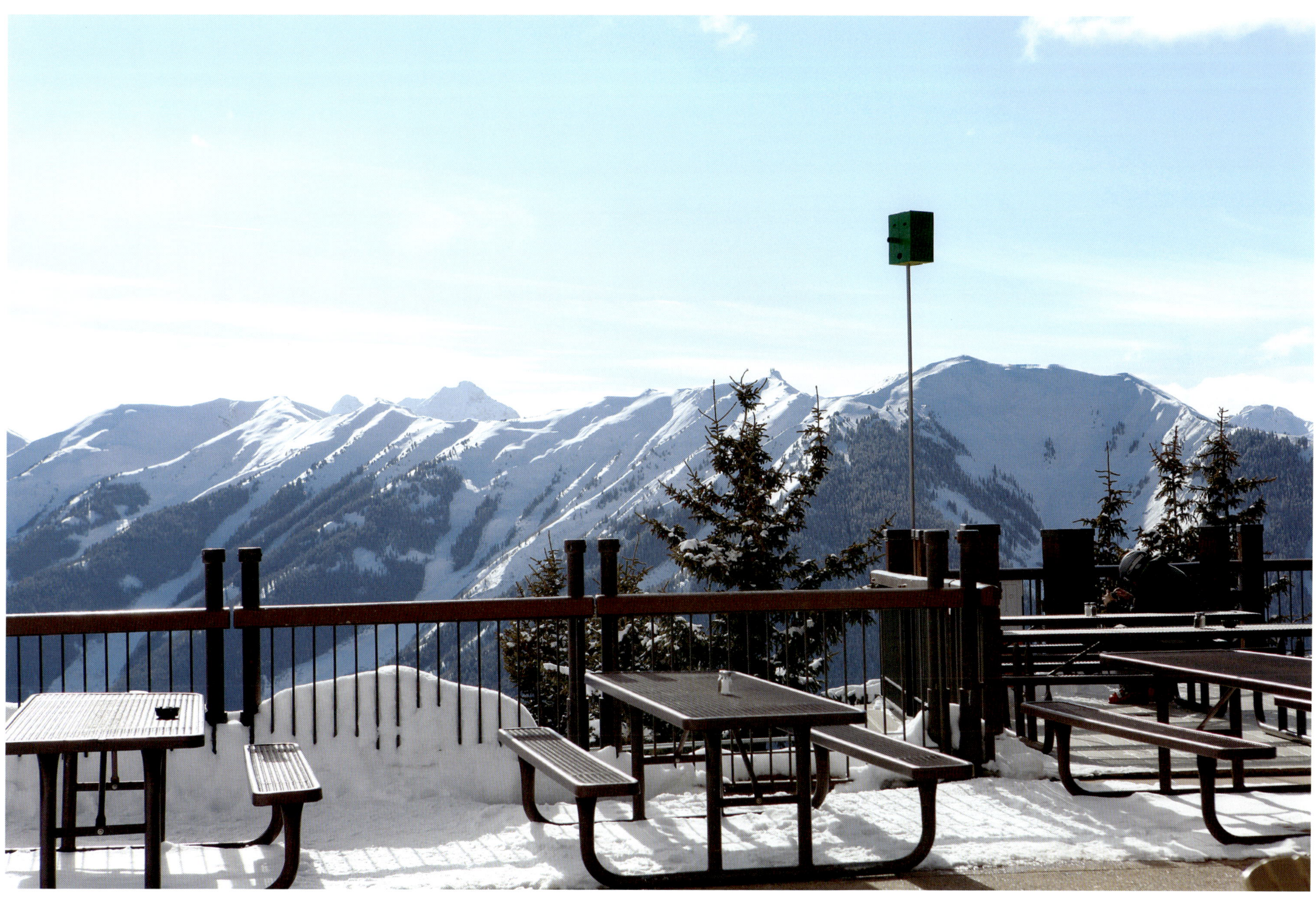

Art in
Unexpected Places II

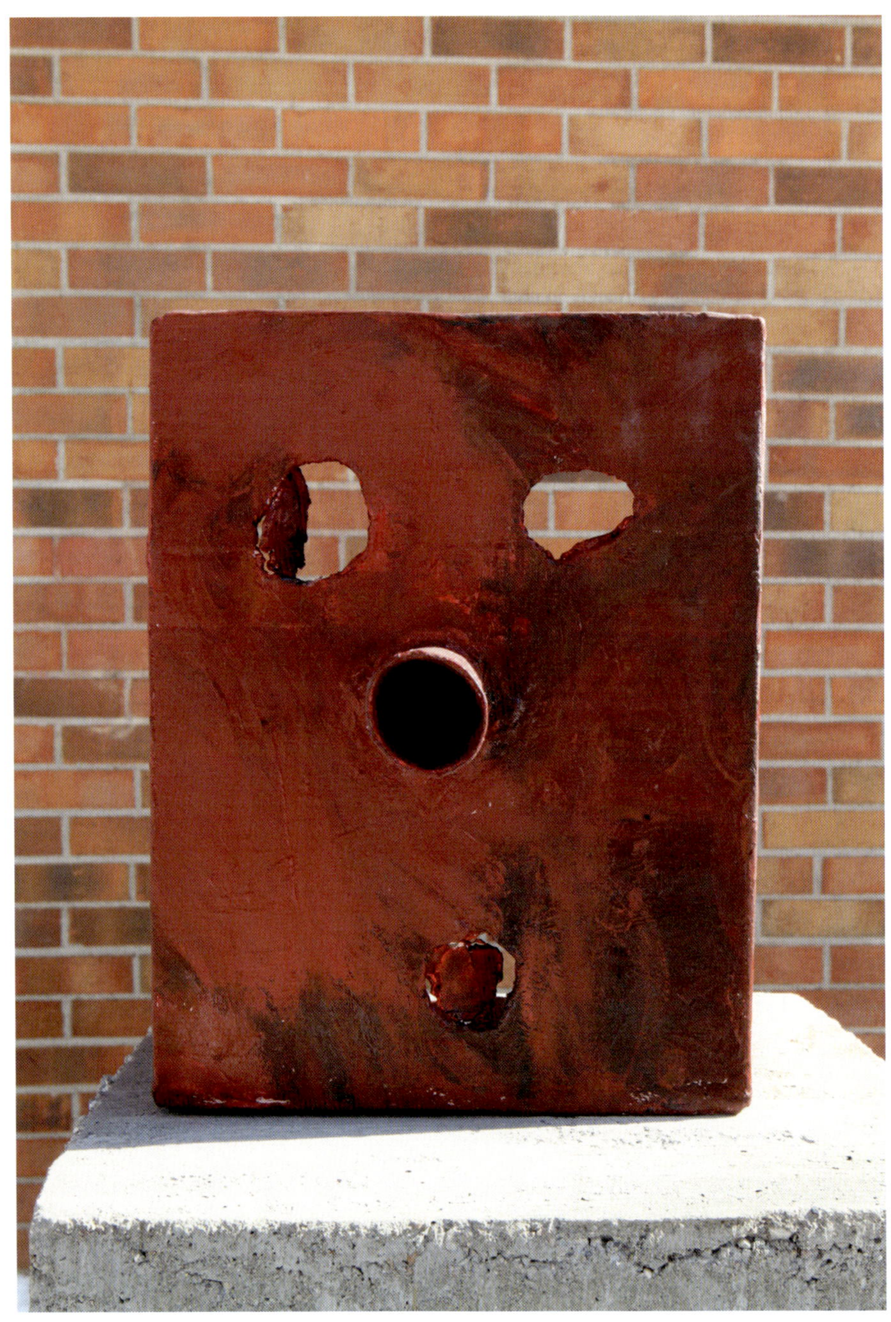

Installation view: Mark Grotjahn, Untitled (Rose Dore Madder Lake Antique Extra and Scheveningen Red Deep Mask M17.a), 2011. Painted bronze, 14 1/2 x 8 x 10 3/4 in (36.8 x 20.3 x 27.3 cm). Aspen Art Museum. Photo: Jeremy Swanson

Mark Grotjahn
2011–12

David Shrigley
2012–13 Lift Tickets

The following interview took place in January 2013 between Heidi Zuckerman and David Shrigley on the occasion of his lift ticket design in collaboration with Aspen Skiing Company.

Heidi Zuckerman
Through the lift tickets you designed for this year's ski season, our Aspen audience is being introduced to your drawing practice. Of course, some people saw your 2006 show here, *To the Wall* [Figs. 1–2], which was a site-specific painting installation with one sculpture in it, but maybe you could start by talking a little bit about your overall practice.

David Shrigley
Was it 2006? That's unbelievable. Time passes. I'm probably best known as a graphic artist, because I publish books, and I'm a de facto cartoonist in the UK. I used to do cartoons for newspapers and magazines.

People identify me with this crude, comic drawing style, but I very much see myself as a fine artist. I make sculpture, animation, and do printmaking. It seems like I've covered almost every media without really intending to. Somehow, my work seems to lend itself to limitless media. I did the libretto for an opera last year, which wasn't something I ever thought I would do in my life. I've also done advertising, fashion photography, and designed clothes. Maybe I'm just not very precious or maybe I'm bad at saying no.

HZ
What do you think pulls together your work in all these different mediums?

DS
I don't know really. I never thought that much about what I do. It's only on occasions such as this that you're invited to contextualize your work within the art world. My ambition as an artist has always been to be able to make art and not have to do anything else—to avoid having a job. I'd never really had a strategy to do anything. I've always liked working in my studio and making things. I do a lot of drawing, but I tend to do it in short bursts. When I get bored of it, I do something else for a while.

People ask me to do stuff, like make a record, and I say yes. That's how things happen. I don't really know why my work seems mutable in terms of form. Maybe because I'm not hindered by being associated with craft. If I was a painter using oil on canvas, I probably wouldn't end up writing a libretto for an opera. Since I use words and images, people don't expect me to render anything particularly well, so I can do anything, in a way.

HZ
Humor is also very present in your work.

DS
Yeah. I don't think I'm a particularly funny guy, though. People say, "Oh, you incorporate humor into your work. What's that all about?," as if it's a color or some material. As an artist, you have a voice. I suppose my voice is a comic one. I don't think my work is that funny. It's not comedy, as such, because it's not quite funny enough. But I suppose there's always a comic resolution to everything I do. It's not that I'm really trying to make anybody else laugh; I'm probably trying to make myself laugh.

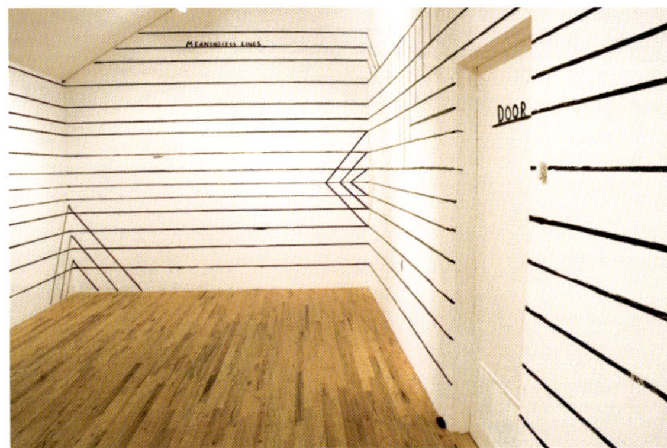

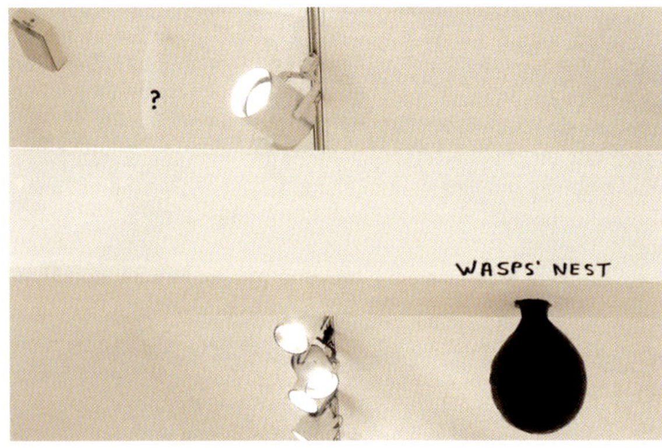

Figs. 1–2
Installation views: David Shrigley, <u>To the Wall</u>,
2007. Aspen Art Museum. Photos: Karl Wolfgang

HZ

Do you laugh when you make the work?

DS

Yeah, I do. I laugh alone in my studio.

HZ

I was recently seated next to someone at a dinner who is a famous comedic actor. When I told people, they asked if he was really funny. But he wasn't particularly; at dinner, he just was a person. Of course, he has a great sense of comic timing, but that's not his personality.

DS

I suppose if you're a basketball player, it's not like you like bouncing things.

HZ

Right. Also, what's humorous or funny to one person isn't necessarily funny to someone else. And the role of humor in art is like the role of beauty in art. They're both things that some people think you have to stay away from. But it's something that I really appreciate about your work.

DS

That it's beautiful…?

HZ

Sometimes it's beautiful. But that it's funny, more often than not.

DS

The thing is, I want the work to be funny. Although not always—sometimes it's far too oblique and minimal to be funny. The problem, in a way, is if it was comedy, then it would have to be funny. For it to be funny would be the *raison d'être*, and that would be really problematic. When I'm making art, the *raison d'être* is to make a finished piece that's finished and somehow engaging and seems to be good enough to show people.

HZ

I would say I have a dark sense of humor, and you often do as well, at least in the work. The humor in your work is more about an isolation of the absurd than it is about anything inherently funny. It makes you think of something that you hadn't thought of before. It's so surprising or unusual that sometimes

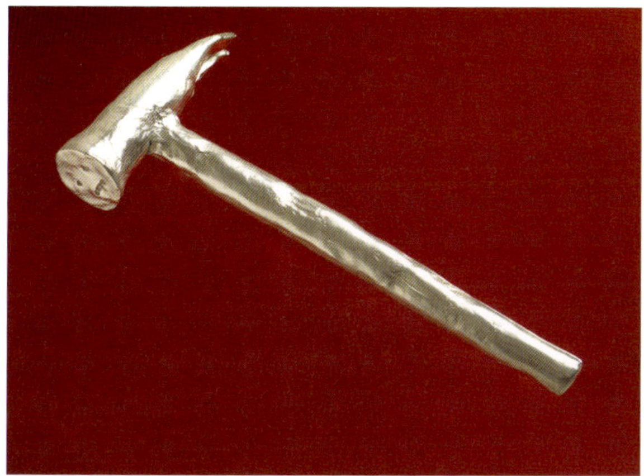

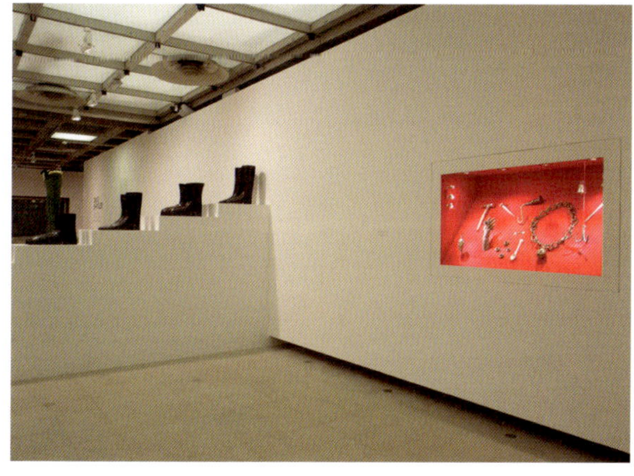

Fig. 3
David Shrigley, Hammer, 2012. Silver-plated bronze, 10 5/8 × 5 1/8 × 1 3/8 in (27 × 13 × 1 3/8 cm). Courtesy the artist and Stephen Friedman Gallery, London

Fig. 4
Installation view: David Shrigley, Brain Activity, 2012. Hayward Gallery, London; toured to Yerba Buena Centre for the Arts, San Francisco, 2012. Courtesy the artist and Stephen Friedman Gallery, London

you laugh because you're embarrassed. Or sometimes you laugh because it's a better alternative to expressing yourself in a less appropriate way. Your work celebrates all of that.

DS
When I first became a professional artist and didn't have to have a job as well, and was at home drawing all day, suddenly I started to accumulate a lot of work. When I stopped to think about it, I suddenly wondered what I was doing, even though I really enjoyed it and was going to do it anyway—I always wanted to make work that was really quite poetic.

HZ
It is, though.

DS
When I look back, it was funny, but it wasn't really poetic. My response to it was not to feel melancholy, it was to chuckle at it. I've maybe given up on that ambition of being a poet, in the sense that I have embraced the comic nature of it. Obviously, hopefully, I can be poetic to a certain extent, but these are things that

have to coexist—I'm more of a comedian than a poet.

HZ
I don't know if the two are mutually exclusive.
I recently saw a sculptural piece of yours that was a series of tools. One of them was a hammer [Figs. 3–4]. On the face of the hammer, it had a little smiley face. I was wondering what you were thinking when you made that piece? Were you thinking about the end point or what the viewer would think when they saw that?

DS
In retrospect, I liked the fact that if somebody used the hammer as a weapon, it would emboss a smiley face onto the victim.

HZ
I didn't think about that. That's good.

DS
I've gone through a phase of making sculptural items that are functional, that don't really deny their function. It is a hammer. You could use it as a hammer.

It's made of cast bronze. You could hammer nails with it. I quite like the fact that this object exists in the real world. The whole group of objects that you saw—some hooks, a bell, a spoon, and a needle—could feasibly be used in the real world. It appeals to me that it's not a sculpture of a hammer; it's a real hammer. I've decorated it in this peculiar way, but these works come about because they're directly cast in wax. Then, they get sent to the bronze foundry and cast. I made a series of coat hooks as well. Unfortunately, once you put them in the gallery, no one wants to hang their coat on them.

HZ

Right, no one wants to use them.

DS

Yeah, but they're supposed to be used. I like things somehow having a place in the real world. The artworks that I really like are interventions. Inevitably, once it's an artwork, people start handling it with white gloves and writing condition reports and don't want to polish it with household products. But at the time I made it, it was a real hammer.

HZ

There's a sculpture of yours that's in a home here in Aspen that's a headless taxidermy cat.

DS

Really, that's here, is it? That's interesting. There are lots of stories attached to my work in taxidermy…

Although, I recently got a puppy— the first pet that was mine. I always hated dogs. Then my wife gave me this little ratlike thing. Suddenly, my heart melted and I became completely in love with the dog and with all dogs. It was a sea change, even though I'm violently allergic to them. But I'm getting over that with medication.

Now, I don't make any more taxidermy. No more headless cats, no more little dogs holding signs saying, "I'm dead." Funnily enough, I got lots of abuse for doing that on social media by people accusing me of killing the puppy. You go to jail if you kill a puppy. You don't go to the pet store and kill a puppy. Also, even though I didn't like dogs, I would never kill another mammal to make an artwork. That would be wrong. For the record, there are very strict rules surrounding the art of taxidermy.

Taxidermy objects have to be dead already, and you're not allowed to have killed them. They have to have died completely independently of the taxidermy process. But people don't realize that. They send me abuse on Twitter and call me all sorts of terrible names.

Anyway, I've made a few headless animals as well—a cat, an ostrich, and a monkey [Figs. 5–7]. So I've got a box of animal heads in my studio at home, and the dog found it. The dog was sniffing around and could smell the animal heads and wanted to get at them. There's no dog head in there, so it wouldn't be too freaky.

HZ

I'm having lots of images of what this could be like…

DS

When I made the cat, they asked if I wanted the head. I said, "Yeah, of course I want the head." And they responded, "Do you want the eyes open or closed?" I opted for the eyes closed because it's cheaper. The taxidermist is in London and I stayed with a friend that night. He

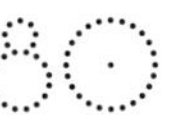

David Shrigley
2012–13

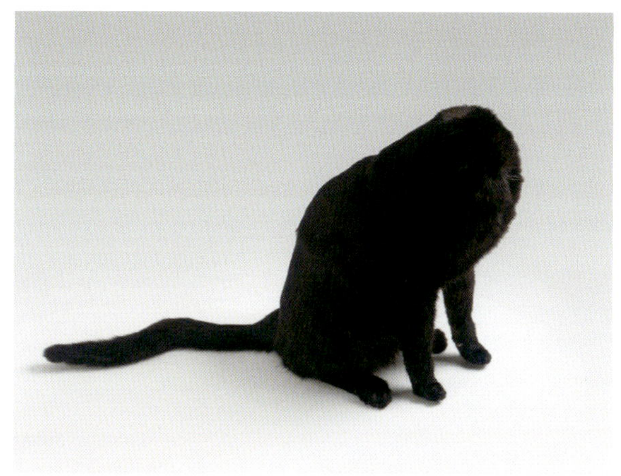

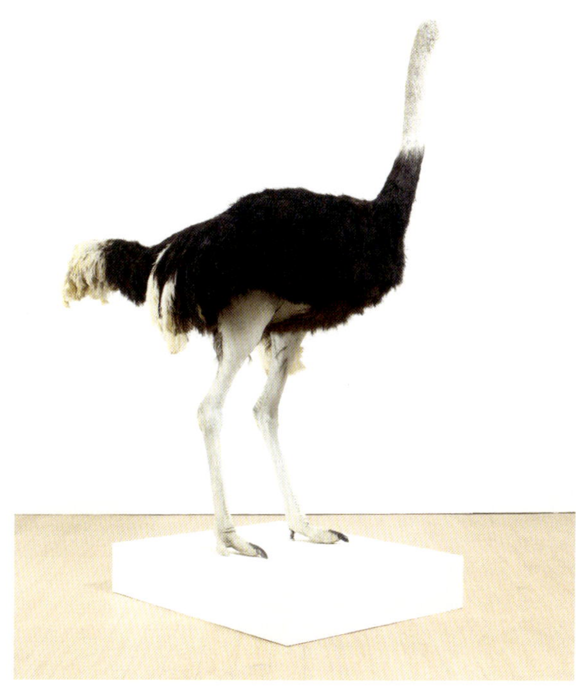

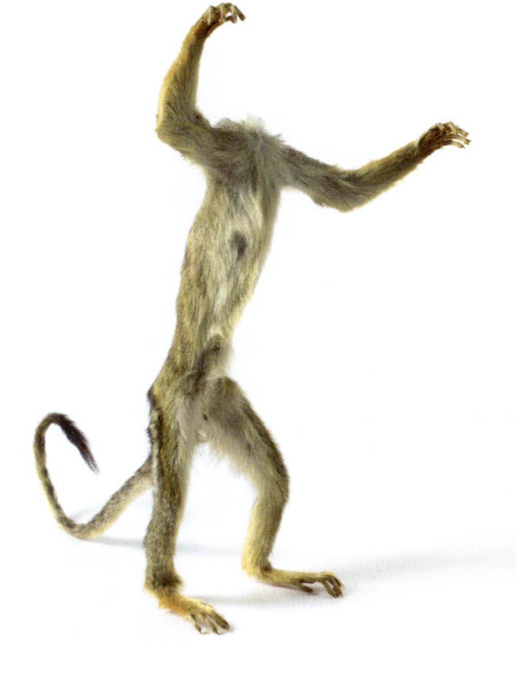

asked what was in the box and I told him it was a cat's head. His son got really excited and pulled the cat's head out, and was poking it in the face of their cat. I was like, "Don't do that. Don't do that. You'll freak the cat out." Obviously, the cat was really freaked out.

HZ
But maybe it was because the object was being pushed in its face, rather than what it was? Or maybe it was self-identifying…

DS
It was bad, the fact that it was a cat's head. If I picked up a human head, I wouldn't have to shove it in your face for you to take exception.

Anyway, they stay in the box now. They're hidden away, where the dog can't get at them.

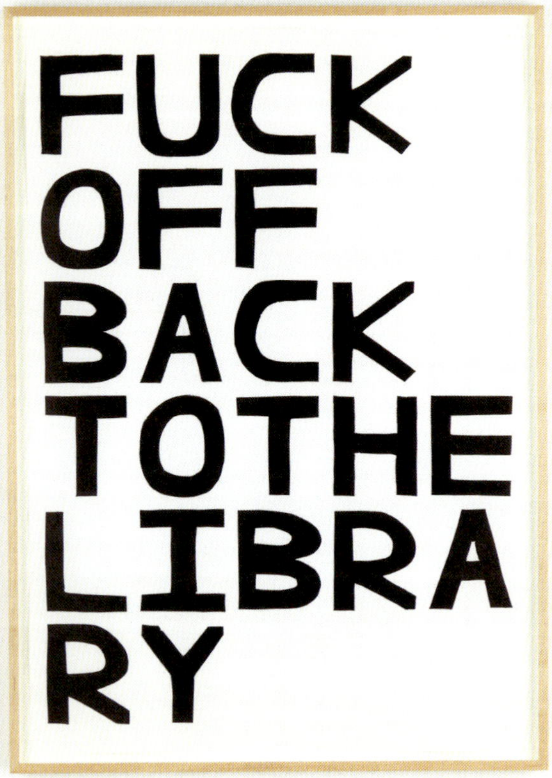

FUCK OFF BACK TO THE LIBRA RY

Fig. 8
David Shrigley, Fuck Off Back to the Library, 2012.
Unique linocut print, 41 3/8 x 28 3/8 in (105.1 x 72.1
cm). Courtesy the artist and Anton Kern Gallery,
New York. © David Shrigley

Fig. 9
Installation view: David Shrigley, Signs, 2013. Anton
Kern Gallery, New York. Courtesy the artist and
Anton Kern Gallery, New York

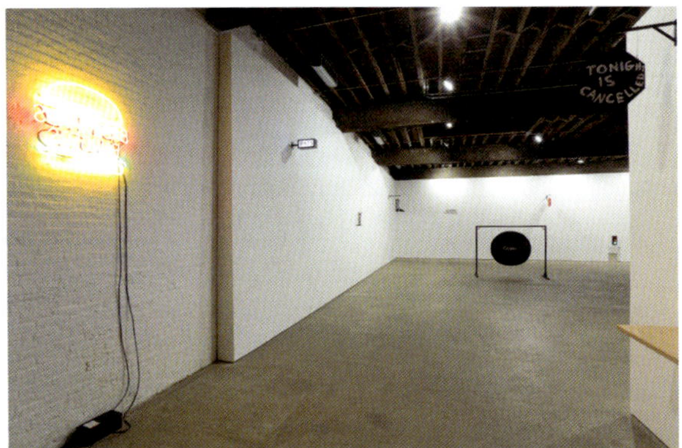

HZ

You have a show that just opened at Anton Kern Gallery in New York. One of the works tells people, with an expletive, to go back to the library [Fig. 8]. I was curious about that one. I particularly loved it, because at least one member of my family goes to the library pretty much every day.

DS

They're closing all the libraries in the UK. It's terrible.

HZ

You've been an advocate against the cuts for arts in the UK.

DS

I have, yes. I think a lot of people don't feel

that our culture should be forgotten about because of the actions of reckless bankers.

But yeah, I made this show of signs for Anton. It was the fifth show I've done with him in New York. He suggested doing a show of signs [Fig. 9]. I thought that would be great, because I'd never done a themed show before. Since my work is so synonymous with my handwriting, I decided that I would make a typeface. I was doing some printmaking with a printmaker that I work with in Copenhagen and decided that I would make a typeface quite quickly with Lino letters. It's a bit like a letterpress and all the prints are unique. But the letters were quite big, relative to the page. You could only really have a five-letter word, so I have all these very short statements or missives, "F off back to the library" being one of them.

I quite liked that it was really constrained, because of the amount of words that I could use, but also because there was a typeface. There was a certain regularity to it, although the letters were quite crude.

HZ

There is often that tension between all the different elements on the page in your work. The letters get really big or they get smaller or things get crossed out.

DS

I have an odd painterly attitude toward making drawing, whereby I never do anything twice. I do things that are similar, but I won't redraw something, unless I've spilled coffee on it or something. I'm into the mark and not doing anything more than once, partly because I feel it doesn't get any better the second time. Because it is in the gesture to some extent, and it's conceptual art, I suppose.

HZ

It's very conceptual, I think.

DS

It doesn't really change. You can change certain elements of it. I suppose it's so nuanced because of the personality of the drawing and the writing. It treads a line between the two things.

HZ

When you draw a person or a figure, are they someone specific or is it a more universal person?

DS

The drawing comes about as a result of a process. It's the residue of a process. I've always felt quite strongly that you should think about the process, rather than the end point in terms of making art. With drawing, it's very easy to do that. I tend to have a set amount of things to draw and I often write a list.

HZ

You keep a list?

DS

I write a list of maybe thirty things to draw, and there'll be thirty drawings that I have to do in that day. And I do all thirty. Sometimes, they start with text, more often with an image, and I'll go back to them and write something or draw something else.

The only rule is that, at the end of the day, they all have to be finished, whether they're good or bad. That's how the work gets made. I focus on that particular task and don't think too hard about whether this drawing could be in an art gallery for sale. I like the fact that the chances are it will go in the garbage. ❋

Born in 1968, in Macclesfield, UK, David Shrigley studied at the Glasgow School of Art, Scotland, from 1988–91, and currently lives and works in Glasgow. Solo exhibitions of Shrigley's work have been hosted at prominent institutions such as the National Gallery of Victoria, Melbourne, Australia (2015); Pinakothek der Moderne, Munich, Germany (2014); Statens Museum for Kunst, Copenhagen, Denmark (2012); Turku Art Museum, Finland (2011); Bergen Kunsthall, Norway (2009); Musée d'Art Moderne et Contemporain, Geneva, Switzerland; UCLA Hammer Museum, Los Angeles (both 2002); and CCS Museum, Bard College, New York (2001). His work has been included in major international group exhibitions such as Drawing Now: 2015, Albertina, Vienna, Austria (2015); Generation: 25 Years of Contemporary Art in Scotland, Scottish National Gallery, Edinburgh (2014); Lightness of Being, Public Art Fund, New York (2013); Danish and International Art After 1900, Statens Museum for Kunst, Copenhagen, Denmark (2012); and The More I Draw, Museum für Gegenwartskunst, Siegen, Germany (2010); amongst many others. Shrigley is the recipient of a Fourth Plinth Commission, Trafalgar Square, London, UK (2016), and was a nominee for the 2013 Turner Prize.

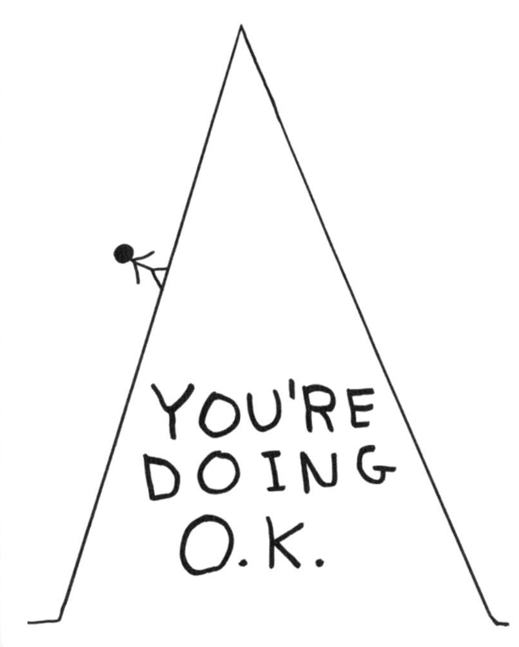

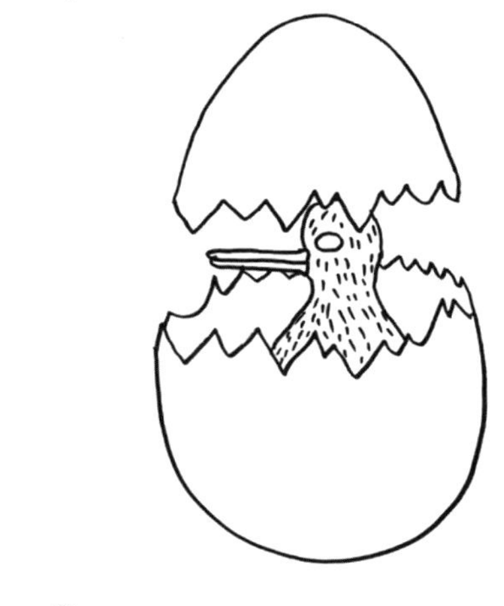

Lift Ticket: David Shrigley, Untitled (You're doing OK), 2010. Courtesy the artist and Galleri Nicolai Wallner. Photo: Anders Sune Berg

Lift Ticket: David Shrigley, Untitled (Welcome to the world), 2011. Courtesy the artist and Galleri Nicolai Wallner. Photo: Anders Sune Berg

Lift Ticket: David Shrigley, Untitled (Please do not show this to anyone), 2009. Courtesy the artist and Stephen Friedman Gallery

David Shrigley
2012–13

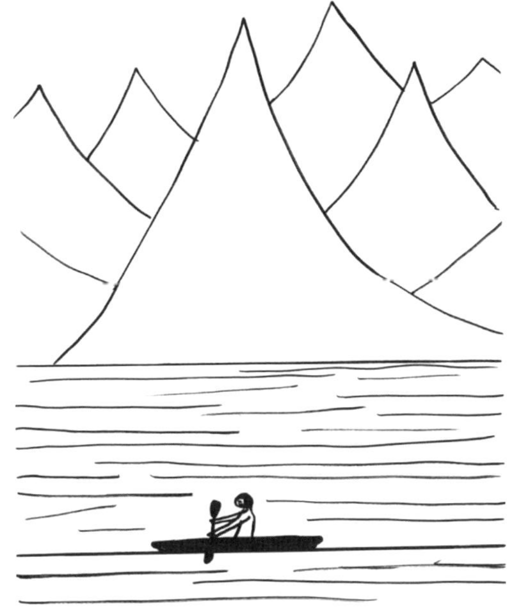

Lift Ticket: David Shrigley, <u>Untitled (I didn't notice the mountains)</u>, 2011. Courtesy the artist and Galleri Nicolai Wallner. Photo: Anders Sune Berg

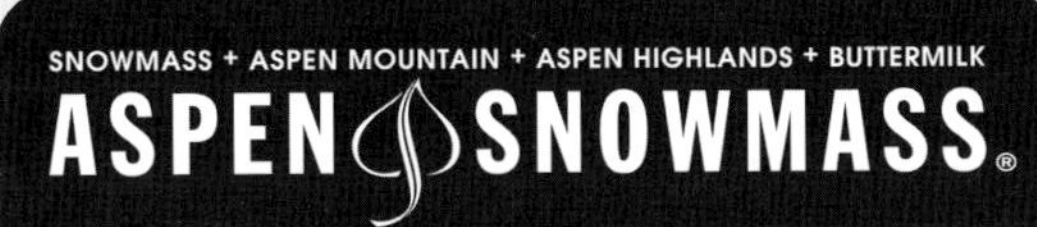
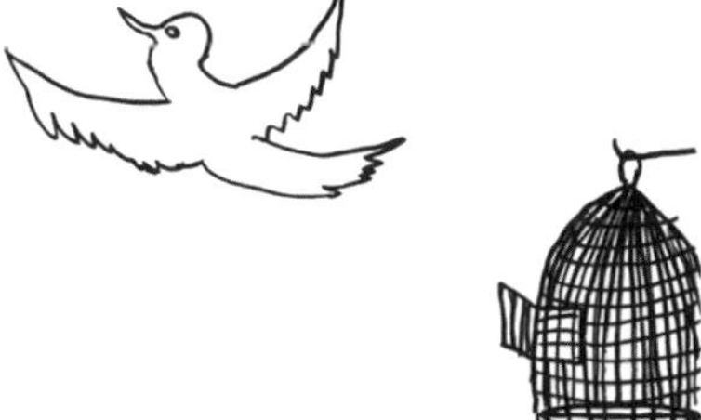

Lift Ticket: David Shrigley, <u>Untitled (Freedom)</u>, 2011. Courtesy the artist and Galleri Nicolai Wallner. Photo: Anders Sune Berg

Lift Ticket: David Shrigley, <u>Untitled (Don't fear the future)</u>, 2009. Courtesy the artist and Galleri Nicolai Wallner. Photo: Anders Sune Berg

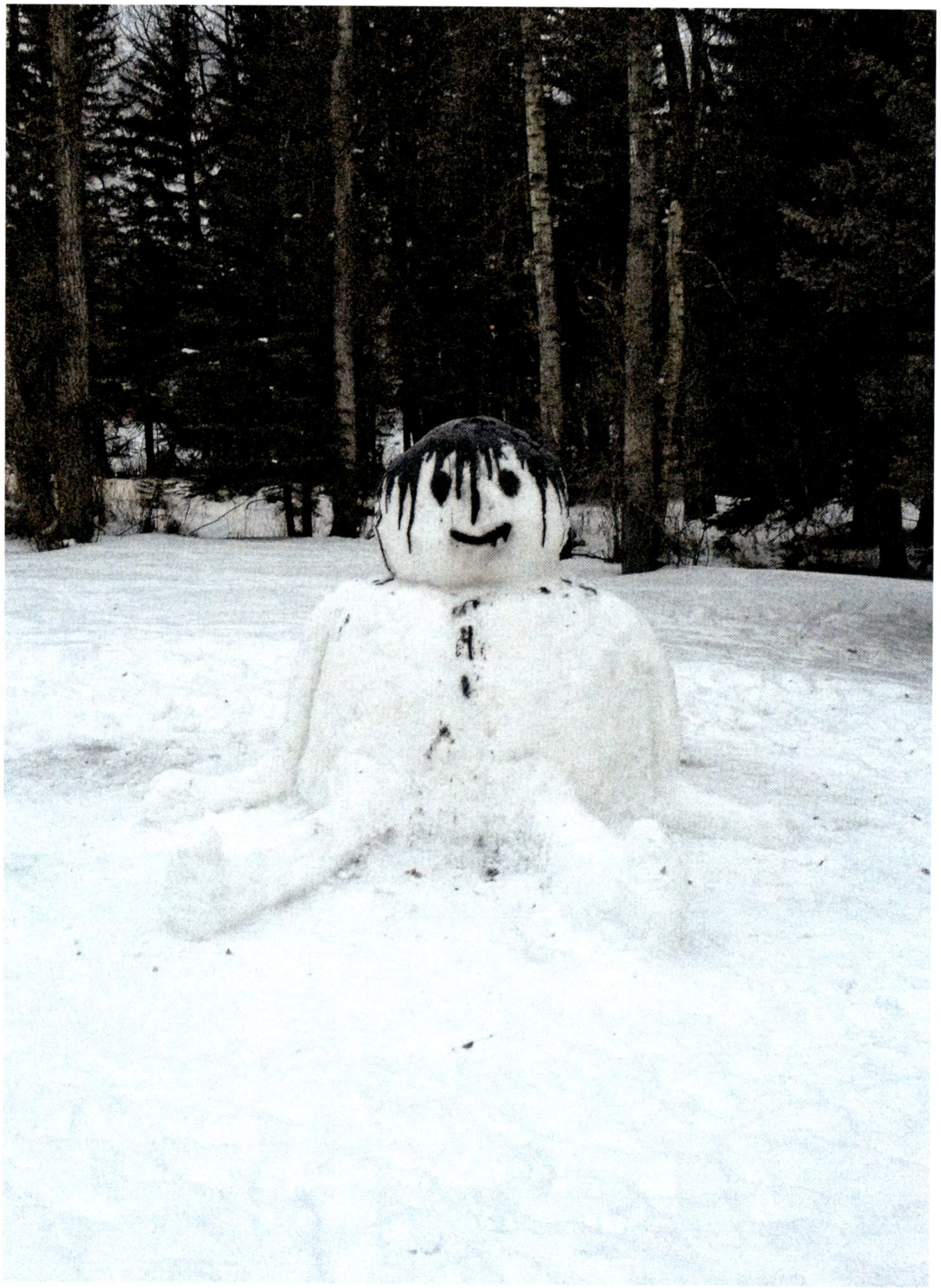

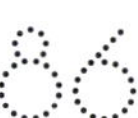

David Shrigley
2012–13

David Shrigley, Snowman Building Workshop,
Aspen Art Museum

Dave Muller

2012–13 Elk Camp Installation & Three Day Weekend

The following interview took place in October 2012 between Heidi Zuckerman and Dave Muller on the occasion of his installation at Elk Camp restaurant in Snowmass.

Heidi Zuckerman
Dave, you are currently making a site-specific wall drawing installation here at the new Elk Camp restaurant on Snowmass Mountain. But before we get into talking about that as well as other parts of your practice, the shirt you are wearing for our interview reads: "I THINK YOUR WORK'S GREAT" [Fig. 1]. It reminds me of one of your T-shirts that I found recently that says, "I ATTENDED THE SUMMER CURATORS' CONFERENCE…   AND ALL I GOT WAS THIS LOUSY T-SHIRT!" [Fig. 2].

Dave Muller
I got asked to make that shirt by Amada Cruz. I did a show at Bard in 2002. They were having a curators' conference there and I thought it would be fun. A *meta* shirt!

HZ
Right. And that conference actually turned out to be a really significant moment in contemporary curatorial practice.

DM
How so?

HZ
It set a collaborative tone that put art, artists, and art objects at the center of curatorial practice. It's something that contemporary curators do every summer now.

Did you make the one you're wearing now?

DM
No. My friend Polly Staple made this to participate in a Three Day Weekend show I put together in 2004. She's now the director of Chisenhale Gallery in London.

HZ
You are doing a Three Day Weekend event here in February, over Presidents' Day weekend. Maybe you can talk about your practice in general and the different ways that it manifests.

DM
When I was a graduate student at CalArts, I found myself interested in what other people were doing. But I also found myself having a hard time understanding what they were doing, because they were sequestered away in their studios. It was almost as though they were being secretive about it.

I tried to figure out various ways to get into different situations. One of the first things I did was set myself up as a visiting artist. I put up the same sign as a regular visiting artist and had people sign up. Most of them knew who I was, but some didn't. I spent a whole day doing studio visits with my peers, so I got to see what was going on.

That developed into one-day shows in my studio. I held a month's worth of one-day shows. Anybody could sign up. First come, first served. I liked seeing my peers' side projects. Providing a space made that easier.

After I graduated, I came up with Three Day Weekend, an artist-run project space that took place on holiday weekends. I didn't have the spare time I could devote to continuously running a gallery. I did

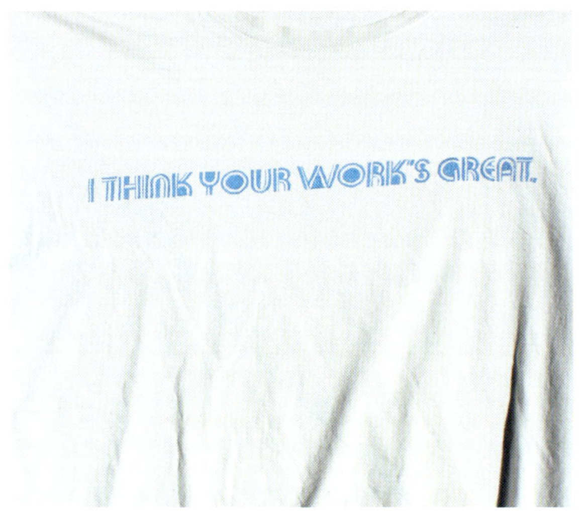

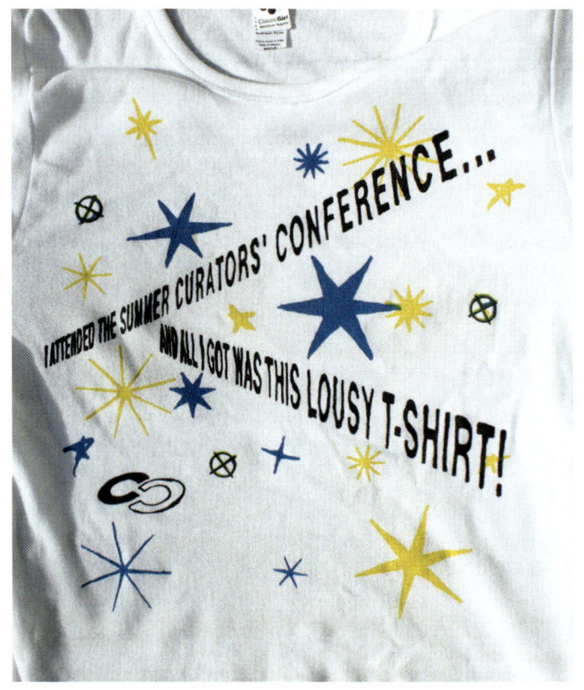

like the idea that you could generate bursts of exuberance for short periods.

HZ

A tenet of your practice is that fascination with what other people are doing. Some of your early work was about finding invitations that you received or other kinds of gallery announcements and re-creating them. Maybe you could talk about that.

DM

My misreading of conceptual art was that you had to do whatever it took to get the job done. I decided to teach myself how to draw, how to make things look the way I wanted. I started making these drawings that looked like they were posters for other people's shows [Fig. 3]. It would work just like an announcement, but it was a one-off. Of course, then they become mementos. But they also were a way for me to comment on things I liked and things I didn't.

HZ

That spirit of generosity is something that continues throughout your work. It's a really important part of your practice.

DM

I'm interested in an expanded economy— a large-scale, long-term economy that encompasses much more than straight transactions. On the whole, you could say *everything* eventually comes back around, and the world is better when people take that into account.

Fig. 3
Dave Muller, I Keep Waiting for Hendrix to Break into the Star-Spangled Banner (White Noise on Red), 1997. Acrylic on paper, 40 x 31 in (101.6 x 78.7 cm). Courtesy the artist and Blum & Poe, Los Angeles. Photo: Dave Muller

HZ

I agree. I always err on the side of being generous. I would put your large-scale wall paintings in that category, particularly the one that you are doing at Elk Camp restaurant in Snowmass. I'm skipping ahead a little bit because it's here for a specific duration and then it will be gone.

DM

That's true. It is temporary. Everybody asks me how I feel about that. I'm most happy when something I make functions efficiently in the environment it's placed. If a project of mine ends up being somewhere for a longer period, great. Some are. It's enough for me that it works, fleeting as that moment might be. That's what it's supposed to do. That's what we're all supposed to do.

HZ

Right. It's the practice of impermanence.

DM

Maybe it also wakes people up. To be enthusiastic about things and take interest in them while they are there. They're not always going to be around.

You've got to take the initiative. You need to get out and be with things.

HZ

Music is also a big part of your work—you've been in bands, you DJ, you record music…

DM

I gravitated toward music very early in life. From the age of five or six, I started listening to my parents' records (the ones they would let me listen to), whereas most of my siblings weren't as interested. I've been obsessed with music almost since I have been functioning in the world—I started playing music in the elementary school bands when I was about nine. It's almost like breathing for me. At this point, it's not just music anymore either; it's more about sound in general. I'm always trying to figure out interesting new sounds.

HZ

One of the things that you do is ask people for their top ten favorite albums or songs of all time. I was wondering about yours and how static or fluid they are?

DM

Oh, mine are always changing. You ask someone what their top ten is and you can give it any kind of context, like *something I thought up under duress,* or *my top ten the last time I was single*. Good qualifiers help narrow it down, but most people feel like they have to come up with the overarching top ten. A top ten for me might last a day in my life.

I've told myself I can make one every week: *this is what I listened to this week, these are the things that !!!!! this week*. I don't always come up with a list per week, but I give myself the opportunity. In theory, I could do fifty-two of those a year.

HZ

When you make paintings of the records, they often appear to be well-loved versions of those albums. Do you paint them from life? Do you own them or do you find them?

DM

I paint my own top tens from life, and generally, it comes from my collection. "Well-loved" is a nice euphemism for throwing your records in crates and taking them to DJ somewhere. Maybe you stick another crate on top of that crate to save space in the car. My collection is an exhibiting collection.

If people still have their records, the LPs, it's nice to use those ones. Some people have better-kept records—Matthew Higgs has the neatest records on Earth. To be honest, it's harder to make pristine records look interesting when I'm painting them, but anything's possible.

HZ

When you've done these, has anyone come up with something you don't have?

DM

Certainly. There was a Yusef Lateef record that I had never heard and I immediately went out and bought it for my collection after painting it. There are all sorts of sounds that I've learned about. It's broadened my horizons, as any good conversation should.

HZ

Absolutely. For your project here, you did a survey of the Aspen Skiing Company employees. You asked them what their top ten favorite albums were?

DM

I just asked them to list as many records as they wanted to. Some people named one. Some people named twenty. The Aspen Skiing Company sent out the email survey to all their employees, and eighty-four people responded [see page 12]. I tallied all that up and figured out as a group what their top ten records were. I took into account longevity—like The Beatles or The Rolling Stones, with so many records, might spread out their votes. Adele or Justin Bieber might concentrate their votes over fewer records.

HZ

Was Justin Bieber on the list?

DM

Not this time. There were over five hundred albums that were listed. I created a graphic chart, where the amount of votes that each one got became little rectangles that sat above the names. The chart suggested topography that ended up looking like mountains (makes sense), which became the backbone of the finished mural. Then, I painted a top ten that would be the top ten vote-getting albums. That framed object

Dave Muller
2012–13

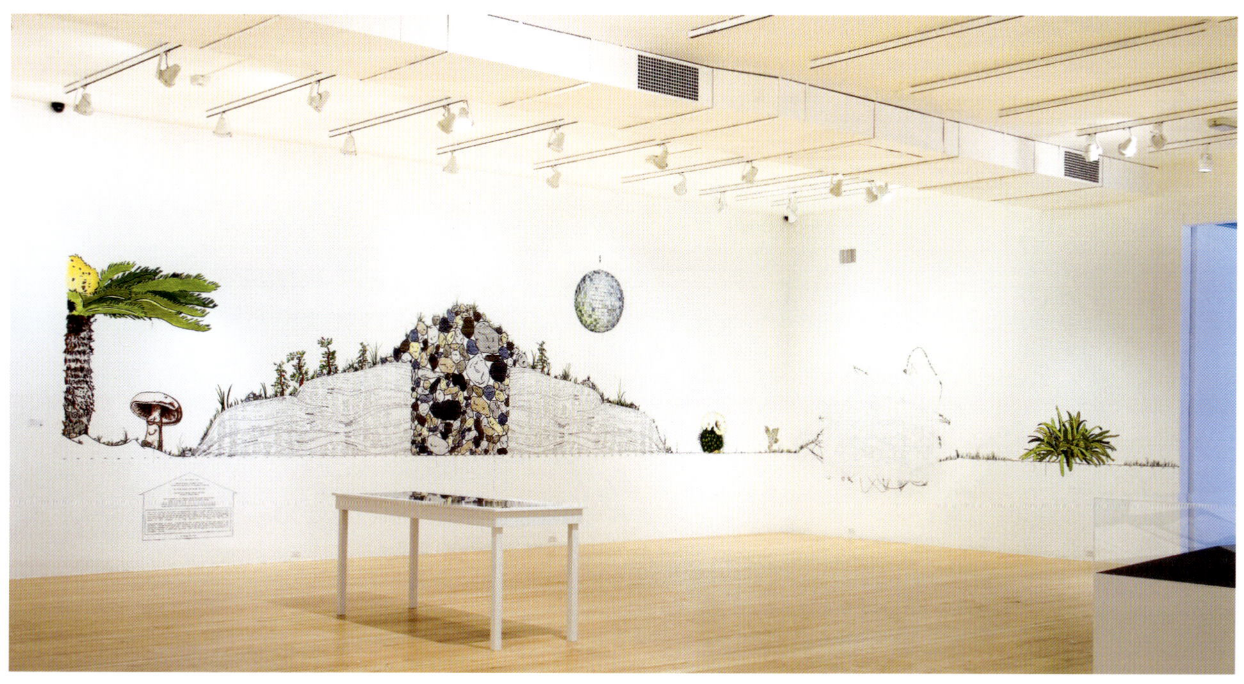

will get plopped on top of this whole thing when I finish [see page 96].

HZ

The survey also asked people for their height. How does that factor in?

DM

With the top tens, the records are rendered as tall as the person who chooses them. In this case, I averaged the height of the eighty-four responders. Their average height was about five feet nine inches. That's how high each record was in this painting.

HZ

I see. You made a previous wall drawing in Aspen, in 2009, that was part of a group show curated by Jeremy Deller, *Marlon Brando, Pocahontas, And Me* [Fig. 4]. Maybe you can talk about the subject of this particular work?

DM

In this case, a rock 'n' roll history timeline was turned into a landscape. I started off with a graphic diagram by Reebee Garofalo that explains the rise of rock 'n' roll as a market contender, from its beginning through 1975. It laid out different rock 'n' roll movements, bands, the British Invasion, Hard Rock, Bubblegum, Folk...

It was an interesting history in a form that I liked. It started looking like hills to me, and I wondered what kind of hill or mound I could make if I created a mirror image to be the other half of a hill. It could stand for the scourge of retro, where everything feeds on itself.

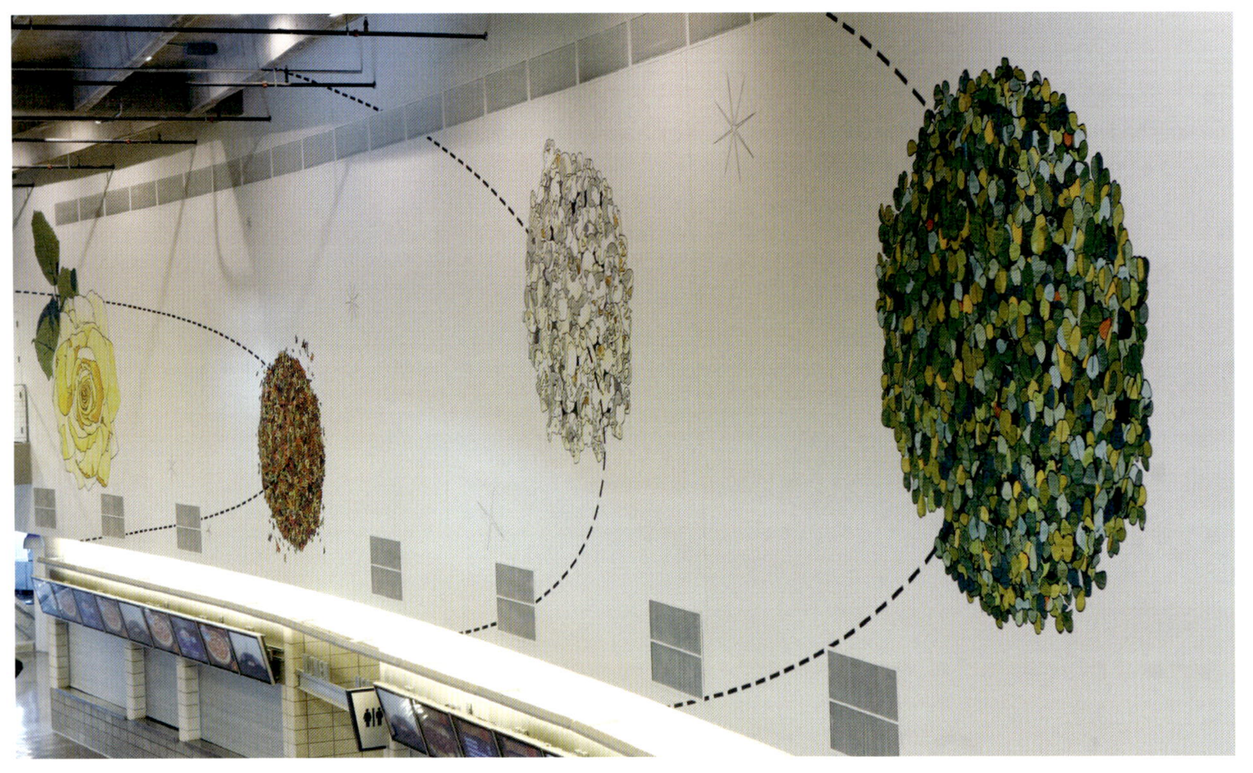

HZ

I thought it was interesting how it started at the edge of the door and then ended with a fragment of a tree.

DM

Right. I like the idea that this might have been a much larger thing, but to fit in this group show with everyone else, it just gets lopped off here and there. It does what it needs to do for the situation, nothing more, nothing less.

HZ

You included a disco ball for context?

DM

In that case, the disco ball would probably signal the death knell of disco. There are different symbols that stand for other musical movements riding the diminishing returns of retro. The snake eats its tail. Then, there might be a cultural wasteland in which we don't know what's going to happen for a while. Until something else interesting gets figured out again—like some new movement blossoms—we're stuck with small snakes, lizards, and scorpions. Waiting for a new enthusiasm.

It could be a historic timeline, in this case. Since *Marlon Brando, Pocahontas, And Me* are Neil Young lyrics, I thought it could function in parallel with what happens with Neil Young through his years as an artist. Everything in the future is completely speculative, so this becomes a fun way of putting a bunch of pictures and symbols into a timeline: a game of a landscape with dates.

HZ
Right.

DM
Solar Arrangement (2008; Fig. 5) is another large-scale wall drawing I did that's at the Dallas Cowboys' Stadium. It's my version of a solar system model. The sun is the yellow rose of Texas. Mercury, a sphere of dead leaves. Venus, being hot and cloudy, is a ball of popcorn. Earth is a clover ball. It's situated directly over a concession stand. While you're waiting to buy nachos and hot dogs, you can spend time with the mural and contemplate your place in the universe. ❋

Los Angeles–based artist Dave Muller was born in San Francisco in 1964. He studied at the California Institute of the Arts, Valencia, the School of Visual Arts, New York, and the University of California Davis. One-person exhibitions of Muller's work have taken place at the Aspen Art Museum (2012); the Institute of Contemporary Art, Boston; Museo de Arte Contemporáneo de Castilla y León, Spain (both 2008); CCS Museum, Bard College, New York (2002); and the Saint Louis Art Museum, Missouri (2001). His work has also been included in group exhibitions such as Abstract Now and Then, Berkeley Art Museum and Pacific Film Archive, University of California (2011); Big New Field: Artists in the Cowboys Stadium Art Program, Cowboys Stadium, Dallas, Texas (2010); Rock – Paper – Scissors: Pop Music as Subject of Visual Art, Kunsthaus Graz, Austria (2009); and Jeremy Deller: Marlon Brando, Pocahontas, And Me, Aspen Art Museum (2008).

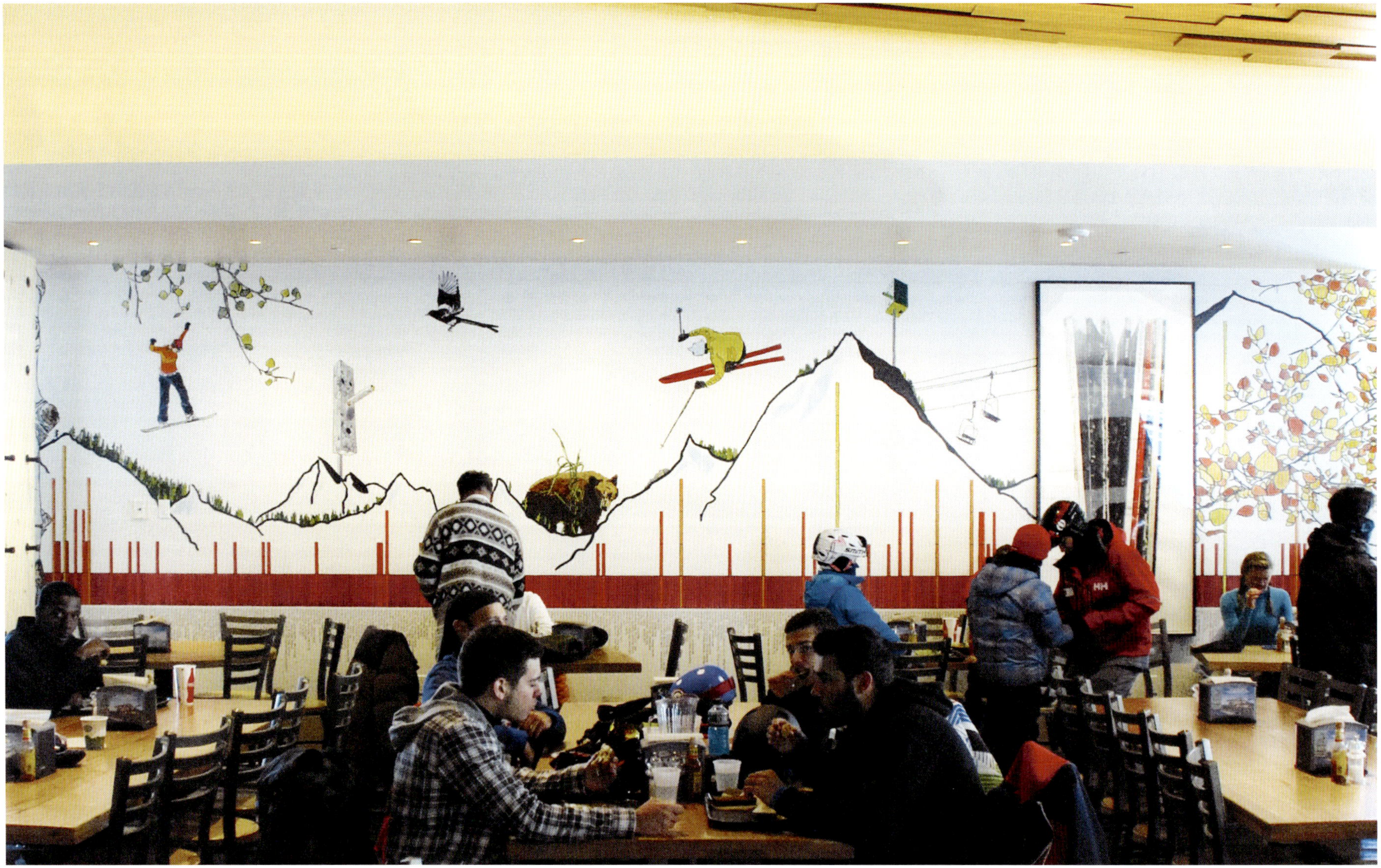

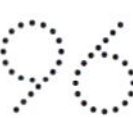

Installation views: Dave Muller, Aspen Skiing Company Music Survey Results and Generated Topography (The Hills are Alive...), 2012. Acrylic on wall, 10 x 29 feet 4 in (3 x 8.8 meters). Aspen Skiing Company Top Ten, 2012. Acrylic on paper, 84 x 36 in (213.36 x 91.44 cm). Elk Camp restaurant. Commissioned by the Aspen Art Museum and Aspen Skiing Company. Courtesy the artist and Blum & Poe, Los Angeles. Photos: Michael Aberman

Dave Muller
2012–13

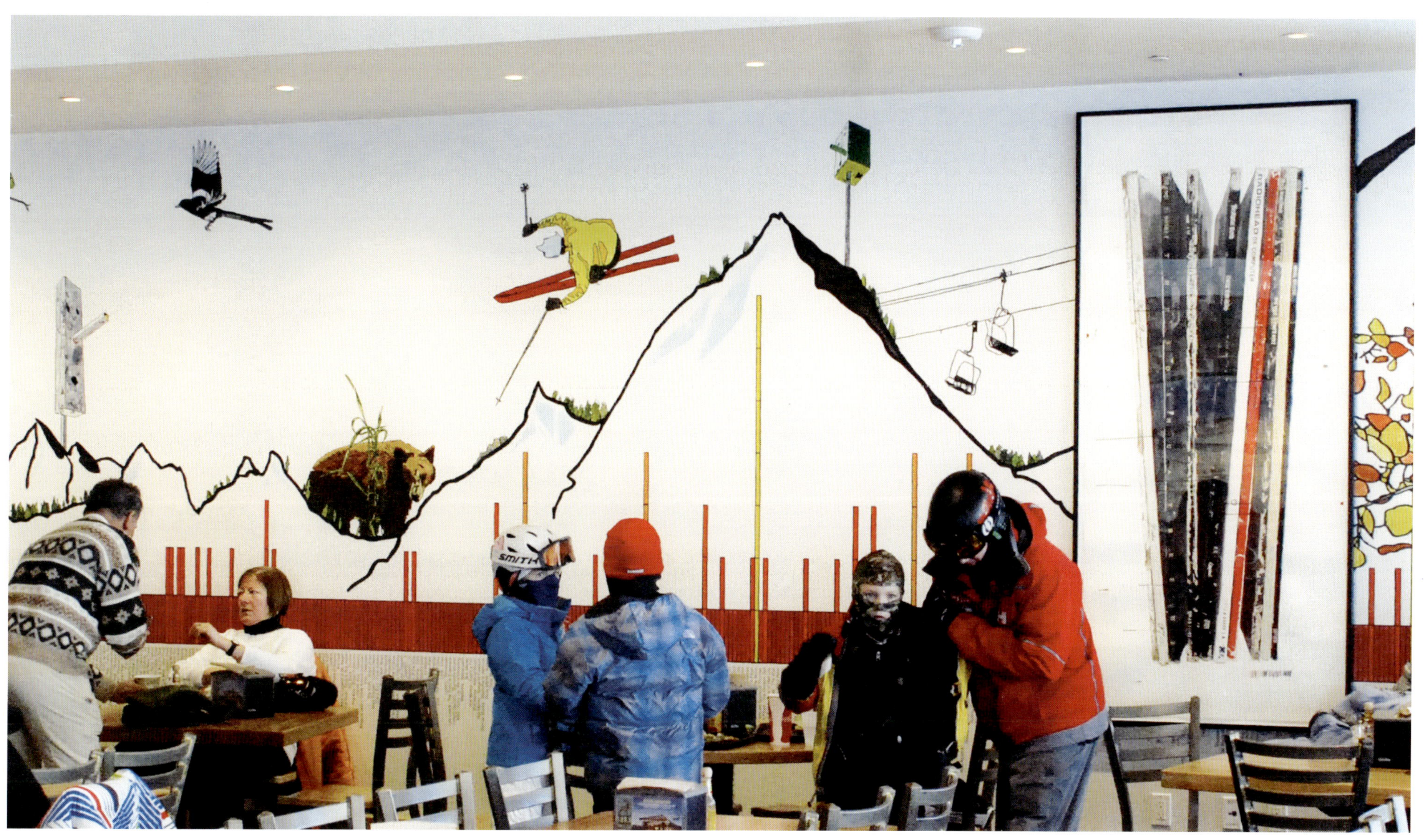

Art in
Unexpected Places II

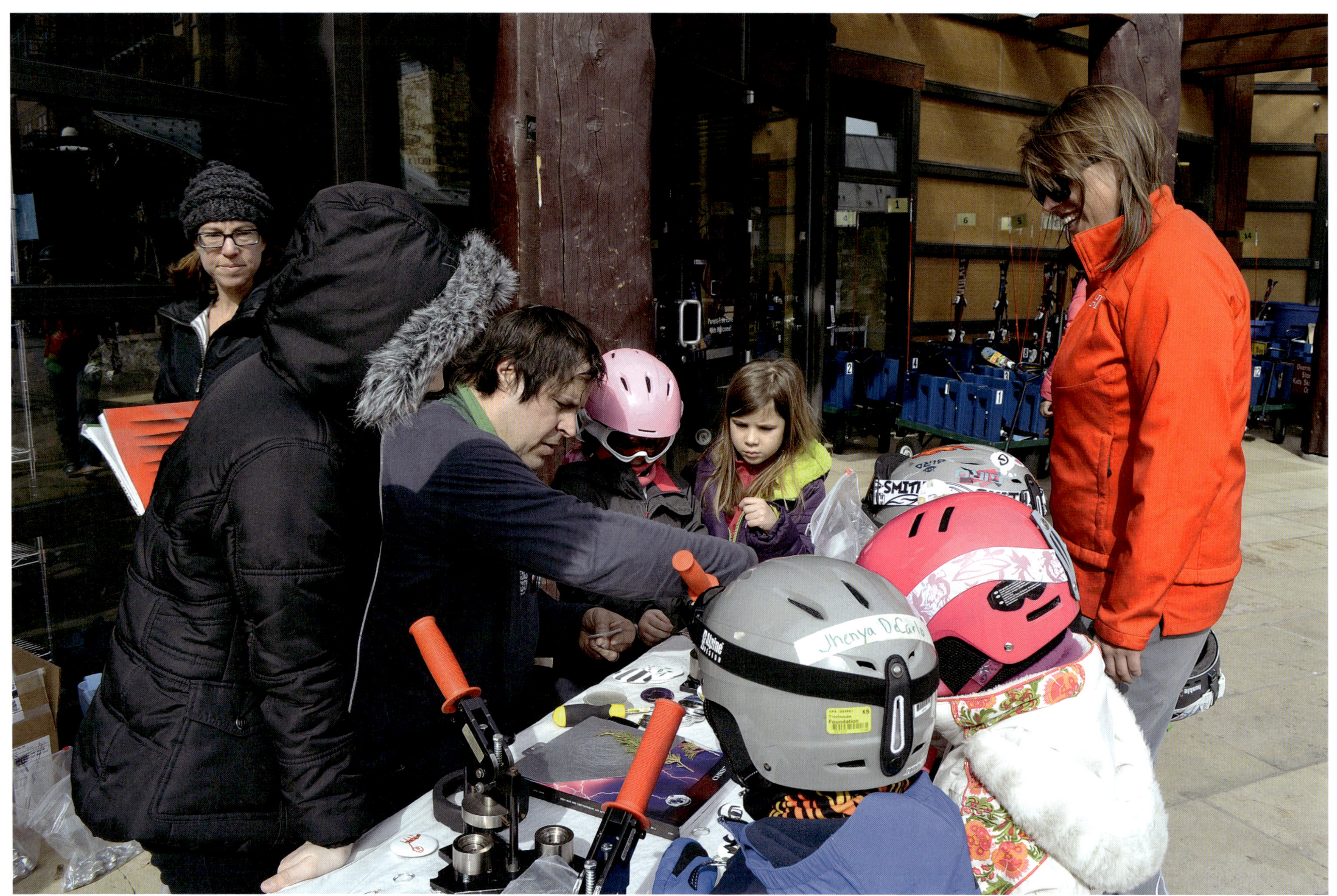

Dave Muller
2012–13

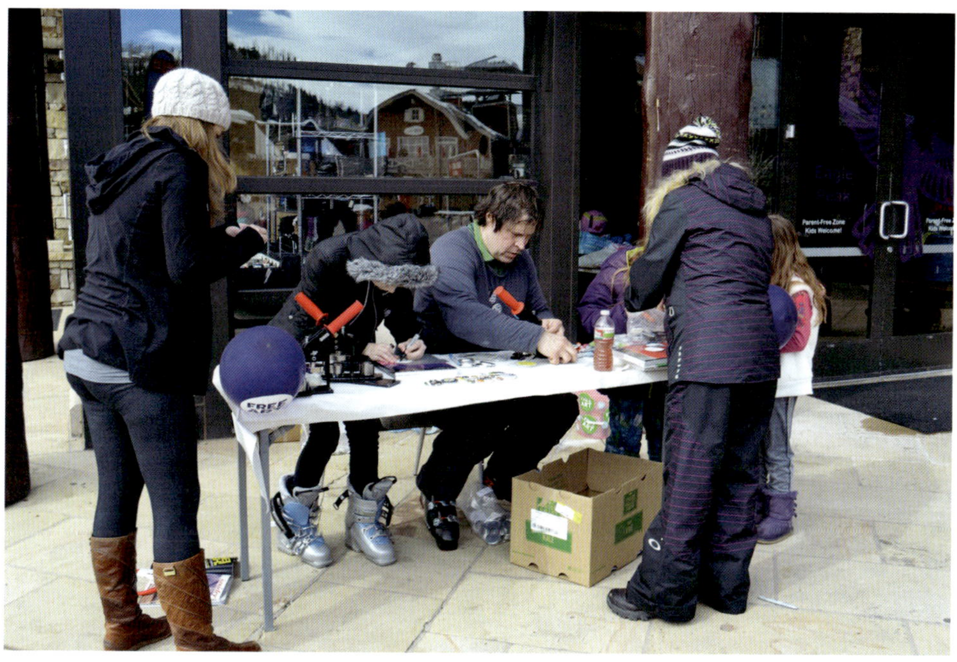

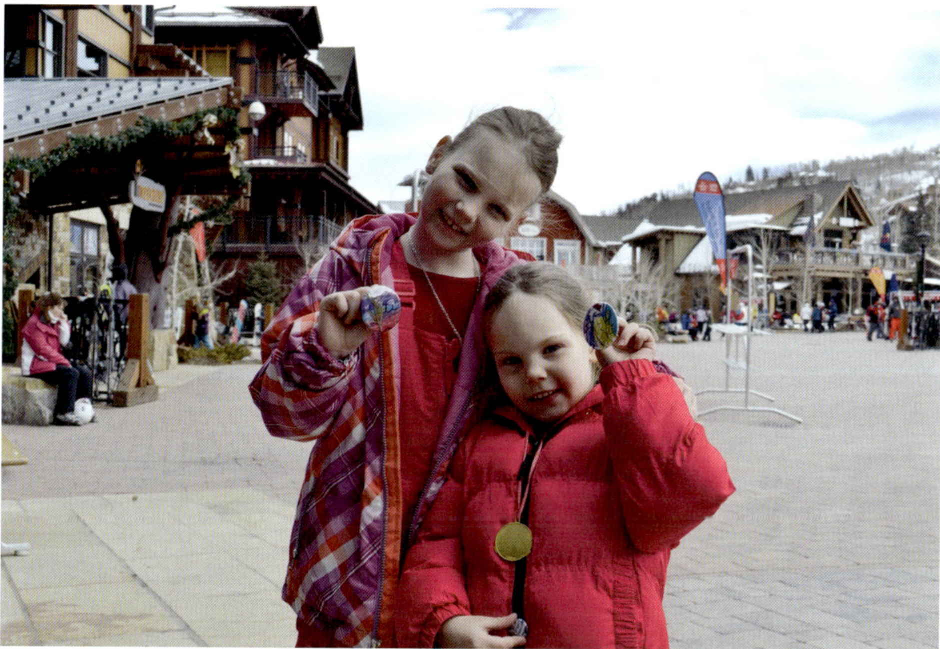

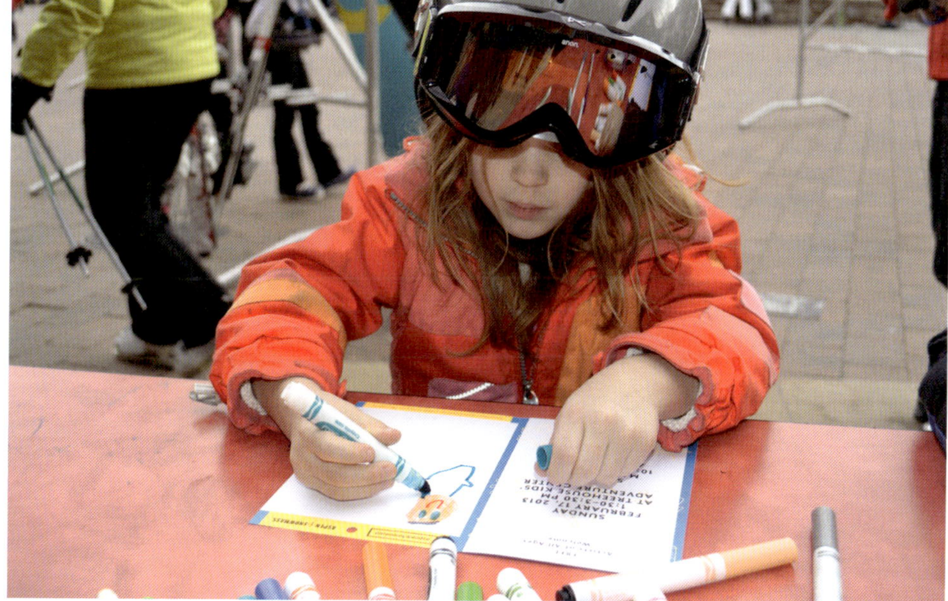

Dave Muller, _Three Day Weekend_, 2013.
Create Your Own Lift Ticket and button making,
Snowmass Village

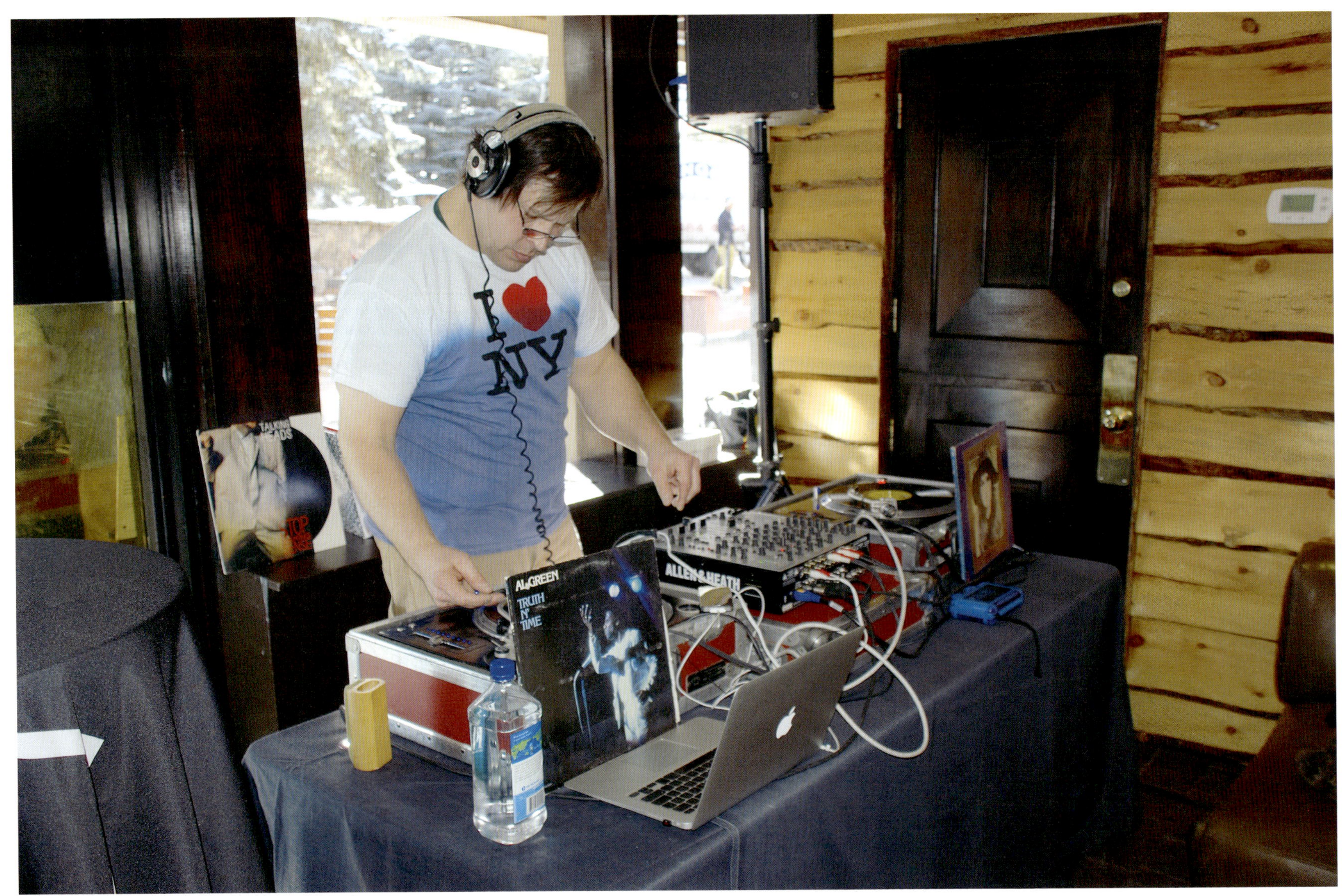

Dave Muller, <u>Three Day Weekend</u>, 2013.
Sky Hotel, Aspen

Dave Muller
2012–13

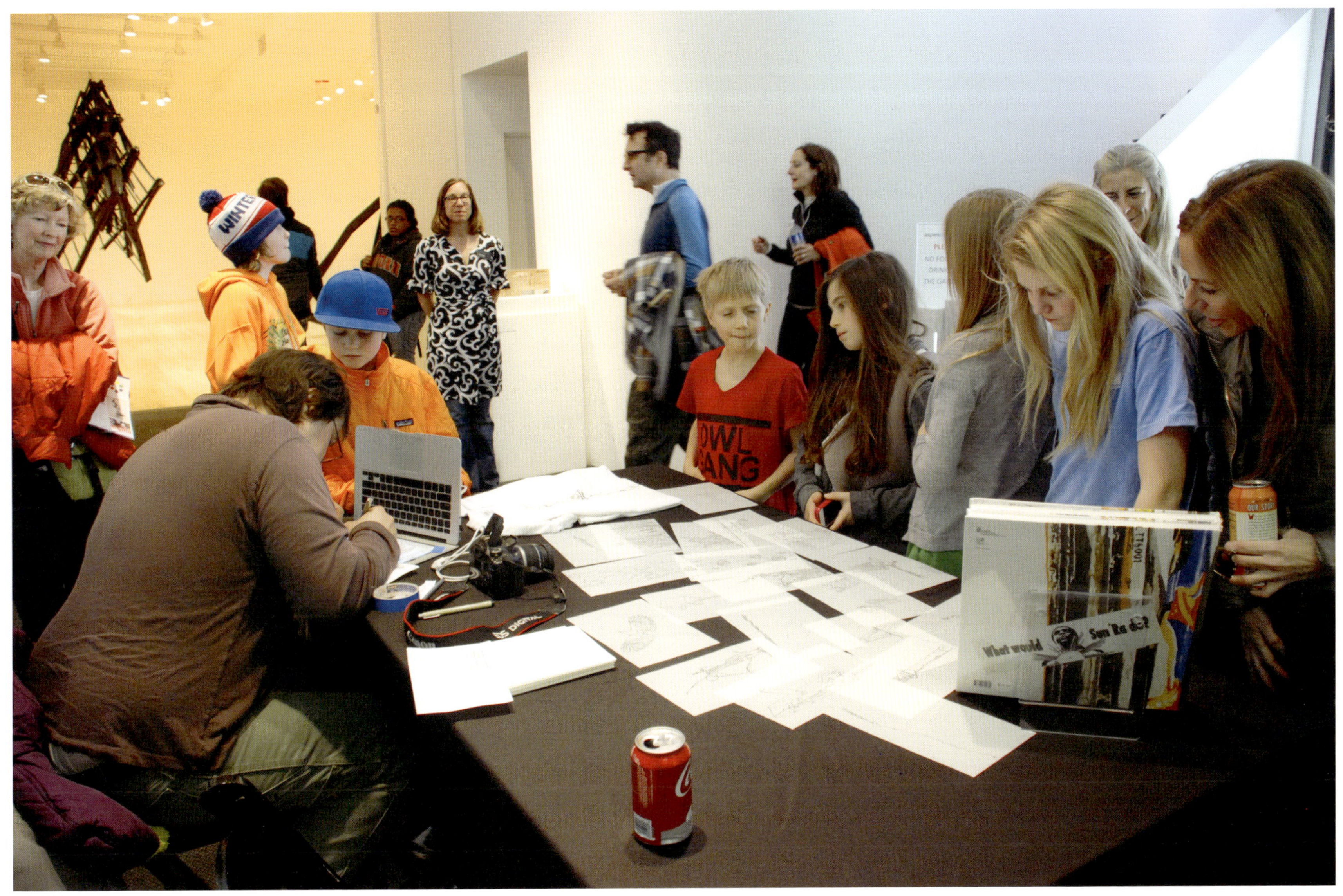

Dave Muller, <u>Three Day Weekend</u>, 2013.
Favorite Things T-shirt making, Aspen Art Museum

Art in
Unexpected Places II

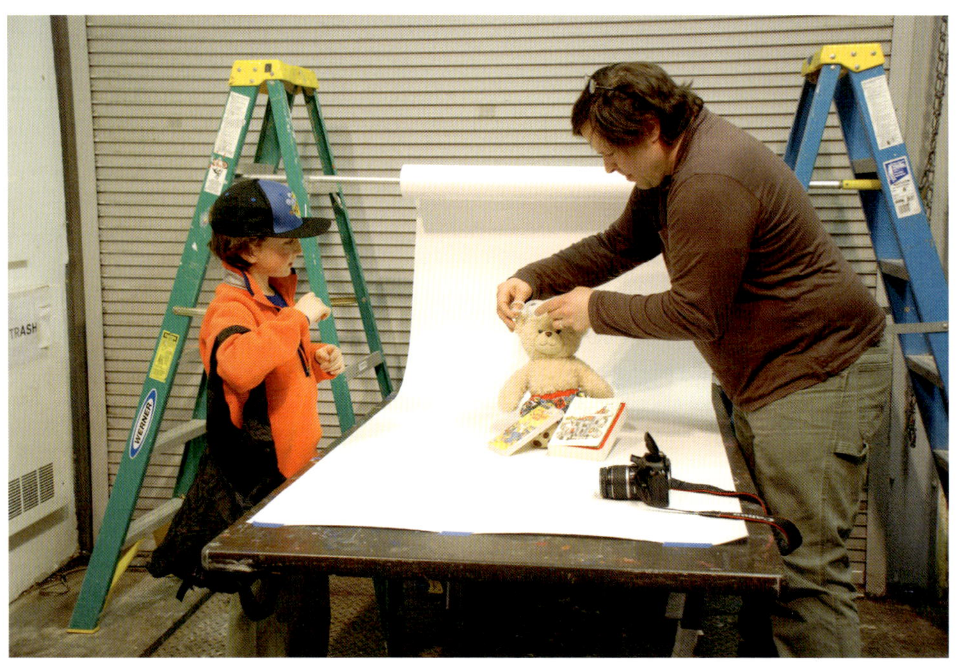

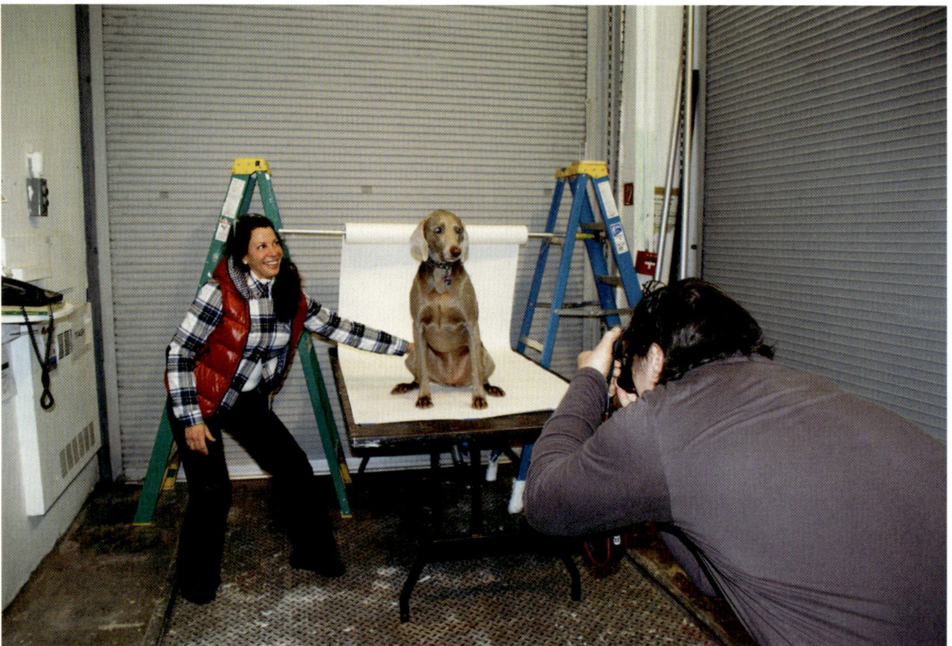

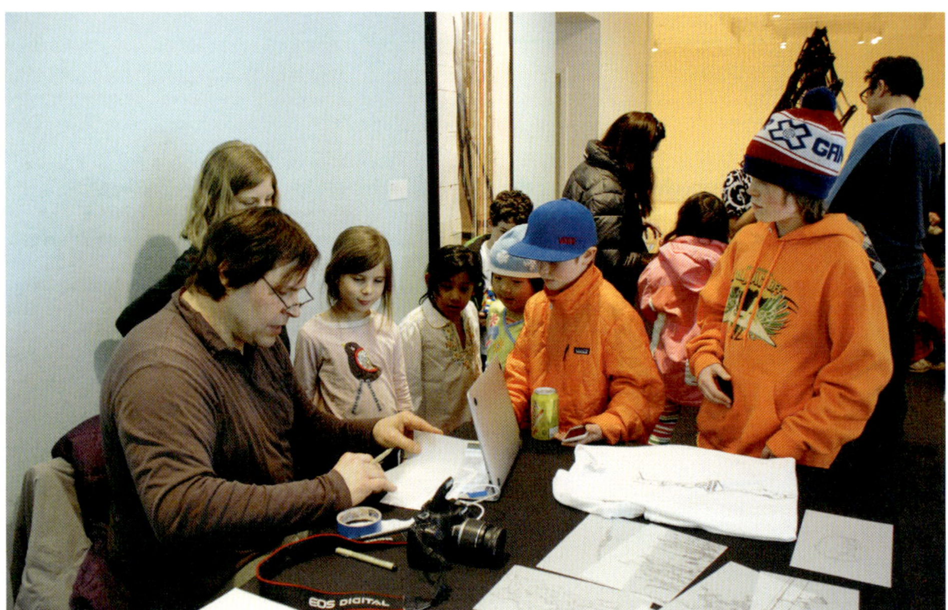

Dave Muller, <u>Three Day Weekend</u>, 2013. Favorite
Things T-shirt making, Aspen Art Museum

Dave Muller
2012–13

Mark Bradford
2013–14 Lift Tickets

The following interview took place in February 2010 between Heidi Zuckerman and Mark Bradford on the occasion of his exhibition at the Aspen Art Museum.

Heidi Zuckerman
I thought we could start off by talking about your practice in general and then we can talk about some of the works that are in the exhibition at the Aspen Art Museum.

Mark Bradford
I consider myself a painter, primarily. The works I make are on canvas and I use a painter's vocabulary, it's very formal: figure, ground, color, composition, weights. I don't use paint, I use paper, or found paper that has information on it, but I've always thought of myself as a painter. Always.

HZ
People refer to your large-scale works as "paintings."

MB
They do, luckily. I don't really know the difference between a collage and a painting. If it's speaking the same language,

I don't think it's necessary to change the description because of the materials.

HZ
For people that aren't familiar with your paintings, how would you describe your subject matter?

MB
I'd probably say that they concern the social condition. I'd probably also say the environment—the social environment. The opposite of where I am now—not in terms of the mountains and the trees, but more the asphalt and the fire hydrants.

HZ
Do you consider your works to be representational?

MB
I've always been an abstract painter, even as a kid. I've never had a figurative moment. I think sometimes there's a push with women and people of color to make a lot of figuration to describe a real condition with real imagery. But I thought that was impossible. You have to go to something abstract to talk about

anything. I don't think that you can describe something through description. Abstraction is the way for me to enter into race, into class, into the things that I'm interested in.

HZ
Your paintings are characterized by a lot of energy. They are kinetic both in terms of the surfaces—which are not flat, they are three-dimensional—and the way that the abstract patterns relate to each other. They're certainly abstract, but they are evocative, more than representational, of some of the energy and subject matter that you're describing.

MB
I'm definitely interested in energy. It just comes out in the painting. I don't start off thinking that I'm going to make a painting really pop and have energy, I just start working. Sometimes, they get a little darker; sometimes, they get a little bit more turbulent. They tell me what's going on with me. Sometimes, I don't like it.

HZ
Yesterday, you were talking about coming

out of art school and trying to figure out how to address your practice as an artist. You talked about going inside and going deeper and farther. It's interesting to hear that you feel your painting directs that action or activity.

MB

I thought that if I was going to do this, then I had to do it 100 percent. I went to school later, so because I had all this experience in the world, I don't think that my practice started when I went to CalArts—it encompasses all of my experiences. Although I had an academic education and reading would inform my work, or trigger something, I always knew that the information was inside of me more than outside of me.

HZ

Did you grow up making art?

MB

I didn't grow up with the words "making art," but I come from a making family, from a family that was always doing something. We were always project-oriented, creative people, but I didn't

come from a background where we described it as art. I thought that was something that existed in museums and outside of what I was doing. I knew that what I was doing was active, and I knew it was creative.

HZ

You've talked a lot about the entrepreneurial spirit or the idea of selling something— being self-reliant and a merchant. I read something about you making signs for your mom's business growing up.

MB

Yeah, I did. My mother is a hairdresser. Early on, I really liked calligraphy, so I was always in charge of making the signs on the wall: Haircut, ten dollars; Blow-dry, fifteen; Perm, twenty-five. Every three or four months or every year, when the prices would go up, I was in charge of remaking them.

I really had this idea of being creative, having a target, doing something with it outside in the world, and doing it based on my own volition. Just being self-motivated.

My mother didn't stand over me. She said, "OK. Here's the paint. There's the

wall. Here are the prices." My creativity has always been active. It's been hermetic in a way, where a lot of my practice goes on in the studio, but I pull so much from things post-studio. I have so many relationships outside the studio.

HZ

The exhibition at the Aspen Art Museum is focused on a body of work that you describe as "merchant posters" [Figs. 1–2]. It's a descriptive term: all the posters are advertising something. They're all a call to action for the viewer to come and buy or test something. These posters, not just in their current state as artworks, but also in their previous state, are additionally about opportunity.

MB

I became fascinated with them in the early nineties. After the riots in Los Angeles, there were so many vacant lots that a lot of cyclone fencing went up. After the lots and the fencing, the merchant posters went up. It was free advertising space.

This whole informal economy sort of sprung up overnight. Both micro and macro: macro in terms of what was going on in the United States or the world, and micro with what was going on in that particular community.

In some ways, they are parasitic conditions. Some of the clients or the customers of these small, quasi-informal businesses couldn't get out to other communities, but at the same time, these businesses were also providing a service that people might not have access to otherwise. It's a very complex relationship. I don't judge it. It's just very layered.

HZ

The layered feature is also quite interesting in the way it relates to your works. Not only philosophically and metaphysically, but also physically. Your techniques for making both your paintings and these merchant posters are unusual. Can you talk a little bit about how you make them and what kinds of tools you use?

MB

I do use a painting vocabulary, but I use non-painting materials. I have a sander instead of a paintbrush. Twine takes the place of graphite pencils and I get my colors from paper that I take from the streets and color-separate in big vats of water. Materially, I have a minimal aesthetic and then I apply very complex, social, academic layers on top of it. I have to narrow the gaze somewhere or I would lose my mind, it would be too much.

HZ

You have talked about how the application of these posters on the cyclone fences had a body reference, because people would walk by them, and the fences were slightly larger, but also had a human scale to them.

The first time I met you was in New Orleans, post-Katrina. You had spent a long time walking—you had just set off from where you were staying. You were discovering the space, discovering the community, in this very physical way.

MB

You see the city differently when you walk. New Orleans has a physicality that's very different from Los Angeles, where everyone is in cars. You can see the markings of culture much more on the buildings. The city doesn't move as fast when you walk—you're able to read the history and process, you can peek through windows. When you're driving by, it moves too fast, you can't keep up with it.

HZ

There's a poster in the exhibition that was made in New Orleans, *Untitled (Corner of Desire and Piety) III* (2008; Fig. 3), but other than that one, they all come from California.

MB

That's right. I spend most of my time in Los Angeles, but I spent over a year in New Orleans so it felt right. I'm not going to travel the city or globe picking up merchant posters out of context and making works about them. I'm not going to globalize it. I don't really like this homogenous global stew. I like things that exist in micro-conditions that have limited range and don't cross over. I want to take that experience and then drop it into another context, but while it still exists in its micro-condition.

HZ

You had said that the merchant posters primarily had a five-block radius. They were targeted for the people that lived

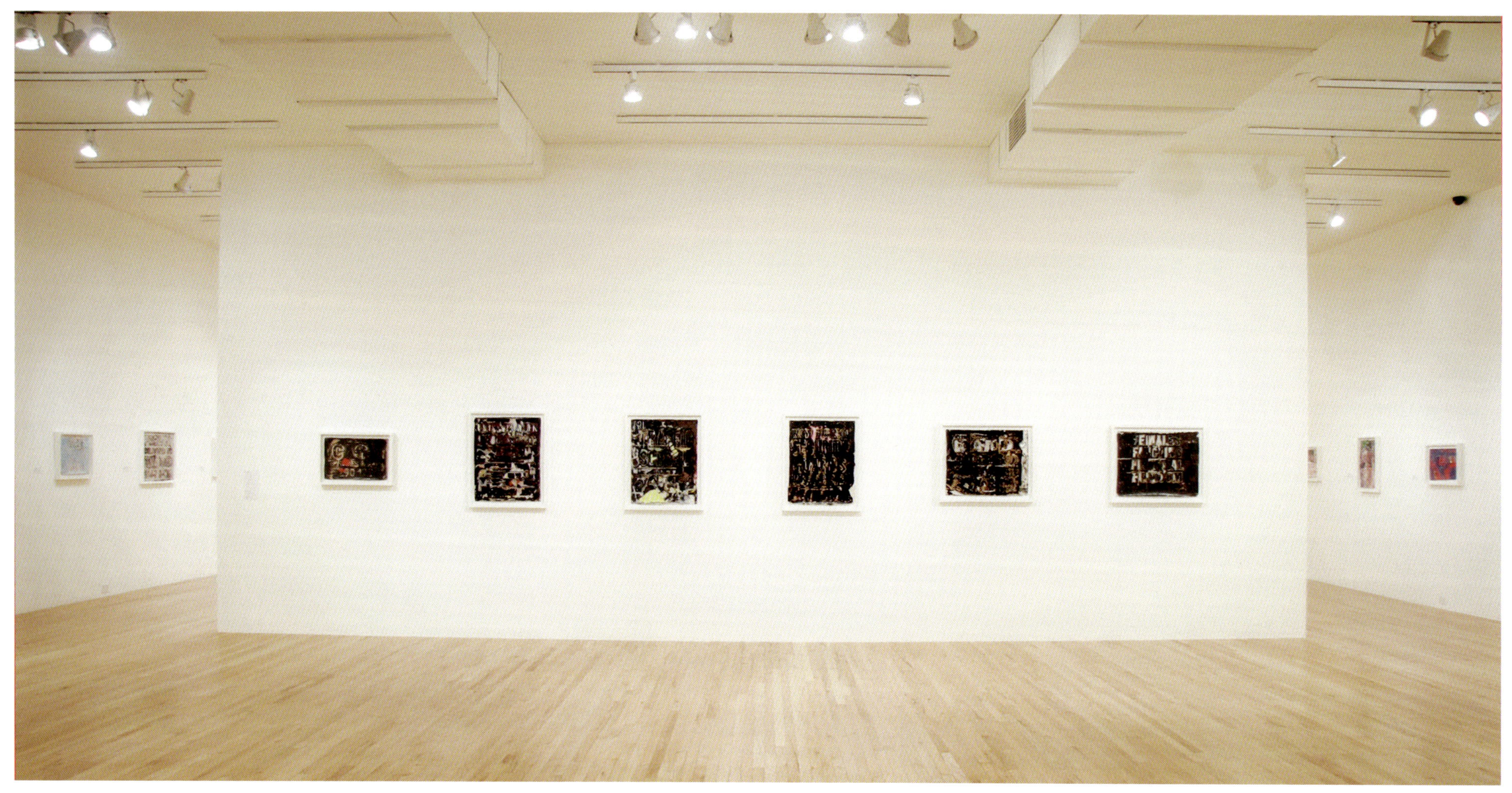

Mark Bradford
2013–14

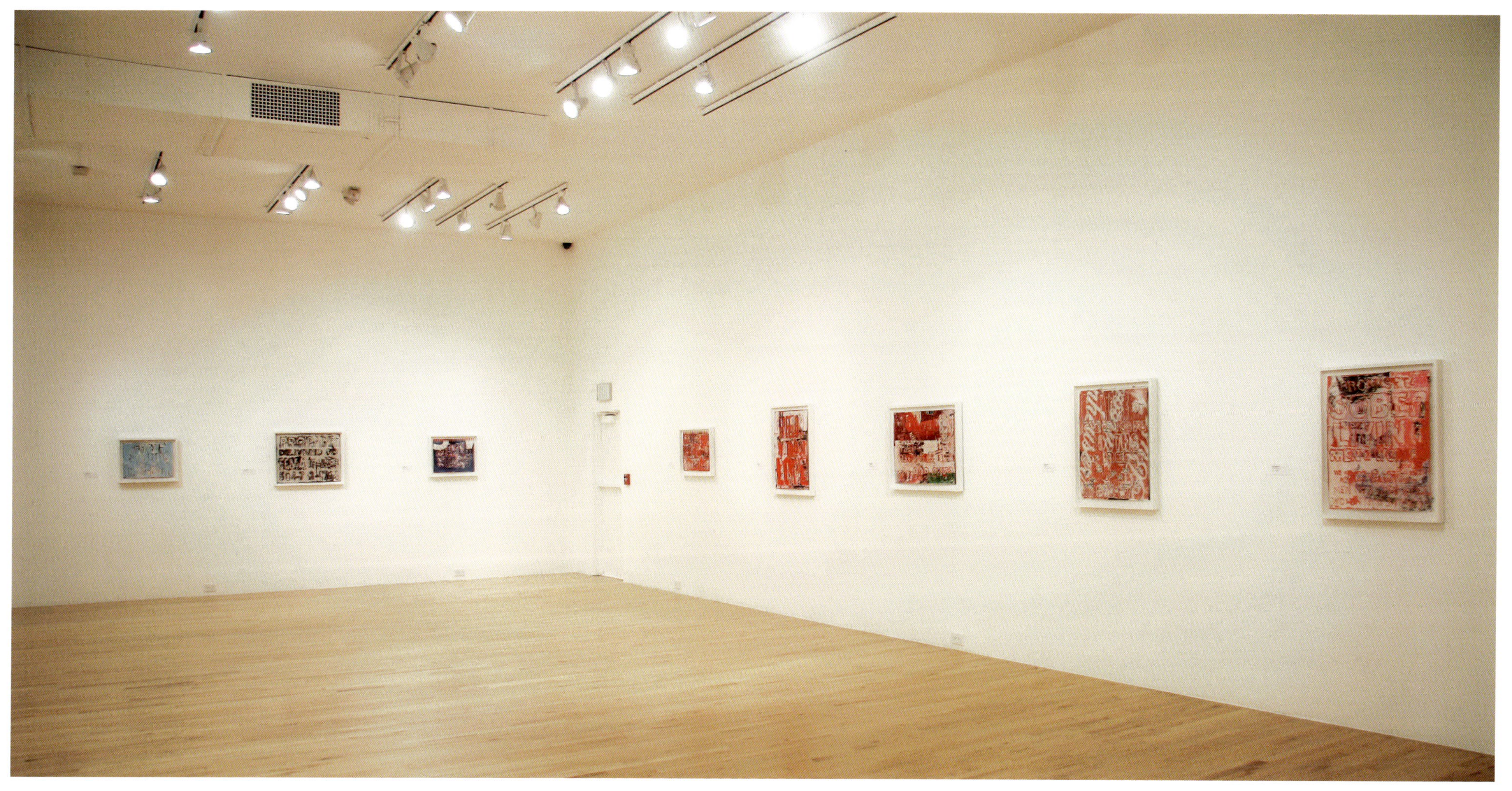

Fig. 1–2
Installation views: <u>Mark Bradford</u>, Aspen Art Museum, 2010.
Courtesy the artist. Photos: Karl Wolfgang

Art in
Unexpected Places II

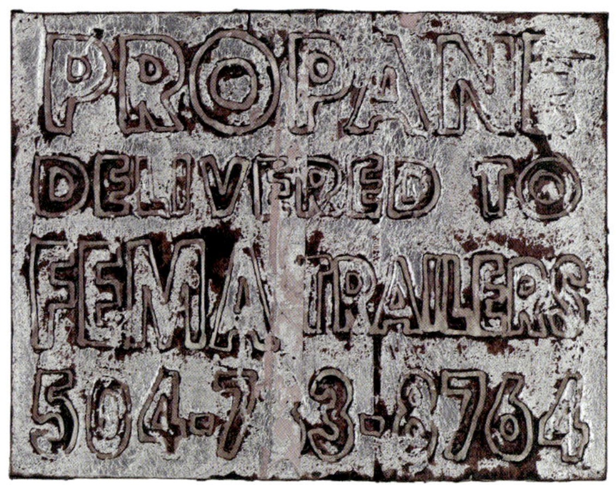

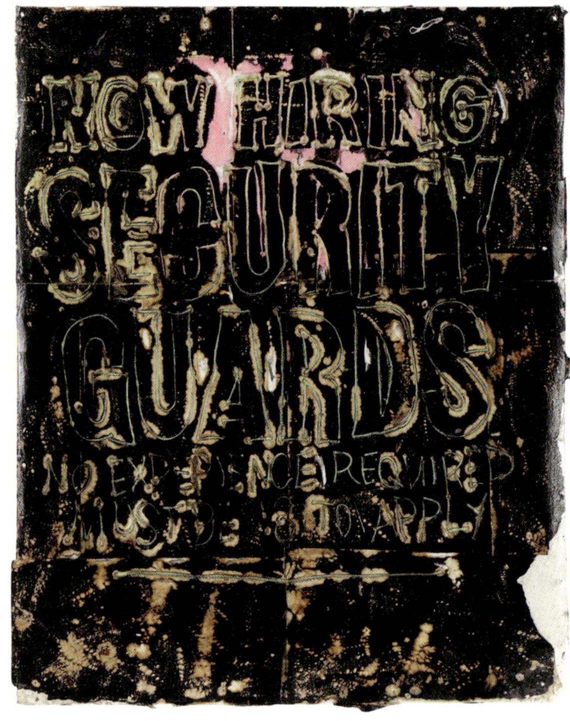

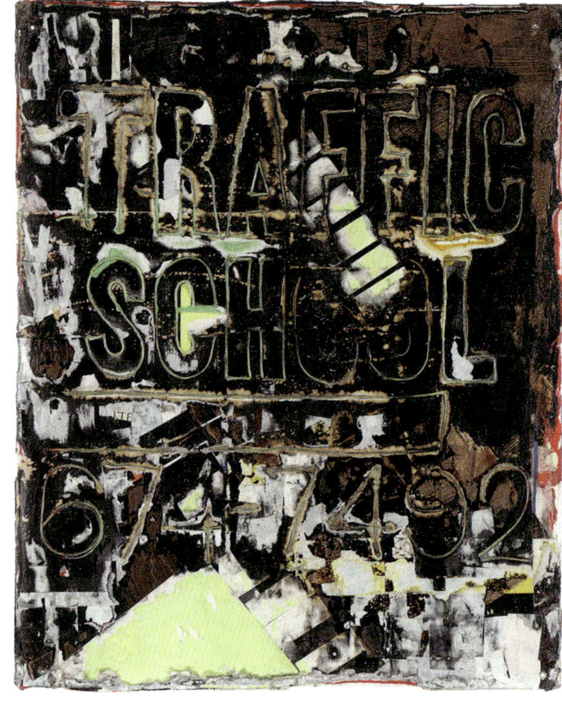

Fig. 3
Mark Bradford, Untitled (Corner of Desire and Piety) III, 2008. Mixed media collage, 22 × 27 3/4 in (55.8 × 70.4 cm). Collection of Liz and Eric Lefkofsky. © Mark Bradford

Fig. 4
Mark Bradford, Untitled, 2009. Mixed media collage, 28 1/8 × 22 in (71.1 × 55.8 cm). Courtesy Nancy and Bob Magoon. © Mark Bradford

Fig. 5
Mark Bradford, Untitled, 2009. Mixed media collage, 28 1/4 × 22 1/4 in (71.1 × 53.9 cm). Collection Elise and Andrew Brownstein, New York. © Mark Bradford

in specific communities, primarily offered by people who also live in those communities.

MB
Little businesses, little money. What's also interesting is that these businesses identify a need. It's not what they always tell you in business school, but it's marketing or advertising 101. The little businesses that I see on the side of the

roads, or in bus and train stations, or flea markets are always specific to the needs of that community. They're always interesting. When you go to another country, another community, it's very, very different.

The New Orleans poster was the only one that I ever really tweaked. It was actually advertising propane. You could buy propane for FEMA trailers. When I was there, a law had been passed that the

FEMA trailers were toxic, and they pulled them all onto this soccer field that people weren't using anymore.

But New Orleans was littered with posters from this business selling propane. This whole FEMA thing was a mess, New Orleans was a mess, so I did this project where instead of the number of the company on the merchant poster, I changed it to the FEMA Office in New Orleans. I imagined all these people calling and thinking that they were calling the propane company not FEMA. It just put a little something on their mind.

HZ

I love that it's a really subtle thing. You also don't even know what effect it had, because you don't know how many people called or what they said. It's a good reminder of all the bad decisions that FEMA made for so many people that were in such difficult circumstances already.

MB

Another piece that has a degree of social layering is an untitled work from 2009 that reads, "NOW HIRING SECURITY GUARDS" [Fig. 4]. It came from South Central Los Angeles, and you begin to wonder who they are hiring. It says, "NO EXPERIENCE REQUIRED." No experience required to be a security guard shows a dead end—maybe they didn't finish high school and they have a police record. I always felt like they've done something that has inhibited their movement through society. I just felt sad for so many young people that don't have more options. It makes you think about the school system and the penal system. It's socially layered. That one always grabbed me; it made me feel sad.

HZ

What about the use of pink in it? Is it a vulnerability to offset the overarching tone?

MB

Yeah, a little bit, because South Central is hard. I'm always infusing the work with a little bit of something different—pink and security guards don't go together.

HZ

It's not that they don't go together necessarily, but it's an interesting choice.

MB

They all feel so vulnerable. I felt like this design felt vulnerable.

HZ

Yeah. Pink is a color of vulnerability for me.

MB

Interesting. Another Los Angeles piece reads, "TRAFFIC SCHOOL," and I was thinking a lot about the city [Fig. 5].

HZ

About a lot of cars?

MB

A lot of cars, and what cars mean to people in Los Angeles—they mean more than houses. You can do a lot with a car in Los Angeles—it's amazing. A couple of times, I've had to borrow a friend's car because my truck wasn't working. It was a fancy car—a BMW or something—I could barely even open the door. I was instantly amazed at the difference driving down the street in a BMW instead of a truck. Los Angeles car culture is the big thing.

Then, for a piece like "GUN SHOW" from 2006, it highlights the gun culture in Los Angeles—not all legal [Fig. 6]. I thought of how I could hold this condition up to itself by mirroring it. I made it backwards into itself, looking in at itself. These are plastered all over South Central.

I don't steer away from the violence of society any more than I steer towards it. It's simply the American condition or the global condition…it's a complex situation. There are days when it becomes more violent and there are days when it doesn't become more violent. There are days when we feel very safe and days when we don't feel safe at all. At the moment, the world feels very vulnerable and unsafe.

It interests me as much as the balloon of years when people felt great and were making a lot of money. I'm more interested in actually putting the complexity on the table; I'm not interested in trying to find a solution—I don't believe that you can find a solution. I think that you can have conversations about the complexity of the lives that we're living. That's all I try to do in the work.

HZ
Another work from 2006 that's really compelling reads, "IS THIS CHILD YOURS? DNA TESTING" [Fig. 7].

MB
It talks about relationships, paternity, who wants children, and who doesn't want children. It talks about economics, court ordered, court certified…

HZ
The government in people's personal business?

MB
Right. I didn't think so much about the two people at war with each other, I thought about the child being caught in between.

HZ
People often forget about the kid, who is in the middle.

Then there are works like "LOCKS OR TWIST" from 2007, which ties back into your mother's hair salon [Fig. 8].

MB
Black people have a long love affair with their hair. This is from a business advertising to do locks or twists, but I re-contextualized it into the locks and twists of society, the sort of crossing, re-crossing, cross-hatching, and cross-weaving of society in general, of a culture, of people. I always look at it as the locking and twisting of different spheres.

HZ
In the upper-right-hand corner, it reads: "GUYS IN LOVE WITH YOU," "EVERYBODY LOVES SOMEBODY," "I'VE LOST THAT LOVING FEELING."

MB
I'm assuming that it's the greatest hits of some Motown advertisement that was in the streets and I liked the text and peeled it down. I love to take language and re-contextualize it. It just blows up the meaning. I love language—the use and misuse of language.

HZ
One of the things that's really interesting about this work and some of your other pieces, too, is the variety. Here, there are obviously a lot of other different sources that come together to make the overall

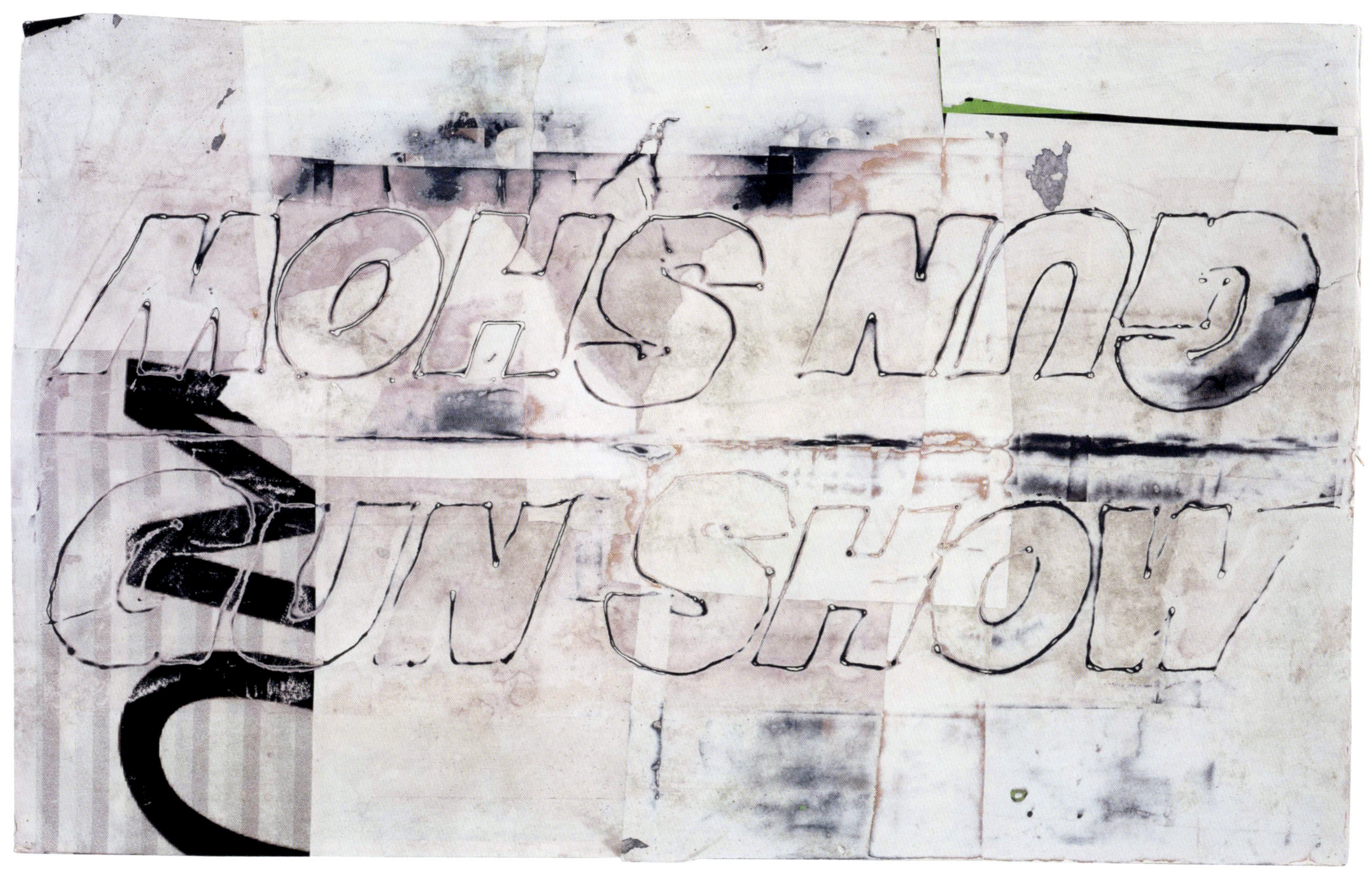

Fig. 6
Mark Bradford, Untitled, 2006. Mixed media collage, 28 x 44 in (71.1 x 111.7 cm). Collection of Dennis and Debra Scholl, Miami Beach, FL. © Mark Bradford

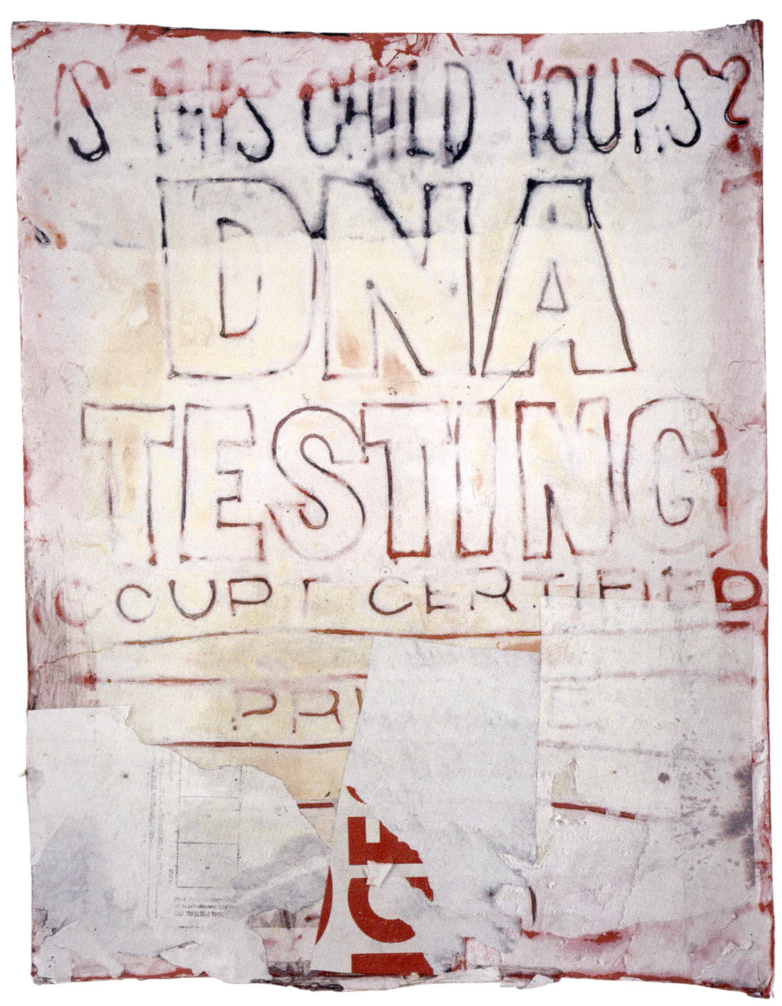

Fig. 7
Mark Bradford, Untitled, 2006. Mixed media
collage, 28 x 22 1/2 in (71.1 x 57.1 cm). Private
collection. © Mark Bradford

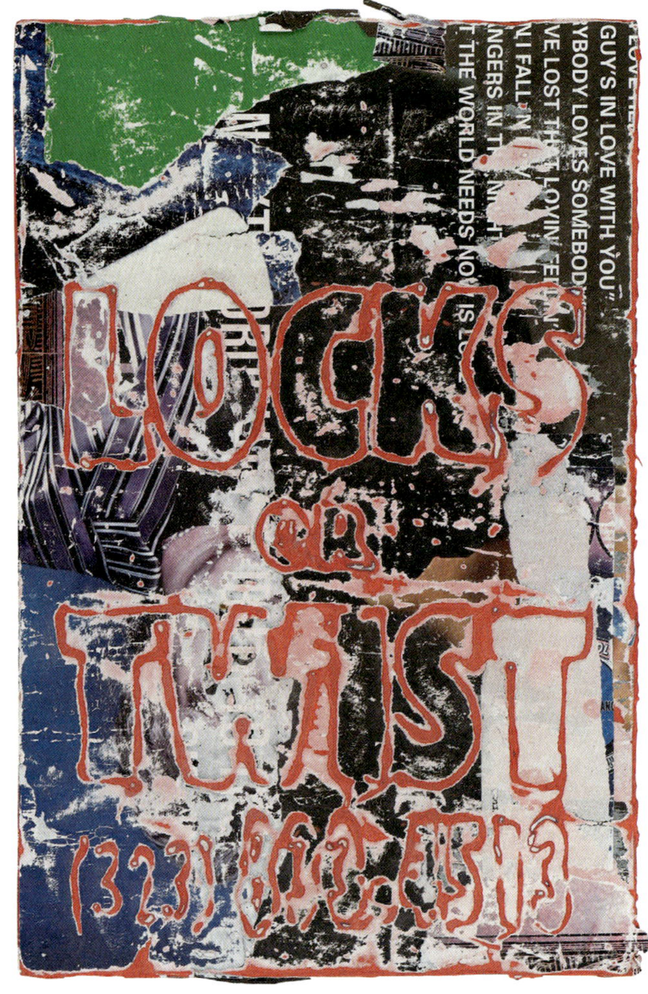

Fig. 8
Mark Bradford, Untitled, 2006. Mixed media
collage, 28 x 22 1/2 in (71.1 x 57.1 cm). Private
collection. © Mark Bradford

Mark Bradford
2013–14

piece. When people look at these, they may see the song titles, they may see a face, or they may be drawn to the text.

MB

That's fine. I think it's ridiculous to think that you're going to control someone's gaze. I know what it means for me and I work that out as best as I can in the studio. Once it becomes part of the public domain, people are going to bring their own histories to the work and they're going to read it in different ways. You have to allow that, you have to let it go.

HZ

Do you know what they're going to look like when you start?

MB

I know what the found piece looks like, but I don't know what they will look like. The easiest way to describe my work, my practice, is that it's like a relationship. Every work that I do, I go through the whole process: you meet a person, you're excited, your heart's pounding, you're on good behavior, you get to know a person, you get a little bit more confident, you

reveal a little bit more of yourself. After that, you show even more, then you get really bold and start to get apathetic. You realize it's not going to work, you get a divorce, and you move on. That is exactly how a work goes for me. I go through all of the different chapters in a relationship to the divorce court and then I go to the next one.

All the relationships have been good, but I do divorce myself. It's funny walking into a space and going through the arc of every single work that I do. They absolutely surprise me. I thought one relationship was going to be easy—we were both the same sign, we both liked the same thing—and it turned out to be the most difficult relationship in the world. Other relationships that I think are going to be very difficult, turn out to be the same thing, it's no different. ❊

Mark Bradford was born in Los Angeles, where he continues to live and work. He received both his BFA (1995) and his MFA (1997) from the California Institute for the Arts. A survey exhibition of Bradford's work premiered at the Wexner Center for the Arts in Columbus (2010) and traveled to the Institute of Contemporary Art, Boston; the Museum of Contemporary Art, Chicago; the Dallas Museum of Art; the San Francisco Museum of Modern Art; and Yerba Buena Center for the Arts, San Francisco. Other solo exhibitions include Scorched Earth, UCLA Hammer Museum, Los Angeles (2015); With That Ass, They Won't Look at Your Eyes, Stanlee and Gerald Rubin Center for the Visual Arts, University of Texas at El Paso (2012); and Mark Bradford, Nasher Museum of Art, Duke University, Durham, North Carolina (2012). He is the recipient of numerous awards including a 2009 MacArthur Fellowship Award, the Bucksbaum Award for his contribution to the Whitney Biennial in 2006, a 2006 USA Fellowship Award, and a 2003 Louis Comfort Tiffany Foundation Award.

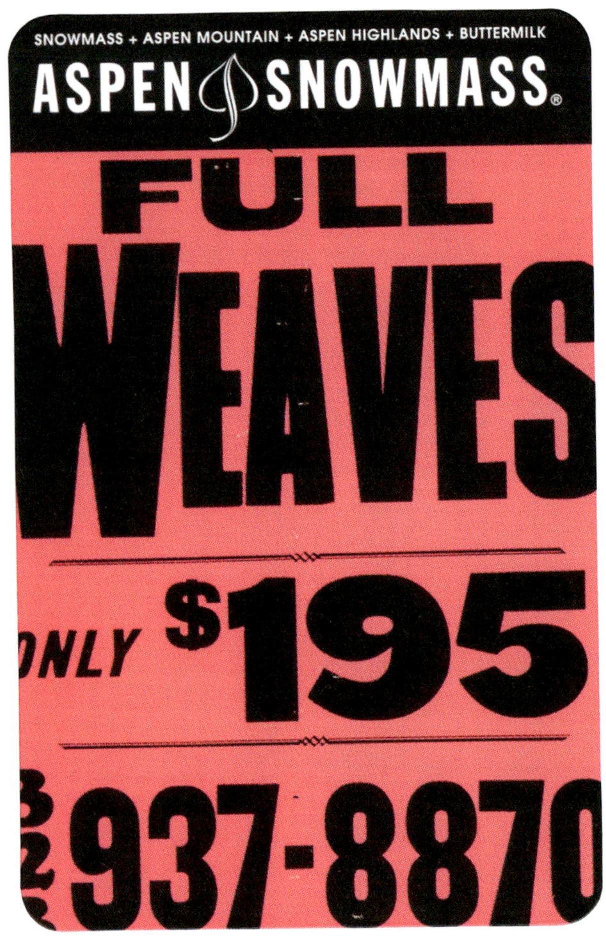

Lift Ticket: Mark Bradford, _Full Weaves_, 2013

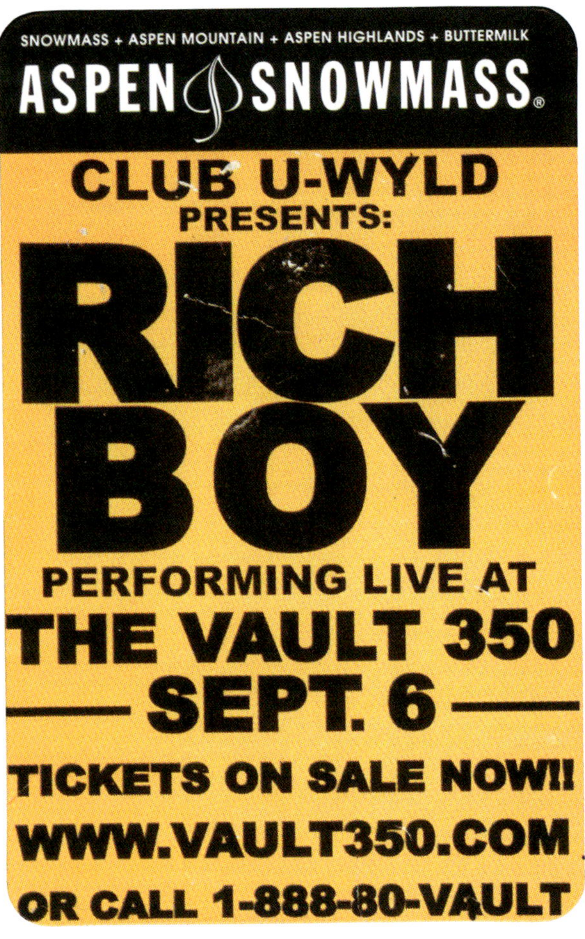

Lift Ticket: Mark Bradford, _Rich Boy_, 2013

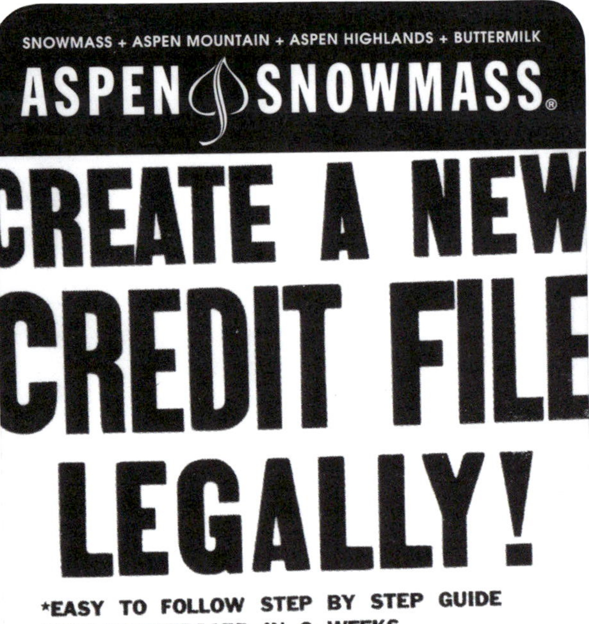

Lift Ticket: Mark Bradford, _Create a New Credit File Legally_, 2013

Mark Bradford
2013–14

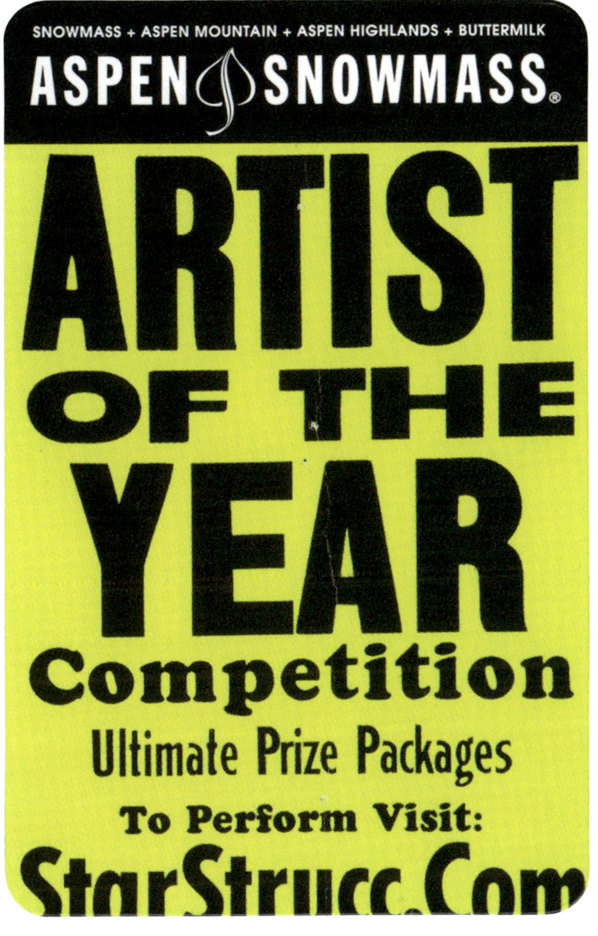

Lift Ticket: Mark Bradford, _Artist of the Year_, 2013

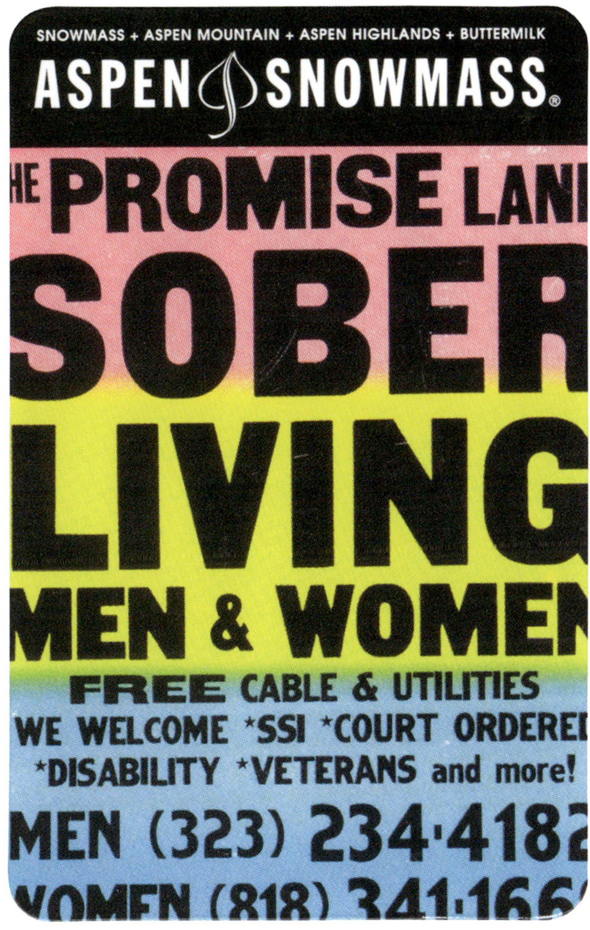

Lift Ticket: Mark Bradford, _The Promise Land_, 2013

All works courtesy the artist. Commissioned by the Aspen Art Museum and the Aspen Skiing Company. © Mark Bradford

Source material for Mark Bradford's lift ticket
<u>The Promise Land</u>, 2013. Poster produced by the
Colby Poster Printing Company, Los Angeles

Source material for Mark Bradford's lift ticket
<u>Full Weaves</u>, 2013. Poster produced by the Colby
Poster Printing Company, Los Angeles

Mark Bradford
2013–14

Teresita Fernández

2013–15 Elk Camp Installation

The following interview took place in July 2013 between Heidi Zuckerman and Teresita Fernández on the occasion of her installation at Elk Camp restaurant in Snowmass.

Heidi Zuckerman
I'd like to talk about some of your work that surveys the last twelve or thirteen years. But it would be great if you could start off describing your practice overall and your approach to art making.

Teresita Fernández
Because my work really depends on the ambulatory viewer interacting with it, I always hesitate to describe experiences and prefer instead to talk about ideas. My process in the studio is completely conceptual. Even though what's seen at the end seems optically seductive and thoroughly visual, it's actually the very last phase of what I do.

A regular day may be reading, writing, walking, researching, traveling to sites, and accumulating images. I have a funny way of working where I start this very blind process of accumulating and layering ideas and images, in large part based on intuition and research that meanders. It's not until something starts to click conceptually that I even start thinking about materials. That comes much later. It's very difficult trying to find materials that I can make transcend their set physical identity and weight in a way that can capture and correlate to the original concept.

It's akin to some kind of alchemy in terms of recognizing when something's important, but not really knowing how it connects until it reveals a connection that isn't necessarily rational or logical. It's really like an aimless search for something that, when it reveals itself, becomes very, very clear. There's lucidity when I get there, but in the middle of the process, I may have no sense of what form it will take.

HZ
We first worked together in 1999, when I invited you to do a show at the Berkeley Art Museum. We talked about what your intention was in creating the works and what you hoped the experience would be like for the viewer. Then, there was a suspension of disbelief, where you weren't sure exactly how it was going to work or how it would be for the viewer. That embracing of the unknown really characterizes your practice.

TF
Yes, it does. In the end, it's a surprise to me as well. I somehow manage to get there. After you've been working for decades, there's a sense that the work has to be elusive to oneself as well. It doesn't get easier; it becomes harder to find ways for the work to be mysterious to oneself.

When I find myself in a place where I can imagine how something may work, but I can't quite convince myself of it, that uncomfortable feeling means I'm onto something. I know I have to inhabit that uneasy position in order to get to the lucid concept. That's when I feel that I may have something to transmit to the viewer.

In other words, it has to happen to me before I can have it happen to you. I have to will something to become more than the sum of its parts, like making something from nothing, where a bunch of ideas get turned into something that moves me in order for me to then be able to move you.

I'm interested in that emotional response from the viewer, as much as I am for myself. It's something that's difficult to talk about, but really, our responses to things are ultimately emotional. There's a very delicate balance of things, there's nothing overt or direct about it, and nothing extra.

That's what I'm interested in both for myself and for my viewers. I think of my viewer as someone who's more like a reader, who's constructing an idea and an image, and a set of important things in their mind. Not someone who's just observing something that I've made.

HZ

I talk about that as the possibility of transcendence. I would say my whole goal in presenting art is creating those opportunities for that experience to happen. You can't dictate that, and you can't prescribe it, but you can offer that as a possibility. When it works, it's perfect.

TF

It's also something that's very difficult to do with sculpture and three-dimensional materials. We're very accustomed to seeing those kinds of transcendent moments in film, photography, or painting—anything where you can control the tone of it. It's not hard to do that in film, photography, or in drawing even, because it's very easy to smudge things or change the lighting to achieve a particular moody tone.

When you're dealing with concrete or a pile of graphite, things just are what they are. I've always been very interested in this narrow niche, questioning how you work with things that are so much what they want to be, and so attached to this obstinate fact of their own physicality. I've done that in the past using cheap materials and low production—making something out of nothing. It's always been a challenge for me.

We did a show together on drawing, *Sculptors Drawing*. Everybody always thinks that sculptors or people who work with materials make drawings to plan the sculpture. For me, it's always been the other way around. I've always wanted to make sculptures that look and feel like my drawings. With solid materials, it's really hard to do that. In the formal aspect of my work, that's been one of the challenges that has kept me entertained for many years; massive, heavy sculptural installations that behave like intimate, ephemeral drawings.

HZ

It's interesting to think about this idea of materials, or objects, or anything being tied to the knowledge of what it is. You made reference to the idea of alchemy and this ability to somehow change something from what it is into something else. That's a real artistic challenge and an incredible feat when it happens, because so many times, it doesn't happen. There's inherent failure, so when there's a success, it's that much more exciting and momentous.

TF

It starts from a very basic point for me. When I make an installation, or something that's going to be shown in a particular city or place, the first thing I ask myself is, "Where am I?" It's a simple question. I think about where I am physically, what happened in this landscape, what the inside of this museum looks like, and when you walk outside, what that looks like. Where am I culturally, historically,

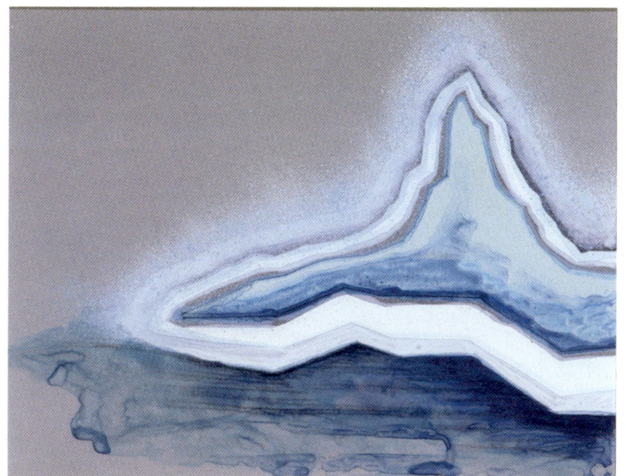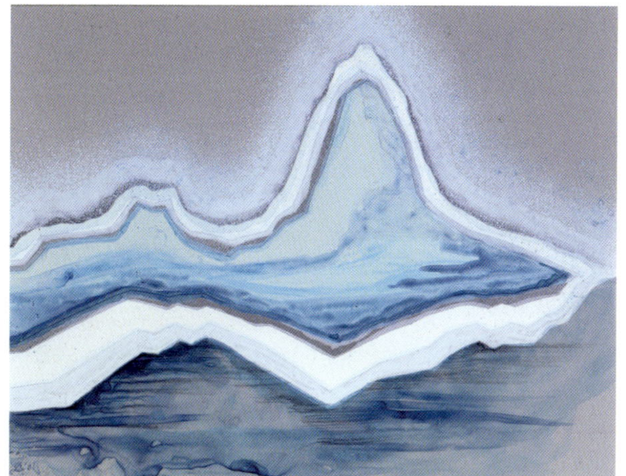

Fig. 1
Teresita Fernández, _Quiet Ice: Soft Breaking Sound_, 2006. Mixed media on paper; diptych, each: 11 x 14 in (27.9 x 35.5 cm). Courtesy the artist and Lehmann Maupin Gallery, New York and Hong Kong

politically—how does this place exist in people's imaginations?

Landscape is a very important reference in my work. I think of landscape as the history of people, not just as a framed vista in front of our eyes, but also what's above our heads and below our feet. The subterranean is a very important reference to me, because if you go up or go down, you're going through or transcending time. When I'm asking myself where I am, I'm also asking myself what happened three hundred years ago underneath my feet. That's also part of landscape. There's that basic question, "What defines where I am right now?" It's often how I start—mining the idea of place. What I do conceptually is an exercise in tangents and where they lead me.

I do that with materials as well. The reason why I used graphite for all of the works in _Sculptors Drawing_ is because I was interested in the history of drawing—specifically landscape drawing, not landscape painting, which we know a lot about [Fig. 1]. Almost all of our limited notions about landscape come from Western landscape painting. There's very, very little that you can talk about in reference to landscape sculpture. It's not even a term. It's not land art. It's a different thing. It has more to do with the imagination and the kind of construction of an image that we usually associate with landscape painting.

When I was doing those graphite pieces, the beginning point was questioning what a landscape drawing even was. In China and Japan, there's a much longer tradition that completely unravels our Western ideas of place. I could trace European ideas about landscape drawing back to one particular drawing by Leonardo da Vinci of the Arno Valley in the early 1500s. It's the first

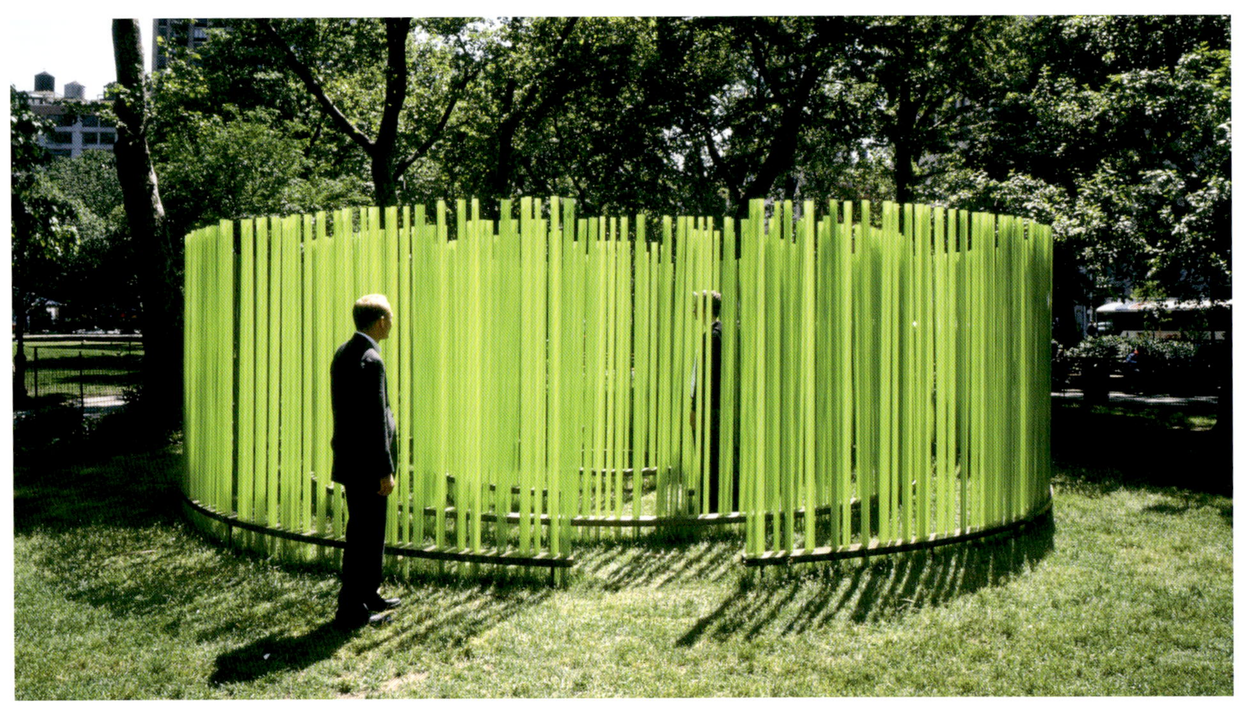

Fig. 2
Teresita Fernández, Bamboo Cinema, 2001.
Polycarbonate tubes and stainless steel, 96 x 332 in d
(243.8 x 843.3 cm d). Courtesy the artist and Lehmann
Maupin, New York and Hong Kong

grazing sheep. I thought of Borrowdale as this place where underneath your feet it was all solid graphite, as though you were walking on a vast landscape drawing.

The leap between sculpture and drawing then became instantaneous. I started to make these immense sculptures out of graphite that I thought of as being big three-dimensional smudges or sketches. The concept was not linear. It was very circular. Ideas rarely make sense logically, but in the end, it takes you to a logical, crystal-clear place. There's a big element of trusting that instinct or excitement.

HZ

One of your earlier works is a piece from 2001 called *Bamboo Cinema* [Fig. 2].

TF

Yes. This work was in Madison Square Park.

I was nine months pregnant when I was installing that piece! I've always loved that title—it was the perfect marriage of these two things that were completely unrelated, but made perfect sense together. I made a labyrinth—concentric circles that were like a maze, sitting in the

drawing that we can look at as believed to be drawn from memory; it's really just a drawing of the landscape for landscape's sake—i.e., not to be the background of a portrait, etc.

I started to think about how to make drawings. You make drawings with pencils. What are pencils made of? They're made out of graphite. Where does graphite come from? From Borrowdale in the United Kingdom. It was first discovered there in the 1500s. Shepherds used it to mark their middle of Madison Square Park.

The sculpture was a very unnatural bright green color, and even though it was in a park full of green, it glowed from a block away. I had polycarbonate tubes extruded and pinstripes embedded into them. You could walk between these concentric circles; it really functioned like an early cinematic device. If you slow down a film, you see a frame projected and then the shutter closing. Another frame is projected and then the shutter closes. If you do that many, many times, you get that rhythm of the projector—what we think of as cinematic. When the first shutter closes, the first image is retained as a ghost image on the back of our retinas. It's why we connect images visually. It has less to do with the projector and more to do with how our eyes work, because we remember that ghost image.

Bamboo Cinema functions very much like that, even though it doesn't do anything—it's very low-tech. If you walked around it, you could imagine that each of the verticals is almost like a shutter closing. This effect created a striated, broken-up view of the surrounding park. If you walked around fast, that pattern of

strobe effects started to happen very fast. If you were standing still and other people were moving, it would also happen. If you were standing there and a yellow cab went by on Fifth Avenue, the car would literally distort and go in and out of the piece. It's the kind of device that constantly warps the landscape and everything else around it.

In this case, I was interested in the viewer becoming not only a spectator, but also a performer, as an element that sets the piece into motion, which is important in the experiential component of my work. The circuit of meaning in the piece only works when it is activated by a participant/viewer.

HZ

The first piece of yours that I ever saw or experienced was the pool at Jeffrey Deitch Projects in 1996. You said earlier that you prefer not to describe or be descriptive about your work, because you want people to experience it—that was what happened to me.

I went there on a regular gallery round and didn't know what I was going to find. I wasn't familiar with you or your work yet, and I had that kind of seductive

experience where you walk in, you're not sure what you're experiencing, and you have these moments of realization. That's when your work is most powerful, when it catches people.

TF

I agree that serendipity is essential. I actually can't talk about the experience itself. I can talk about my research. I can talk about the conceptual development. I can talk about the ideas. But I can't talk about the experience. You can't pre-empt experience—its value lies in a kind of mute, unexplained lived moment that is fragile and can be easily disrupted.

HZ

Right. And it's not the same for anyone else. What I was feeling in the space was different from anyone else, I'm sure. It was this opportunity to know myself, my physical self in relation to space, in a way that was different, mesmerizing, and transformative.

TF

By not giving you instructions or descriptions, you are prompted to find your own way—it's that moment of self-reflection and engagement that is at the heart of what I am after. When experiences are described beforehand there's an anticipated expectation for the viewer. It's like a spoiler. It prevents you from actually having an authentic, deep unraveling of that nameless thing that you're experiencing. When an image is preplanted in your mind's eye, there's no room to create your own images, even words become distractions, like when someone describes how great a movie or piece of music is.

HZ

Or, that Aspen is so beautiful.

TF

Right. It's such a cliché that sets you up: all I've ever heard about Aspen is that it's so beautiful. When I got here, I realized that it is indeed beautiful. But it was about an experience of what that meant to me, rather than just the description of it—they are entirely different. Again, you can't pre-empt experience and lived reaction. There's really nothing that substitutes it.

HZ

Somehow, it cheapens it if you go in anticipating that you'll be moved.

TF

It creates a self-consciousness that cheats you of the work that you have to do. I actually don't believe that successful, effective works of art depend solely on their measurable parts or what the artist has done. I think that there needs to be a willingness on the part of the viewer. That's the kind of viewer I'm interested in, one that's willing, engaged, and actually wants to do the work and invest in building an image and meaning.

HZ

You have to be open to it.

Another great piece is *Seattle Cloud Cover* (2004–6; Fig. 3).

TF

That's a huge piece; it's about the length of a New York City block. There was nothing there when Seattle's Olympic Sculpture Park was started, just brown fields. I was going on the description of what the site would eventually become. I really fell in love with this particular location because the pedestrian overpass where the piece is sited is over train tracks. These trains are still in operation—they're the way in and out of Seattle.

I loved the idea of making an elevated walkway where there would be one kind of movement superimposed on another. Almost like when you walk up an escalator, where there's the movement of your feet superimposed on the movement of the escalator itself.

I spent a lot of time in Seattle trying to take the images that made up this photomontage, but there were no colorful epic clouds, it was just gray. I ended up going to Miami and getting really great cloud images, thousands of them, which were then turned into this final image that's made up of a lot of different moments of the Miami sky.

The piece also has clear openings, almost like a Ben-Day pattern, throughout the whole thing. I always say my work is really figurative. There aren't any figures in it, but you're the figure. All the components in it are related to those proportions. To the right, you can see the Olympic mountain range and Puget

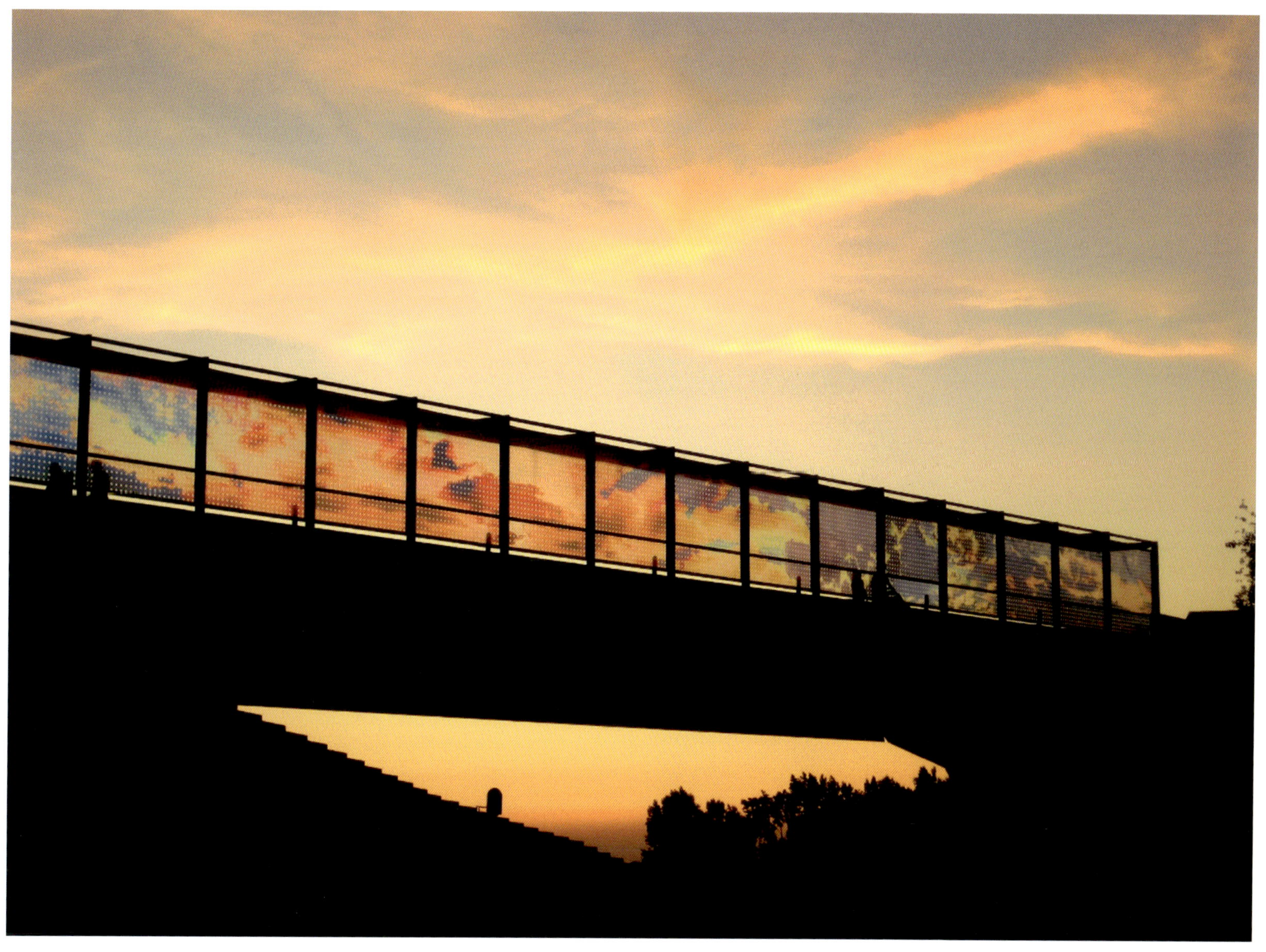

Fig. 3
Teresita Fernández, <u>Seattle Cloud Cover</u>, 2004–6. Laminated glass with photographic design interlay, 114 x 2400 x 75 in (289.6 x 6096 x 190.5 cm). Commissioned by the Seattle Art Museum for the Olympic Sculpture Park, Seattle, WA. Courtesy the artist and Lehmann Maupin, New York and Hong Kong

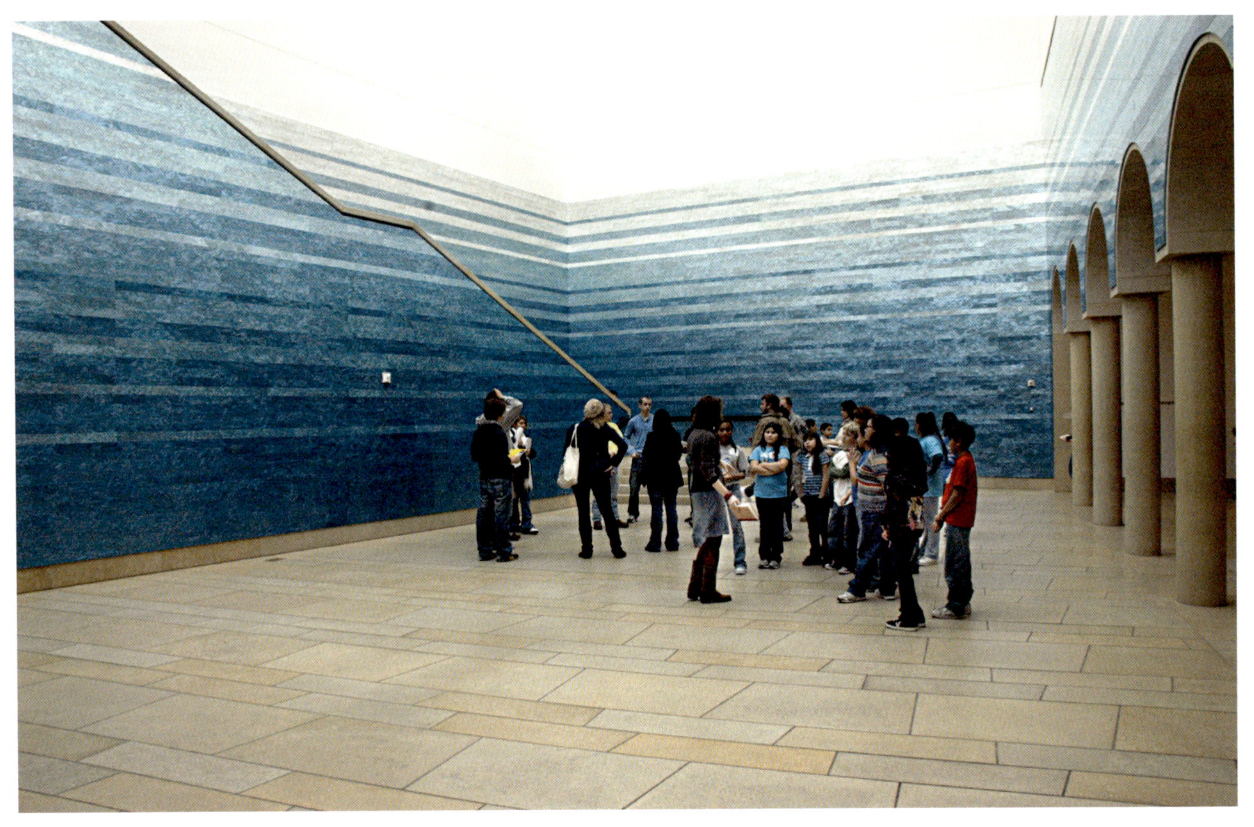

the round openings are that image that pops in and out. As you're walking, your pace controls that almost cinematic understanding of the Seattle skyline appearing in and out of those little holes. It changes depending on where the sun is and the time of the year; it can look almost invisible, like a watercolor. If you look at this piece from where the Richard Serra is in the sculpture park, you don't see anything at all. All you'll see is this line of the armature like an "L." I was very interested in the idea that this block-long piece could disappear entirely from certain angles, which it does. In the context of a sculpture park full of iconic, heavy, outdoor sculptures, mostly made by men, the idea that my monumental piece could appear and disappear felt like a secret, a way of exerting a presence that uses the opposite strategies to being big, heavy, and grounded.

Sound. To the left, you can see downtown Seattle. If you're walking through the overpass, you basically see the city appearing in and out of those clear openings that puncture the saturated colorful cloud images.

This piece is very much related to *Bamboo Cinema*, because in this case, the whole colored part is the shutter and

HZ

Another large-scale piece is *Stacked Waters* (2009; Fig. 4) in Texas.

TF

Stacked Waters is in the atrium of the

Blanton Museum of Art. When I first saw the space, I thought it was one of the most architecturally alienating places I'd ever seen. It was also huge, with skylights and an odd arcade and columns. I kept thinking of Donald Judd and of the Texas light, which was the one really beautiful part of this space—the skylights meant it was always full of natural light.

I ended up thinking of the space as almost being like an ancient Roman cistern that I could fill up with water. I couldn't get away from the arcade—I had to somehow use it. I visually filled it up with water. I had strips of acrylic cast for me in very specific colors. The installation is like a painting in the sense that the colors were made for me. The gradation slowly moves from blue to white as the acrylic goes up the wall. It's really like a series of waterlines. As you're moving, that waterline changes in relation to your moving body. In order to get to the main galleries, you go up the monumental staircase, which has fifty steps. The waterline became a way of marking that ascension into the main gallery. By the time you get to the top of the stairs and you step up that last step, the "waterline"

is at about your ankles, as though you're stepping out of a pool.

The title *Stacked Waters* was a bit of an inside joke because Judd, of course, has such a presence in Texas. My piece almost felt like what would happen if you were on the inside of one of Judd's stacked blue pieces. There was a kind of sensuous implication to it, as well. It was a way of making visitors animate the space and project imagined water—water moving over skin and people drenched in the shifting Texas sunlight that turned all of the lined walls into reflective mirrors where viewers could see themselves superimposed on that watery surface. ❈

Teresita Fernández was born in 1968, Miami, Florida, and currently lives and works in Brooklyn, New York. She received her MFA from Virginia Commonwealth University and her BFA from Florida International University. Fernández has received international commissions for her large-scale installations and recent solo exhibitions include As Above So Below, MASS MoCA (2015); Modern Art Museum of Forth Worth, Texas; Blind Landscape, MOCA Cleveland, Ohio (both 2011); Centro de Arte Contemporaneo de Málaga, Spain (2005); Castello di Rivoli, Turin, Italy (2001); and the Institute of Contemporary Art, Philadelphia (1999). Fernández's works have been exhibited extensively at institutions such as the MCA Denver; Saint Louis Art Museum, Missouri (both 2013); Dallas Museum of Art, Texas (2010); Aspen Art Museum (2007); and Miami Art Museum (2006); amongst many others. She is a 2005 MacArthur Foundation Fellow and the recipient of many prestigious awards, including a Guggenheim Fellowship, a National Endowment for the Arts Artist's Grant, an American Academy in Rome Affiliated Fellowship, and a Louis Comfort Tiffany Biennial Award.

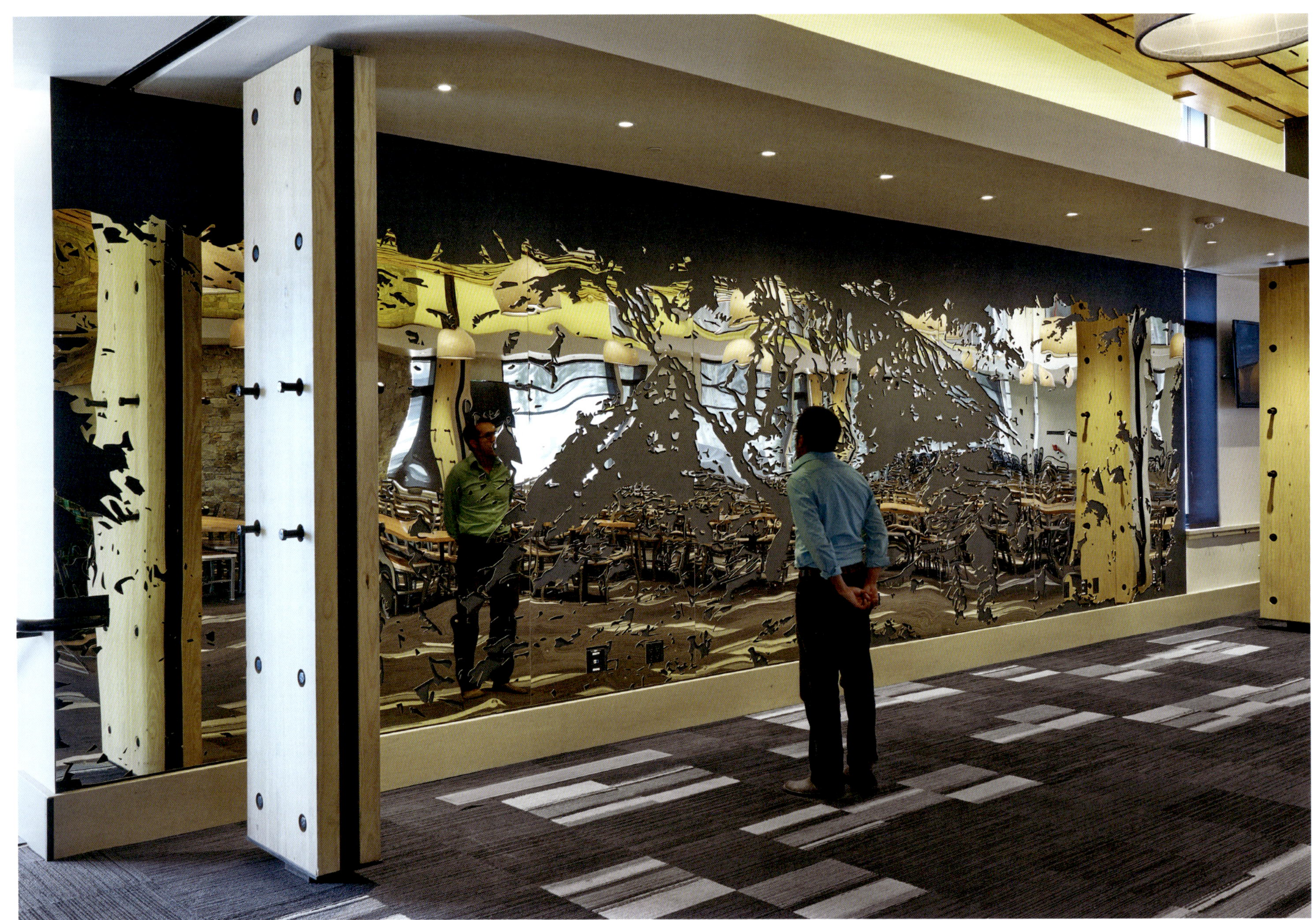

Teresita Fernández
2013–15

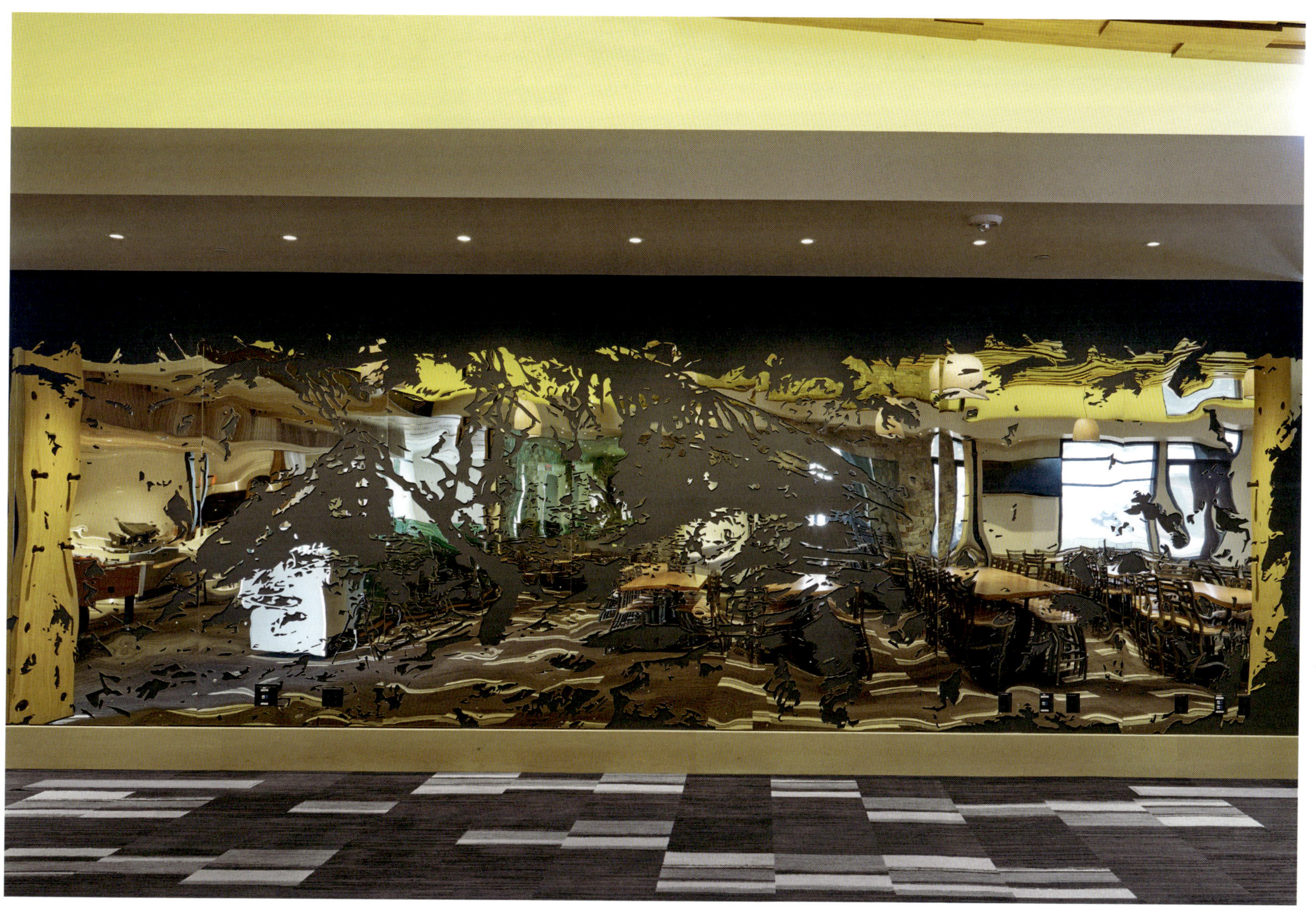

Installation views: Teresita Fernández, _Golden Panorama (Snowmass Mountain)_, 2013. Precision-cut plastic, paint. Elk Camp restaurant. Courtesy the artist and Lehmann Maupin, New York and Hong Kong. Photos: Jason Dewey

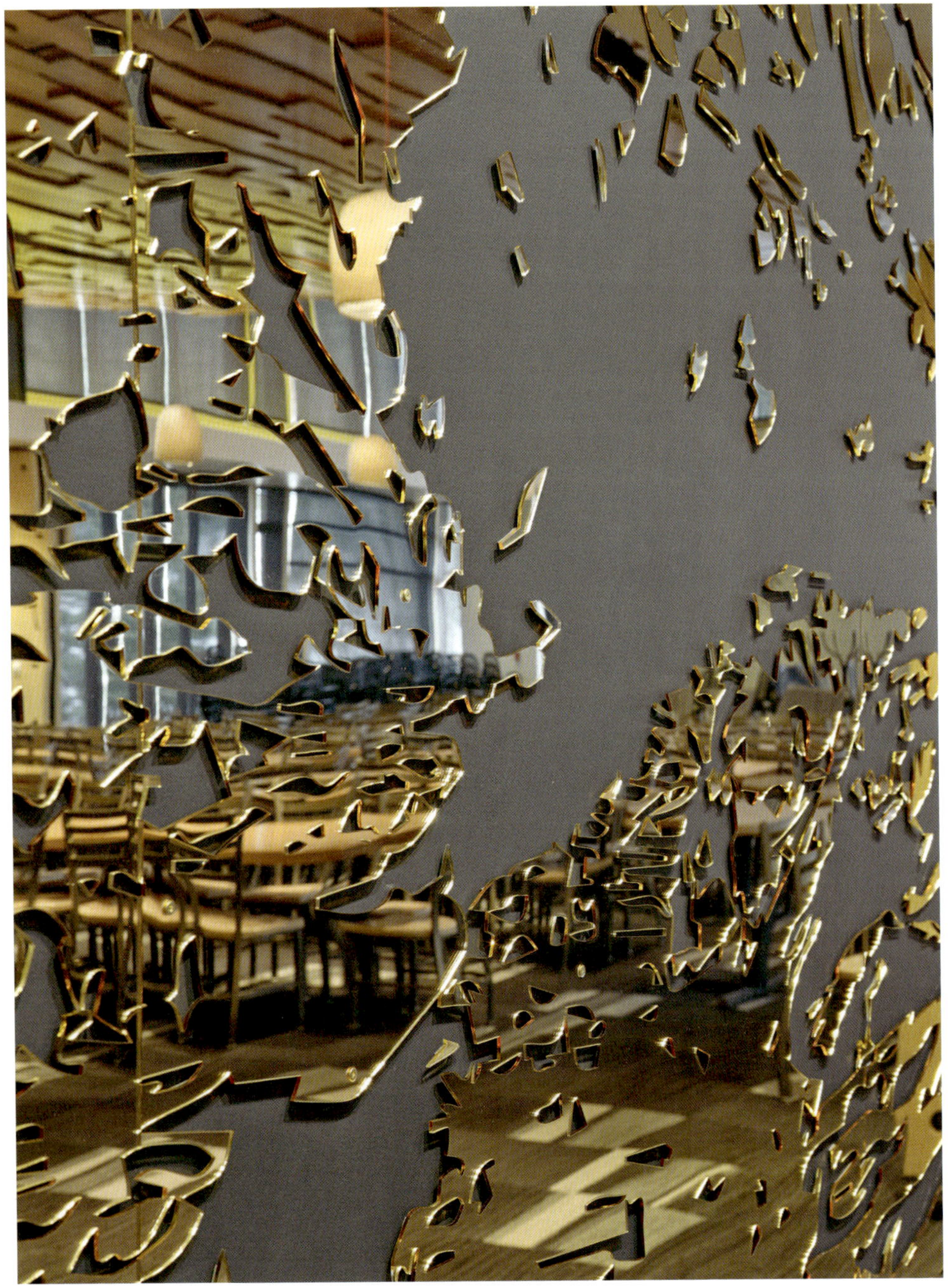

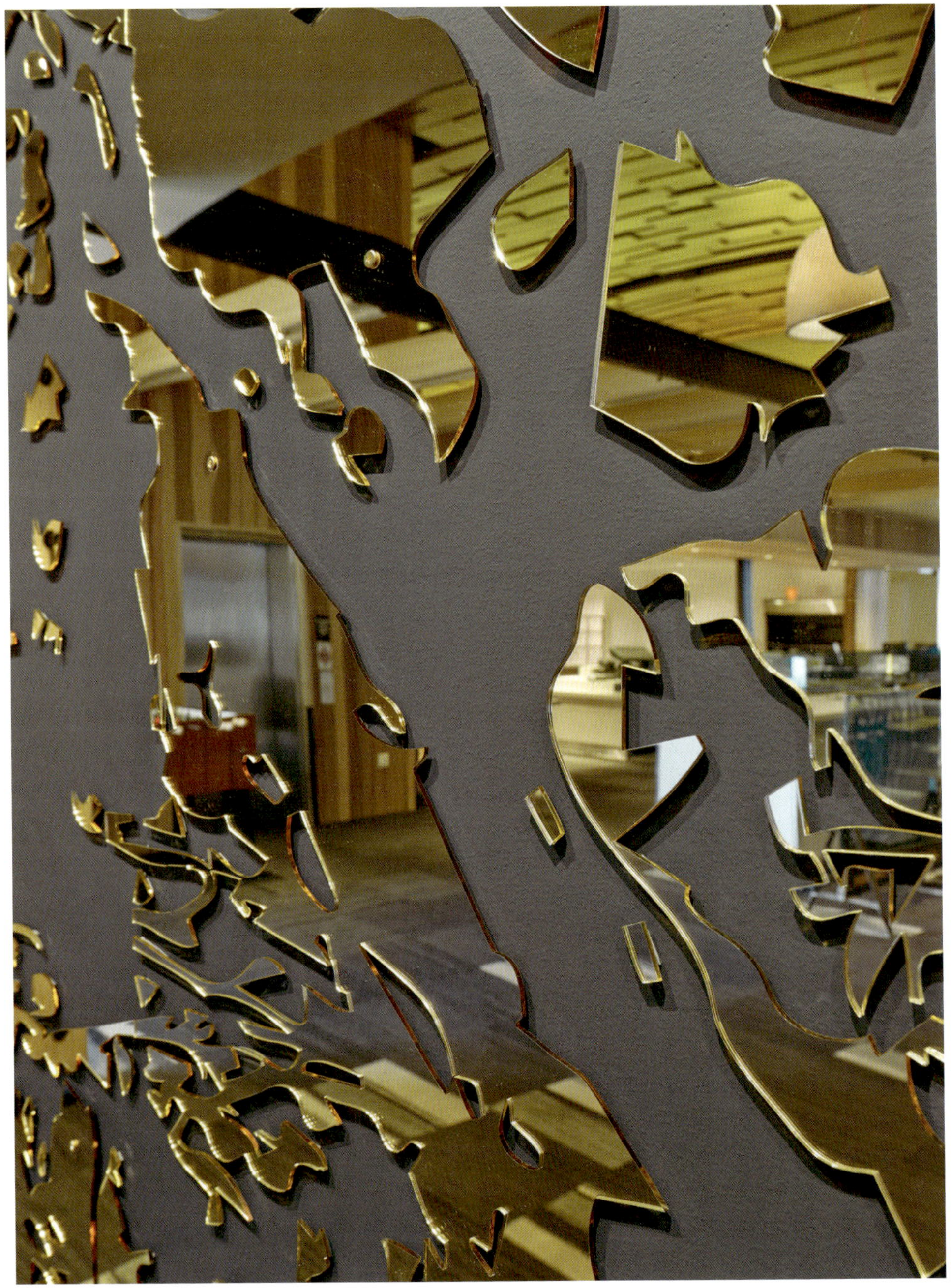

Teresita Fernández
2013–15

Cai Guo-Qiang

2014 Aspen Mountain Explosion Event

Cai Guo-Qiang, one of the most celebrated Chinese contemporary artists working today, is known predominantly for his gunpowder drawings and firework displays, which he refers to as "explosion events." Through the use of gunpowder—one of China's most important inventions alongside printing, paper, and the compass—Cai Guo-Qiang takes a historically destructive force and reconfigures it into one of creative fusion and transformation. In traditional Chinese belief, the world is populated by a vast number of spirits, both good and evil. Because evil spirits seemingly have an aversion to light, many rituals involving fire developed, including the use of firecrackers. At once conceptual, site-specific, ephemeral, and interactive, Cai Guo-Qiang's explosion events showcase the artist's interest in "opening up a dialogue with the universe" and exploring our relationship with the earth as well as with each other.

Invited to present work as part of the inaugural series of exhibitions at the new Aspen Art Museum, Cai Guo-Qiang created a daytime explosion event titled *Black Lightning* (2014). A black lightning bolt struck twice against the dramatic backdrop of Aspen's blue sky and the city's iconic mountain, Ajax. An extraordinary presence seven hundred feet high, the lightning was accompanied by a loud, thunderous crack that emphasized the connection between the museum and the surrounding landscape. Over in a matter of seconds, *Black Lightning* was a moment of natural energy and spontaneity, blurring the boundaries between mind and matter, science and faith, beauty and violence.

Cai Guo-Qiang says of his events, "Before and after the explosion, there is a change from the invisible to the visible, an expectation of the transformation of energy. The ritual in fire and gunpowder is related to the ancient practice of fortune-telling and the fate of the artwork. When seeing the process, the audience feels connected to the artist's fate." He continues, "This model is quite different from performance art, because people know a performance is the result of many rehearsals. In an open production, viewers not only watch a performance, but they also become connected to the explosion. Everyone senses the uncertainty while waiting for the result together, wondering whether this work will succeed or not. What they care about is the unfolding of the concept the artist creates." Striking and thought-provoking, Cai Guo-Qiang's *Black Lightning* brought everyone who witnessed the dark thunderbolt together, leaving its mark in the memory of each viewer and forging an unforgettable connection between the artwork and the mountain. ✳

Cai Guo-Qiang, born in 1957, in Quanzhou City, Fujian Province, China, studied stage design at the Shanghai Theater Academy and currently lives and works in New York. His many solo exhibitions include There and Back Again, Yokohama Museum of Art, Japan (2015); Sky Ladder, Museum of Contemporary Art, Los Angeles (2012); Saraab, Mathaf: Arab Museum of Modern Art, Doha, Qatar (2011); his retrospective I Want to Believe, Solomon R. Guggenheim Museum, New York (2008), traveled to the National Art Museum of China, Beijing (2008), and the Guggenheim Bilbao (2009); and Cai Guo-Qiang on the Roof: Transparent Monument, Metropolitan Museum of Art, New York (2006). Guo-Qiang was awarded the Japan Cultural Design Prize in 1995, the Golden Lion at the 48th Venice Biennale in 1999, and was also among the five artists to receive the first US Department of State Medal of Arts Award.

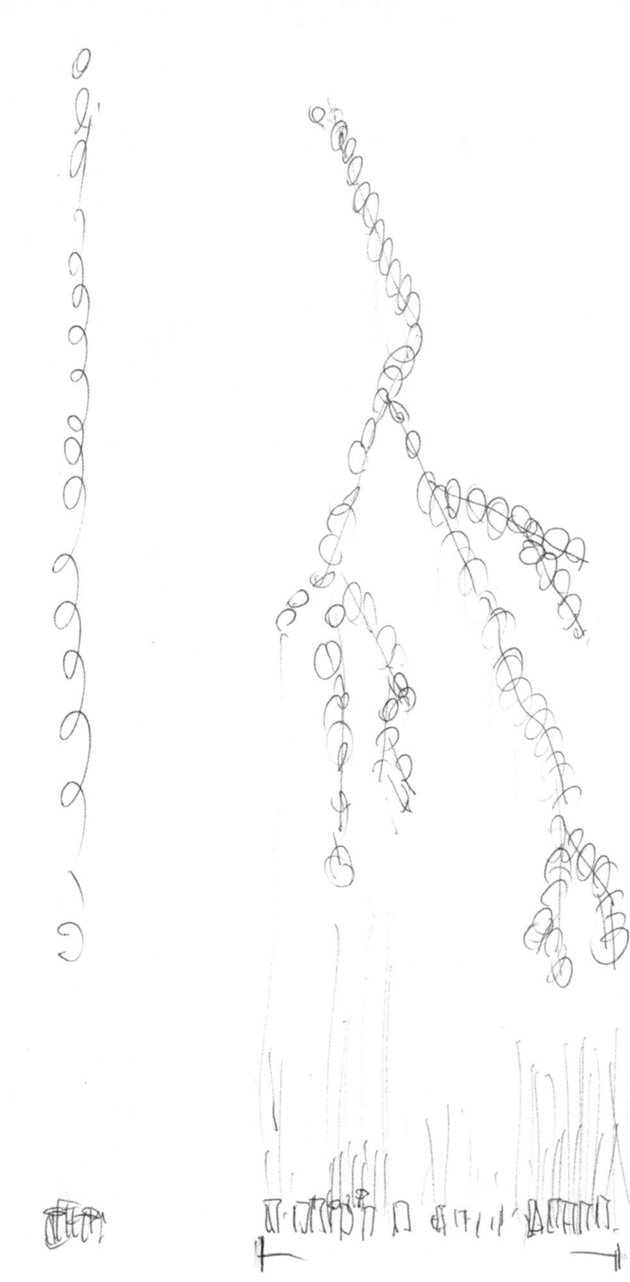

Cai Guo-Qiang, Preparatory
Drawings for Black Lightning, 2013.
Courtesy the artist

Cai Guo-Qiang
2014

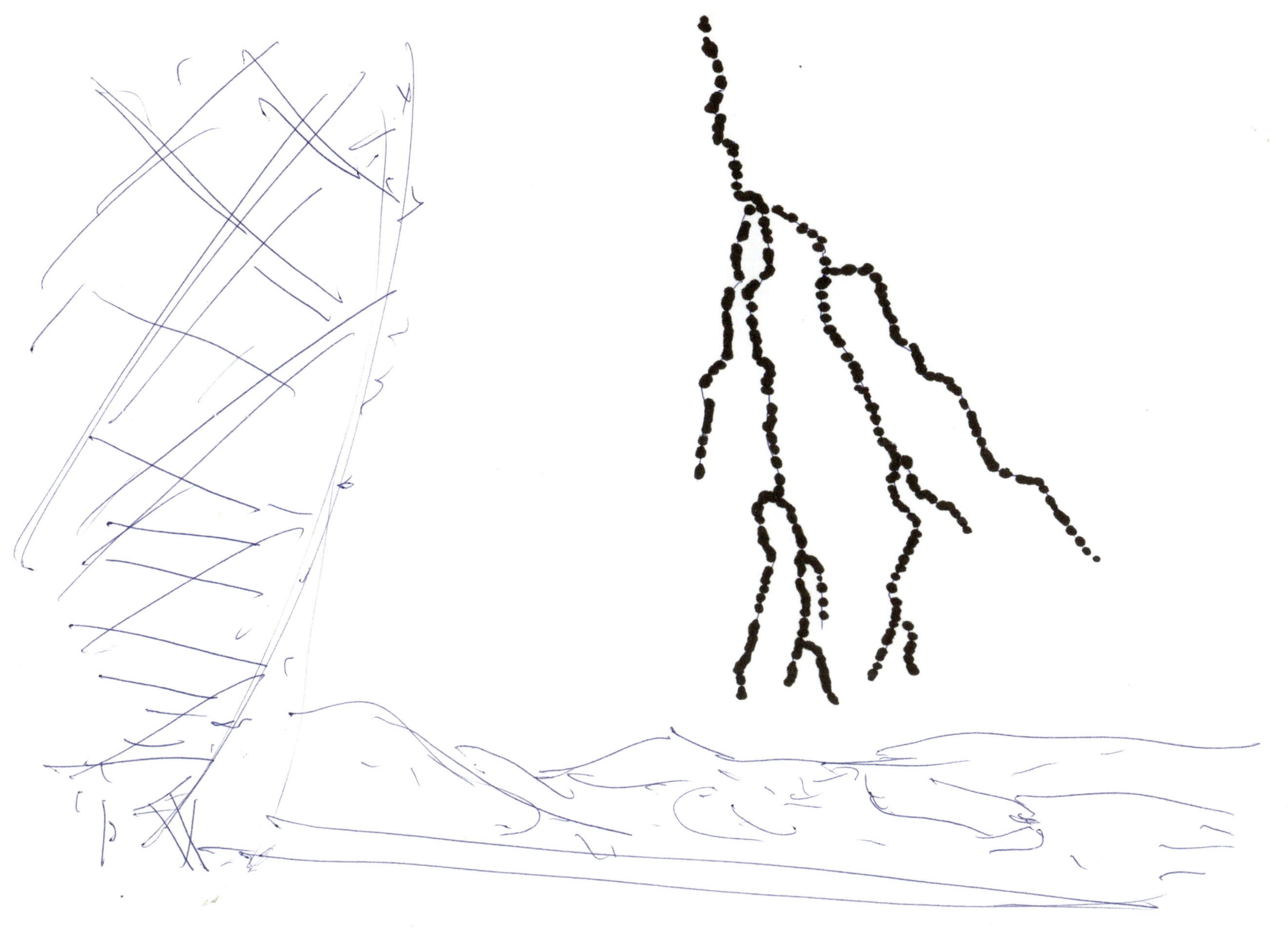

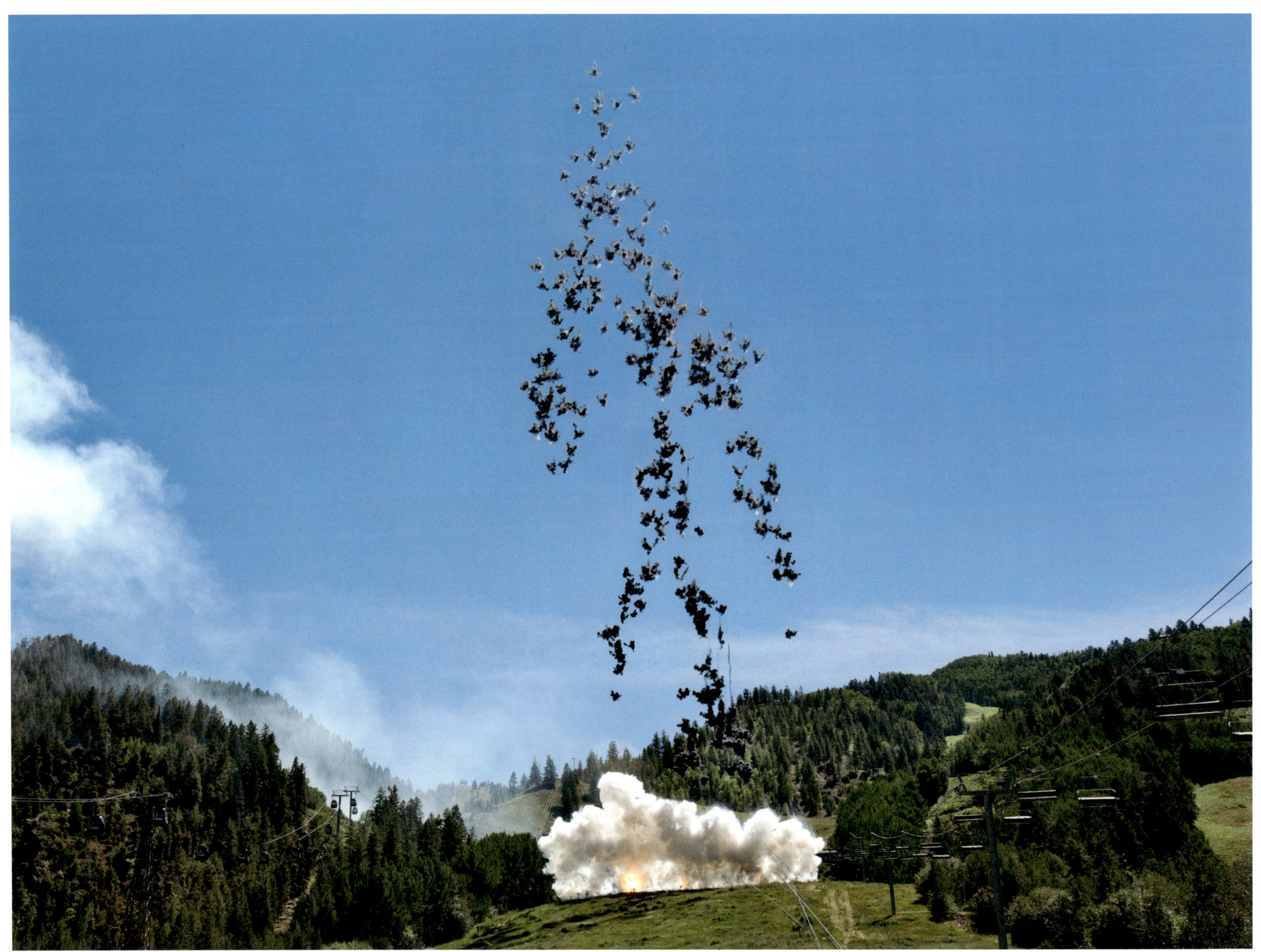

Cai Guo-Qiang
2014

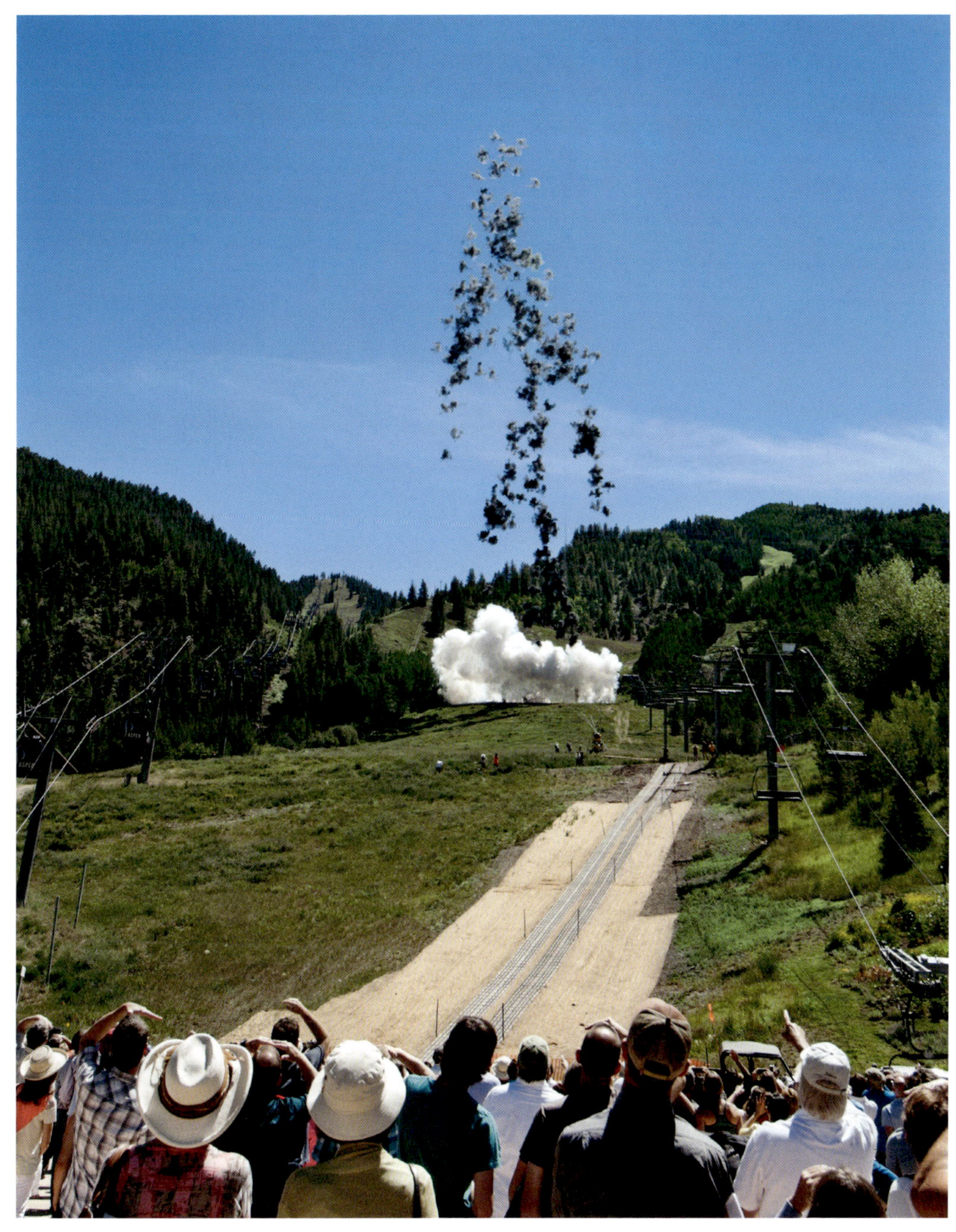

Cai Guo-Qiang, <u>Black Lightning</u>, 2014. Explosion event. Commissioned by the Aspen Art Museum, Colorado. Courtesy the artist. Photos: Tony Prikryl

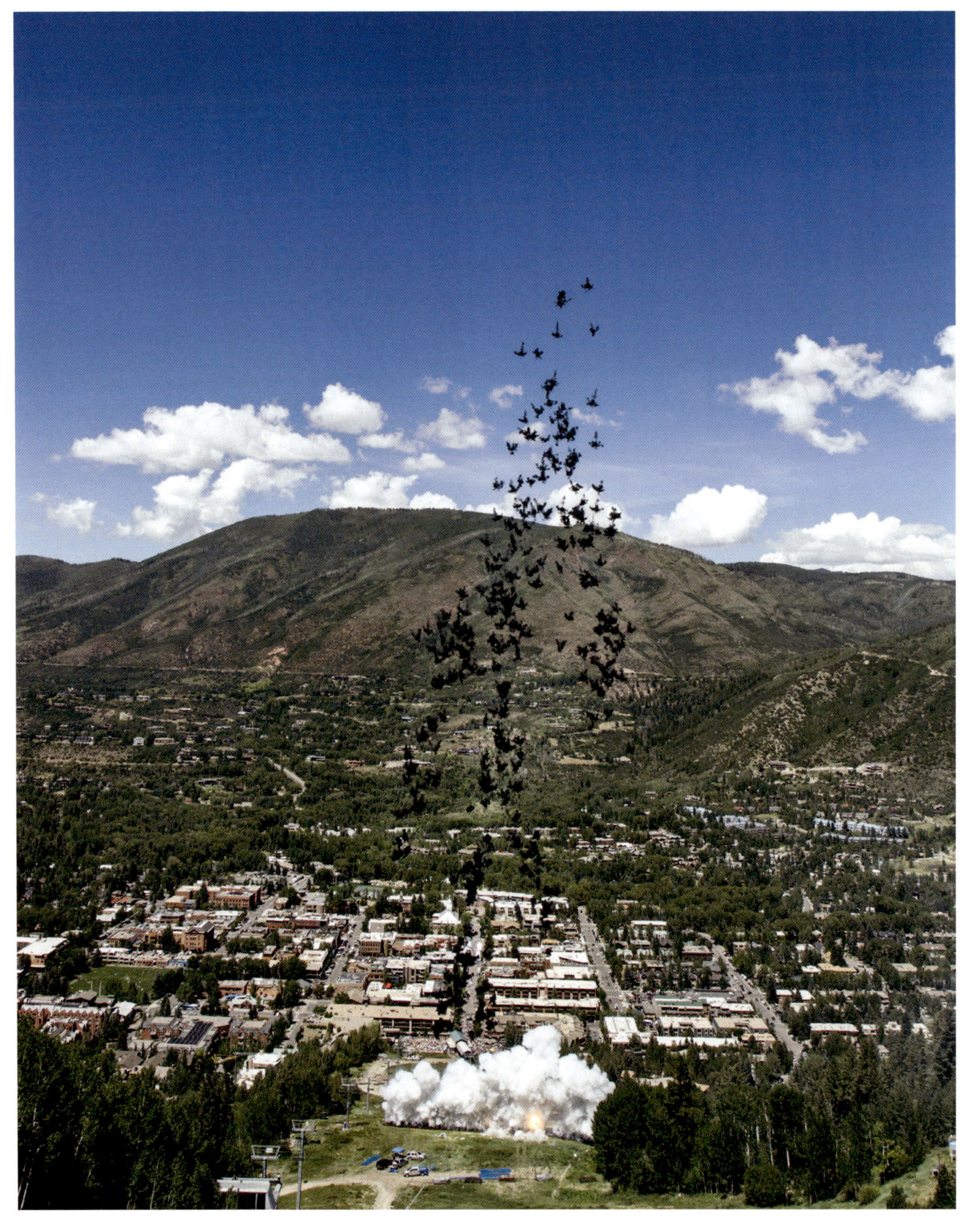

Cai Guo-Qiang, <u>Black Lightning</u>,
2014. Explosion event. Commissioned
by the Aspen Art Museum,
Colorado. Courtesy the artist.
Photo: Seth Beckton

Cai Guo-Qiang
2014

Anne Collier
2014–15 Lift Tickets

Artist Anne Collier produced three unique photographs of the famous record single "Ain't No Mountain High Enough." Written by Nickolas Ashford and Valerie Simpson in 1966 and originally recorded under the Tamla Motown label, "Ain't No Mountain High Enough" was also recorded by Diana Ross and Marvin Gaye. Collier's series included images of the Ashford/Simpson, Diana Ross, and Marvin Gaye albums, which were featured on the 2014–15 ski season lift ticket.

Heidi Zuckerman

Your work turns the camera lens on objects already present within popular culture—books, record albums, magazines, and film stills—and you often photograph items that have had past lives, that have been handled, used, or discarded. Do you feel that by focusing on these artifacts, they help us to learn and understand more about our present moment?

Anne Collier

One of the things that I am interested in is our personal relationship with images, and how we partly construct our identities based on the images we encounter. Some of the photographic imagery that appears in my work is sourced from objects and artifacts from the seventies and eighties—the years of my childhood, adolescence, and early adulthood. The resulting pieces aren't necessarily autobiographical *per se*, but they are rooted in my own experience. I'm also interested in how these earlier "analog" images reverberate in the present—and to what extent I can, as an artist, negotiate the sensations of melancholia or nostalgia that such images invariably conjure up. I'm interested in the tension between an image's original intent and how that same image operates in the context of my own work.

HZ

You have said that you do not necessarily see your work as nostalgic, but "as a form of melancholia…a reconsideration and recuperation of the recent past." In addition, scale plays an important role in your practice. Can you speak about these elements in relation to the invitation to create a lift ticket that is distributed to skiers/snowboarders of all ages and from all walks of life?

AC

In a number of my works, I have made images of vinyl records, a medium that became effectively obsolete in the late eighties and early nineties, but is currently undergoing something of a renaissance. I'm drawn to how, as a medium, vinyl has negotiated its own obsolescence to become relevant again. I'm also interested in how images of specific recordings—e.g., their sleeves, or in the case of the lift ticket, their labels—can trigger strong personal, emotional, or psychological associations.

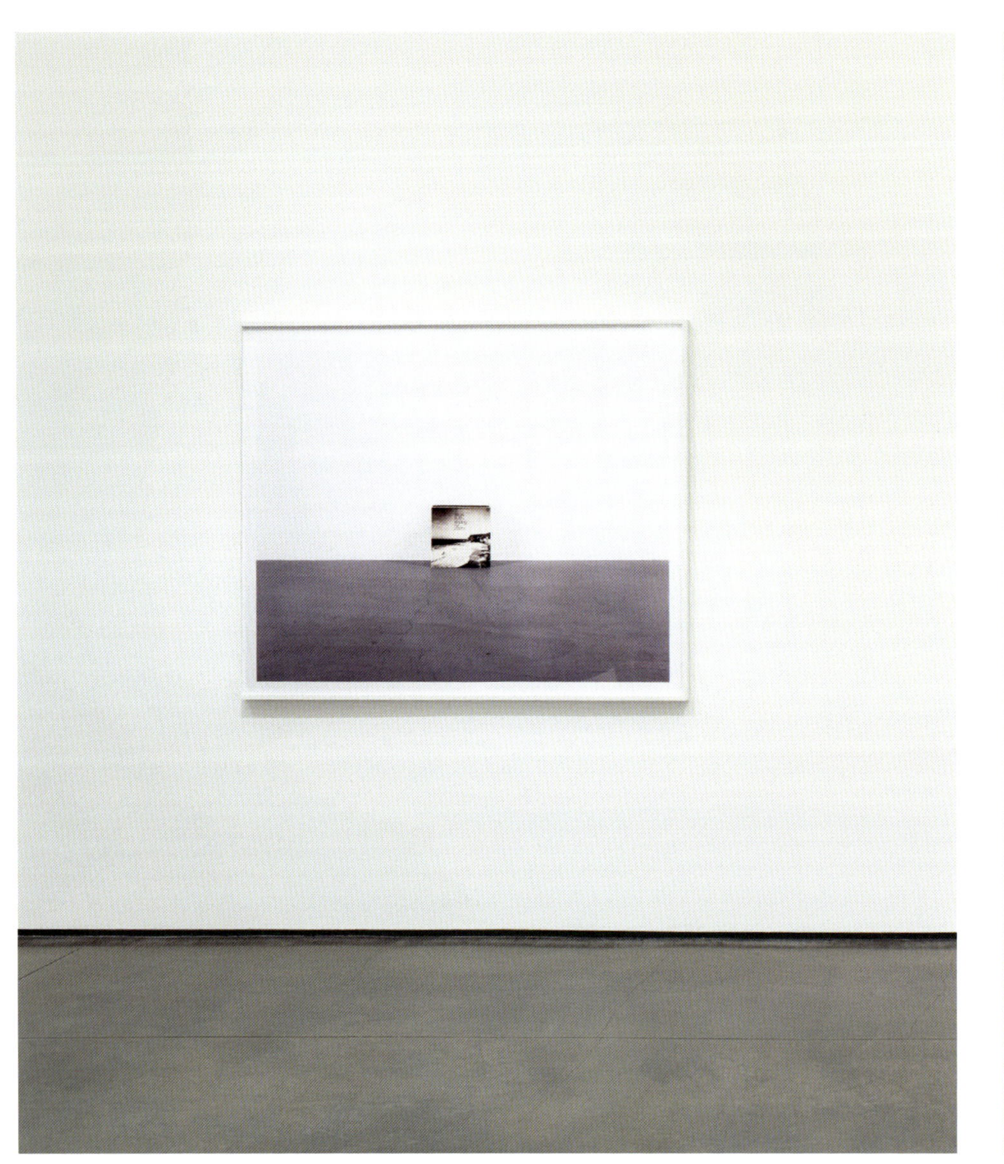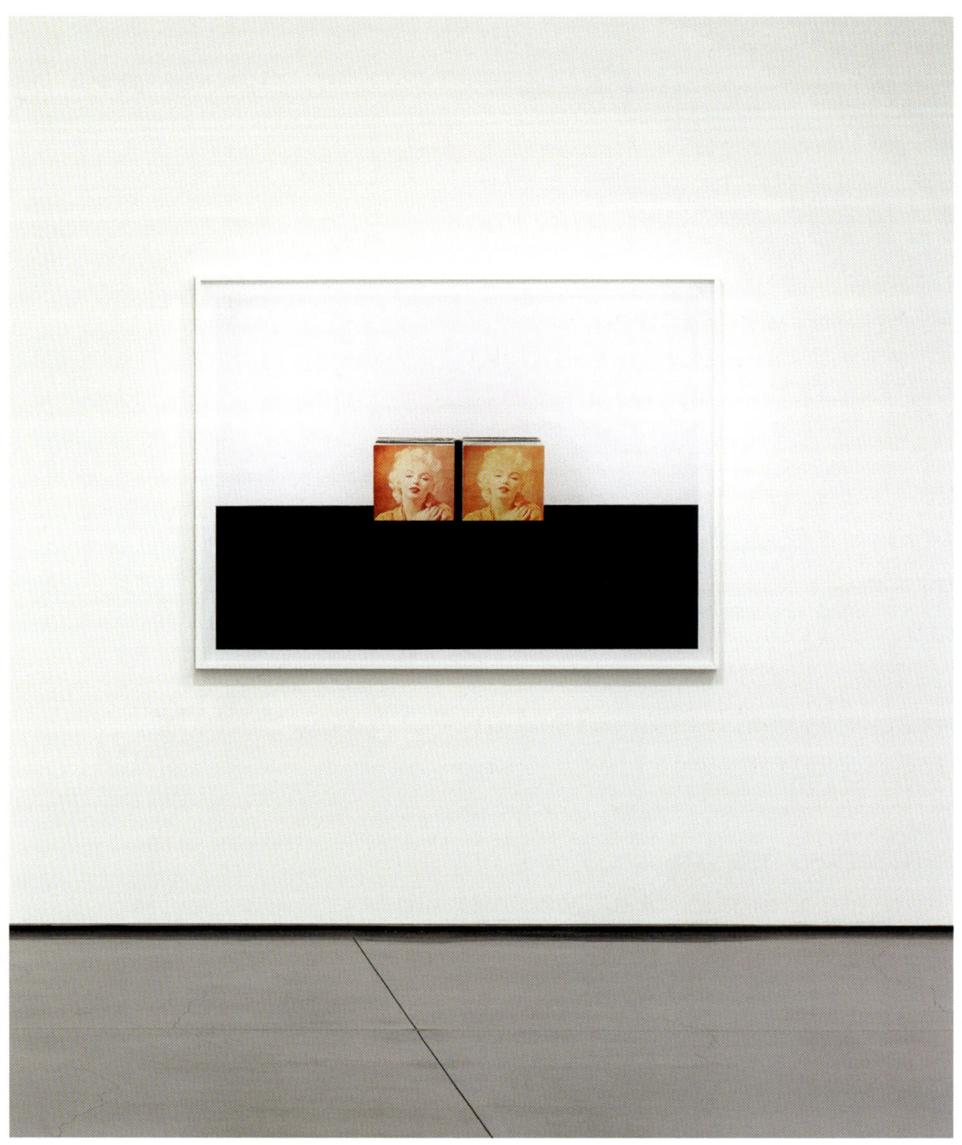

Installation views: <u>Anne Collier</u>, Aspen Art Museum, 2015.
Courtesy the artist. Photos: Tony Prikryl

Anne Collier
2014–15

I had not made a site-specific work before, so the invitation to make a piece that would appear on the Aspen lift tickets was an intriguing problem. I was interested in what kind of imagery would make sense at such a small scale, as my photographic works tend to be very large—whereas the lift ticket fits comfortably in a pocket.

I started to think about songs that used the idea of "mountains" metaphorically, where the idea of the mountain stood in for an emotional obstacle. I eventually focused on the song "Ain't No Mountain High Enough," which I think remains sufficiently well known to be in the popular unconscious. I wanted to use a song with which all kinds of people, across different generations, might have a relationship. There are a number of different versions of this song by different artists so I simply photographed the labels of a number of these records. Three of them became the imagery that appeared on the three lift tickets I designed, so there ended up being different "versions" of my work out on the mountain at any given time. ❋

Anne Collier was born in Los Angeles, California, and currently lives and works in New York. She studied at the California Institute of the Arts and the University of California, Los Angeles. Solo exhibitions of her work have been presented at numerous institutions, including the Art Gallery of Ontario, Toronto, Canada; Aspen Art Museum (both 2015); the Museum of Contemporary Art, Chicago; CCS Museum, Bard College, New York; the Modern Institute, Glasgow, Scotland (all 2014); Artpace, San Antonio, Texas (2009); Bonner Kunstverein, Bonn, Germany (2008); and the Institute of Visual Arts, University of Wisconsin, Milwaukee (1998). Her work has also been featured in numerous major group exhibitions including UGO RONDINONE: I ♥ JOHN GIORNO, Palais de Tokyo, Paris, France; America is Hard to See, Whitney Museum of American Art, New York; Photo Poetics, Solomon R. Guggenheim Museum, New York (all 2015); and More Love: Art, Politics, and Sharing since the 1990's, Ackland Art Museum, University of North Carolina at Chapel Hill (2013); amongst many others.

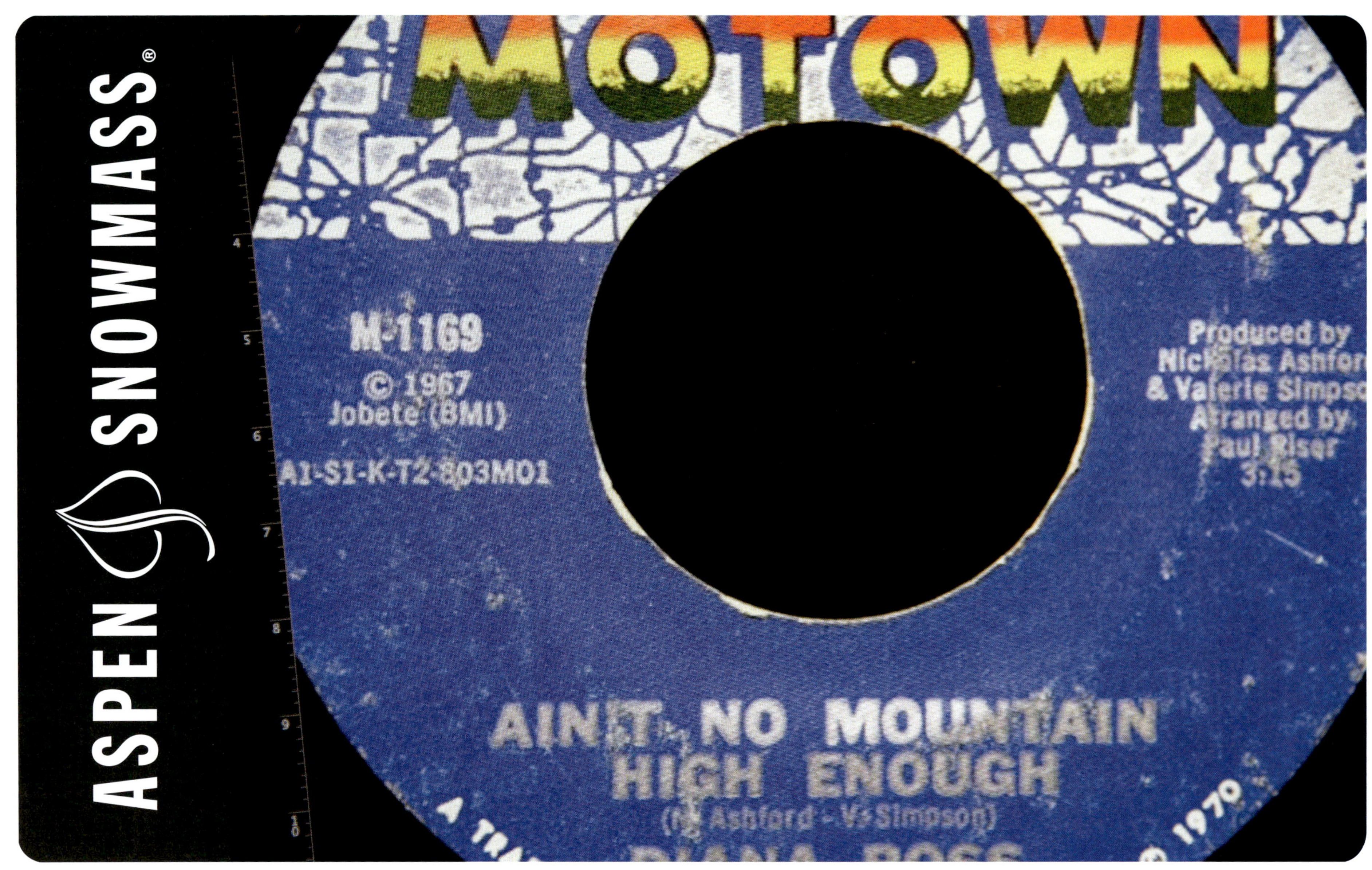

Anne Collier, <u>Ain't No Mountain High Enough (Diana Ross)</u>, 2014.
Commissioned by the Aspen Art Museum and the Aspen Skiing Company. Courtesy the artist

Anne Collier
2014–15

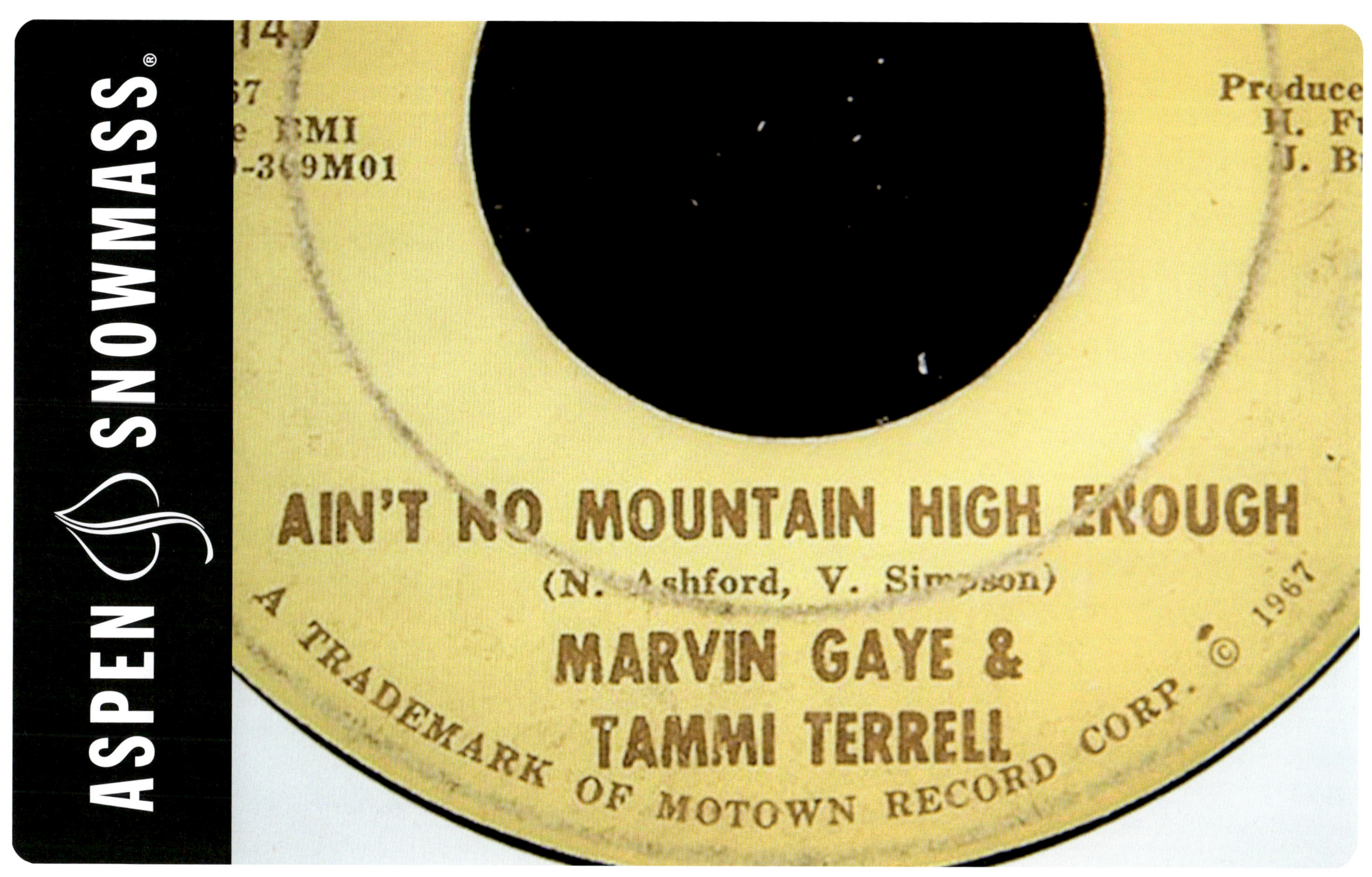

Anne Collier, *Ain't No Mountain High Enough (Marvin Gaye & Tammi Terrell)*, 2014.
Commissioned by the Aspen Art Museum and the Aspen Skiing Company. Courtesy the artist

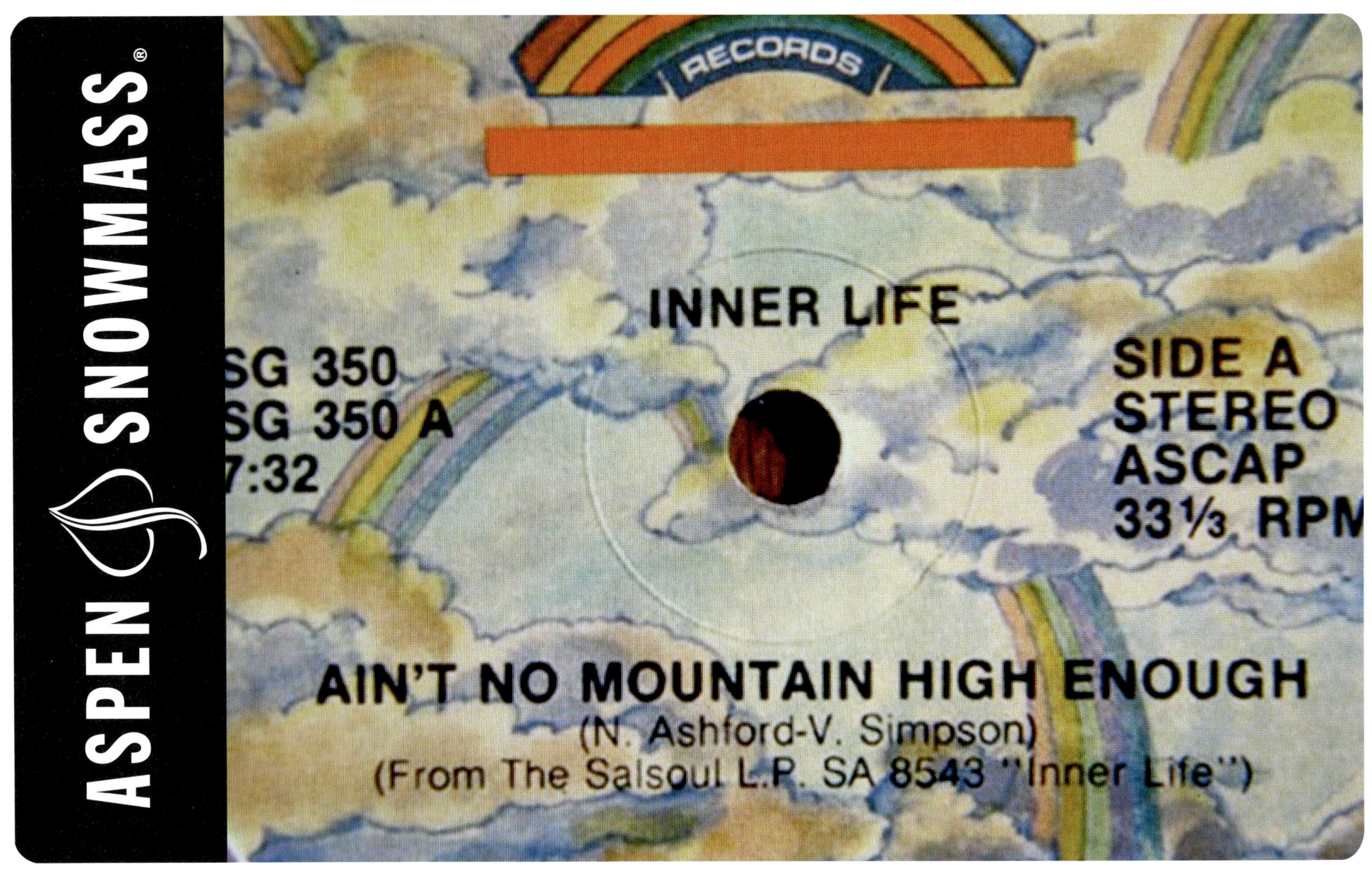

Anne Collier, _Ain't No Mountain High Enough (N. Ashford - V. Simpson)_, 2014.
Commissioned by the Aspen Art Museum and the Aspen Skiing Company. Courtesy the artist

Anne Collier
2014–15

Takashi Murakami
2015–16 Lift Tickets

150

The Tokyo-based artist Takashi Murakami combines highly refined classical Japanese painting techniques with distinctive Pop sensibilities. Known for his "Superflat" style, directly influenced by manga and anime, the artist creates works that explode with color and playfulness. Brightly colored, whimsical, and futuristic, Murakami's cast of characters, like "Mr. DOB," "Smiley-Face Flowers," and colorful mushrooms, push the boundaries of what we define as Eastern and Western, or high art and popular culture.

In 2002, Murakami was invited by fashion designer Marc Jacobs to collaborate on a line of bags for Louis Vuitton. Following this successful fashion–art partnership, the artist went on to design album artwork and a music video for Kanye West as well as work with Comme des Garçons and Vans, constantly blurring the lines between art and commerce. For the 2015–16 ski season, in collaboration with the Aspen Skiing Company, Murakami produced four unique images for the lift tickets, each embodying his trademark visual aesthetic. When asked how he approached the project, Murakami explained, "I first heard the name Aspen when I learned of the solo exhibition that Mark Grotjahn had at the Aspen Art Museum. I liked the way it sounded when spoken aloud and thought it was a fine name for a town. If I were to compare it to Japan, the image I have in my head is that it is similar to the town of Karuizawa. I'm a person who is very sensitive to the cold and so have zero understanding of people who enjoy doing outdoor winter sports. This left me feeling a little awkward about doing the designs, but I hope everyone enjoys them. In the future, I would like to visit Aspen with my sketchbook and draw the snow-covered mountains."

Two of Murakami's lift tickets feature his "Smiley-Face Flowers," a motif that he has been working with for over fifteen years. In an interview, Murakami said of the flower design, "Every flower is smiling, but it looks more like the sign for a smile. So my message for the kids is to 'please find out what is real.' If your parents are laughing or not laughing…maybe their hearts are sad or something different. When I created this flower design, I wanted to approach the kids, not the serious art fans…I realized I could get a great reaction from kids." The third lift ticket features Murakami's best-known character, "Mr. DOB," who functions like a self-portrait of the artist with a round head and large circular ears. The final lift ticket is a cartoon drawing of the artist's own dog, POM, sitting on a mountain nestled in the clouds. Each ticket design is an unexpected pop of bold color and patterns, an exciting interruption within the white, snow-filled landscape of Aspen's mountains. ※

Born in Tokyo in 1962, artist Takashi Murakami received a BFA, MFA, and PhD from Tokyo National University of Fine Arts and Music. He has had numerous solo presentations, including his large-scale retrospective ©MURAKAMI, Los Angeles Museum of Contemporary Art, which traveled to the Brooklyn Museum, New York, and the Museum für Moderne Kunst, Frankfurt, Germany (2007); Kaikai Kiki: Takashi Murakami, Fondation Cartier, Paris (2002); Summon monsters? Open the door? Heal? Or die?, Museum of Contemporary Art, Tokyo; Takashi Murakami: Made in Japan, Museum of Fine Arts, Boston (both 2001); and Second Mission Project Ko², MoMA PS1, New York (2000). His work has been included in numerous major international group exhibitions including Sold Out: The Artist in the Age of Pop, Tate Modern, London, UK; Mapping the Studio, Palazzo Grassi, Venice, Italy; Red Hot: Contemporary Asian Art Rising, Museum of Fine Arts, Houston, Texas (2007); and Surprise, Surprise, Institute of Contemporary Art, London, UK (2006); amongst many others.

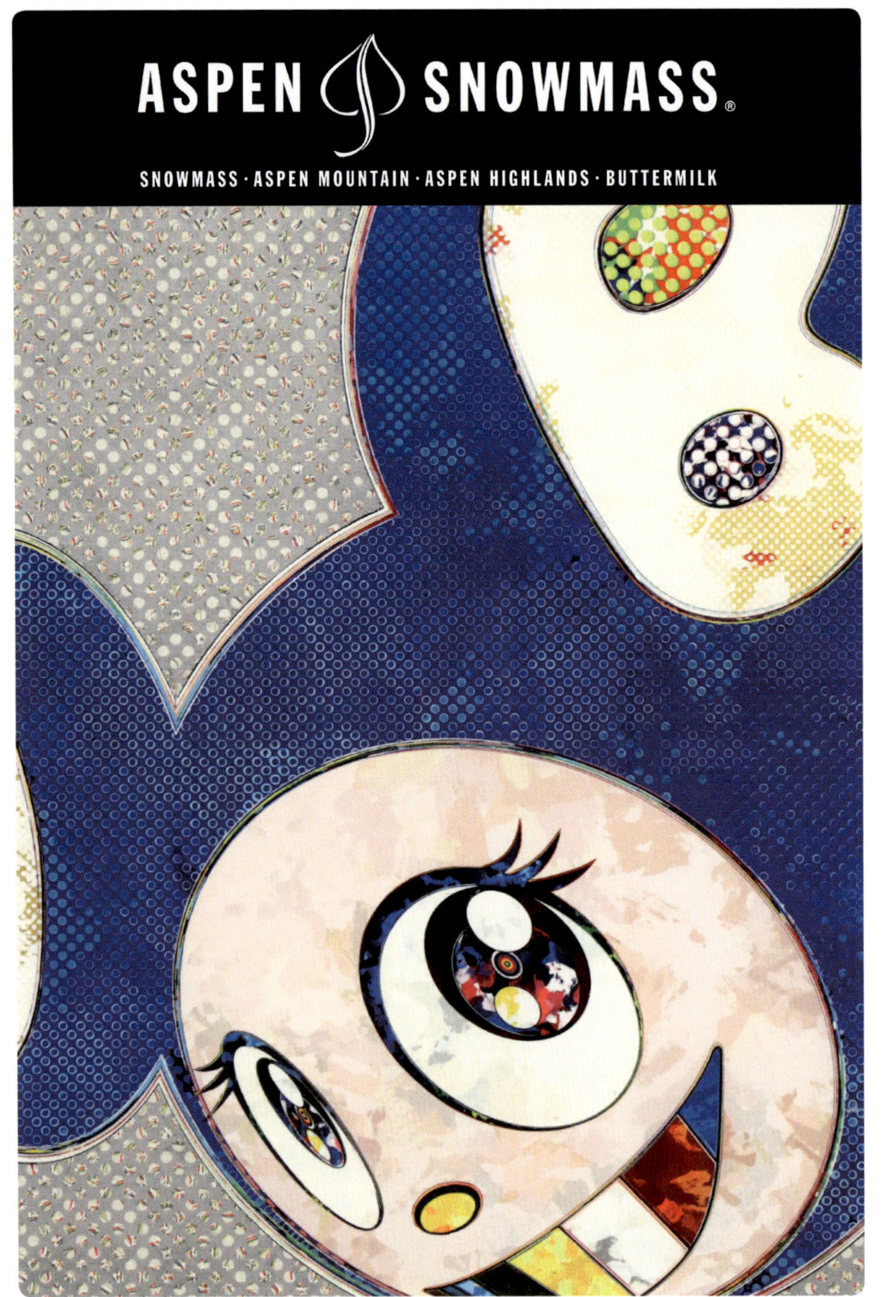

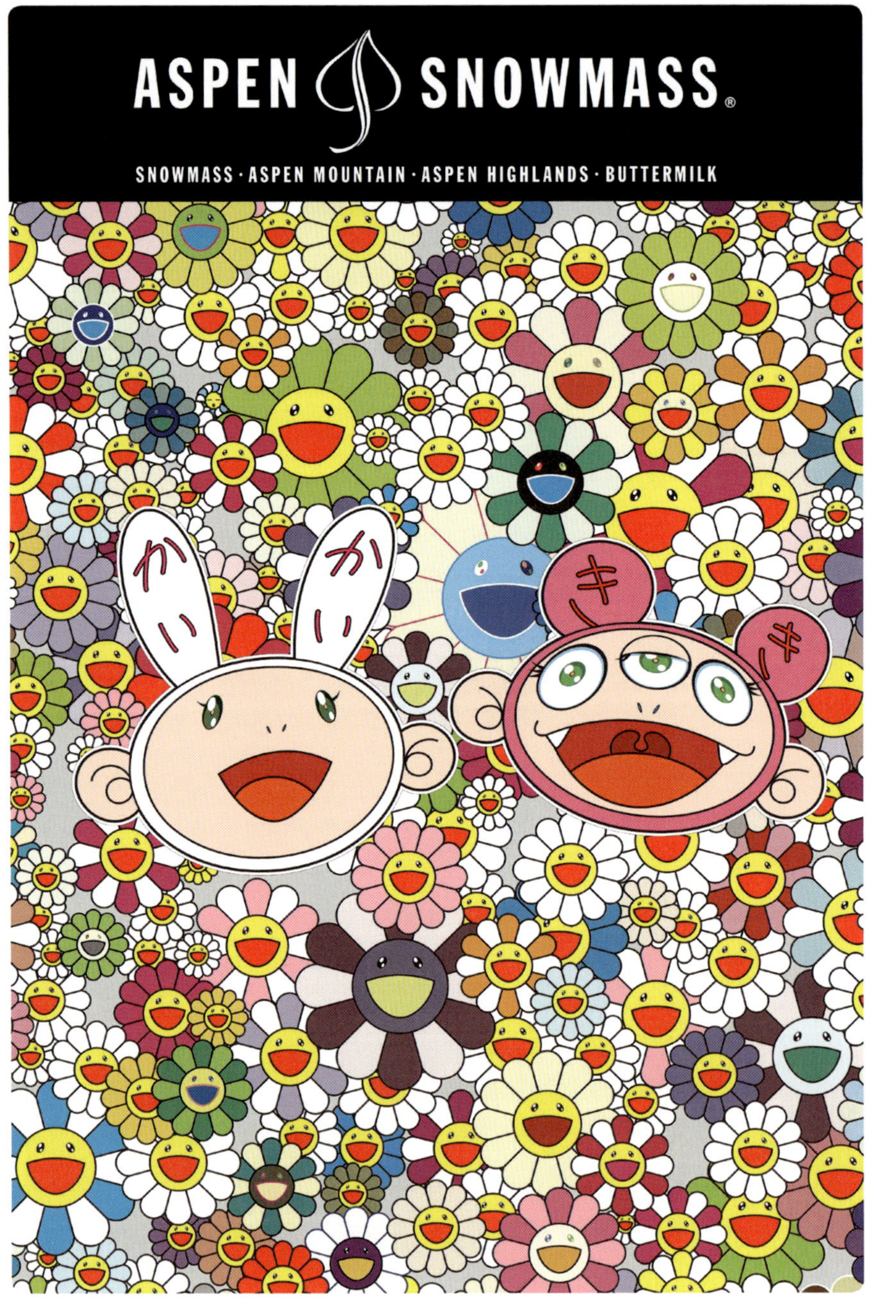

Takashi Murakami
2015–16

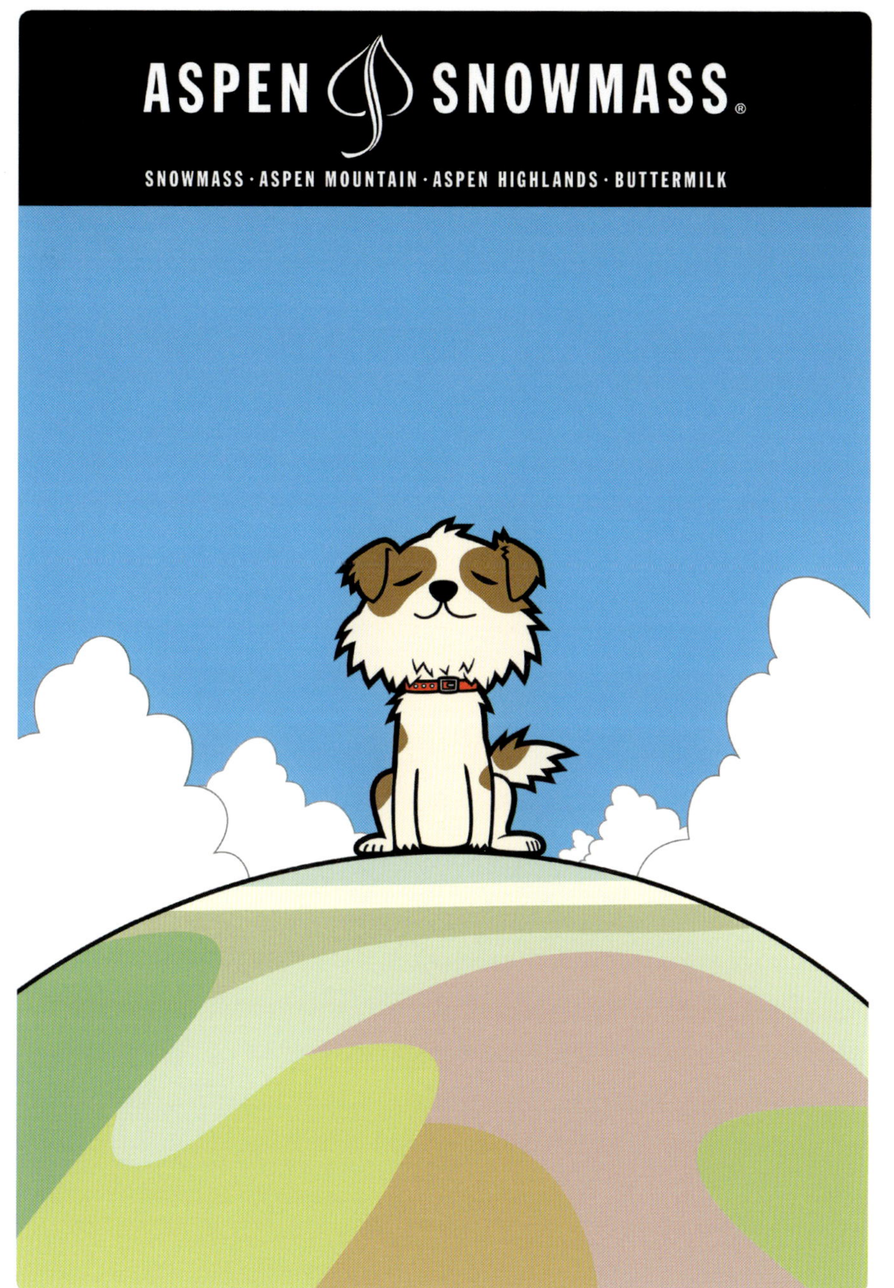

ASPEN SNOWMASS.
SNOWMASS · ASPEN MOUNTAIN · ASPEN HIGHLANDS · BUTTERMILK

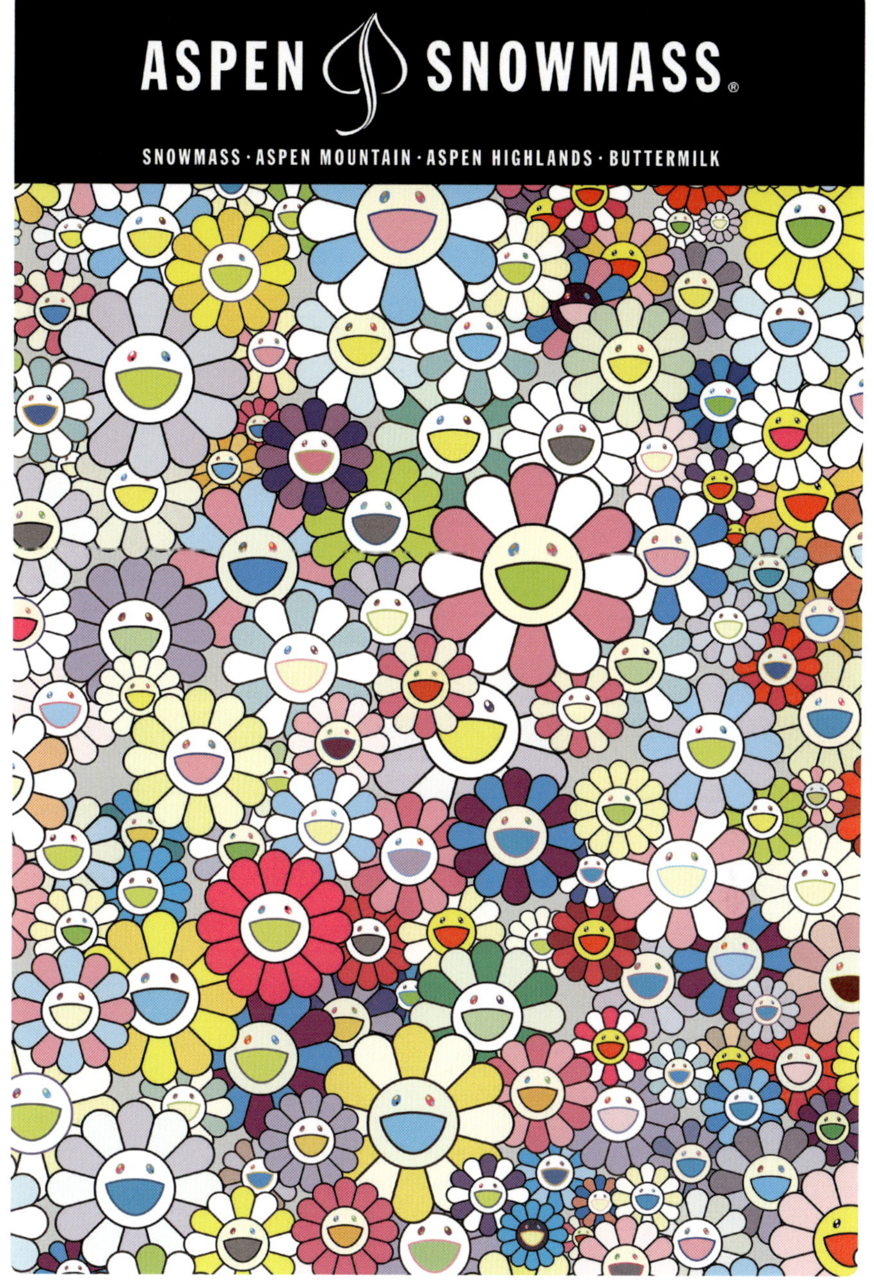

ASPEN SNOWMASS.
SNOWMASS · ASPEN MOUNTAIN · ASPEN HIGHLANDS · BUTTERMILK

Takashi Murakami
2015–16

Shinique Smith

2015–16 Elk Camp

Installation

Heidi Zuckerman
Shinique, you were invited to come and create a site-specific wall drawing in the Elk Camp restaurant. Could you start off by talking about how the title relates to the work and also how your initial concepts relate to the finished product?

Shinique Smith
I was really pleased to receive the invitation to come here and create a mural. I saw images of the space, but I had never been to Elk Camp before, so my first inclination was to make something a little different, something that could be one big object on the wall.

I have a lot of clothing and fabric that I've collected over the last eleven years—Mike called me a hoarder, and he's right, to a degree. Some come from people I know, my grandmother's linen closet, some from my own closet, sometimes Goodwills, and through my travels to do exhibitions, especially across the US. In preparation for this installation, I assembled a bunch of my favorite bits.

When I got here, the space became a part of it, too—the energy and environment were freeing. I also wanted to do something that was expressive and emotional, but would be in harmony with the room—it wouldn't assault you when you came in. There would be a lot of information because I use a lot of stuff, but no extra information because I only use the stuff that I need.

It takes me a while to title pieces, and I only do it after they're made. It's like naming something that was born. I was really picking up on the vibes around here—the slopes, the landscape, and the energy of movement, like waves of energy. That's why it's called *Resonant Tides*—I wanted it to allude to that.

Mike Kaplan
What initially struck me about your work was that sense of movement; that compelled me and drew me in. I was excited to see how this new work really conveyed the movement of this place, through the setting, the act of skiing, or the hiking. There are also a lot of elements of surprise in it—the more you look, the more you see.

SS
I like that you see different things every time you look at it and that there's surprise. Working abstractly, there are a lot of concepts that I'm inspired by, like a romantic idea of pastoral scenes and Utopian farm life. For example, I'll use fabric with a woodland scene and eagles soaring, which is a very American textile. But as I'm creating each piece, I don't have an exact idea of how it will turn out. There isn't a sketch, *per se*—I'm discovering as I'm making. And I'm

hoping that viewers are tuned into or connected to my process so that they're also discovering as I'm discovering.

HZ
You were up here by yourself, morning until night, for a week. It was the off-season so there weren't any people, but you knew that you were creating a work for a public space—and a specific kind of public.

You've created work in the public realm before, like your mural in Philadelphia. Maybe you could talk about that work and if the people you expect to encounter your pieces influence the decisions that you make.

SS
I don't like to presuppose who might see the work or what lens of experience they might have. I approach my public work, paintings, and sculptures all the same way so that they might have a connection to a broad range of people.

When viewers are looking at the finished work—whether they like the piece or not—there is an exchange of energy between me and them, there is some provocation and questioning. I don't really impose any kind of judgment other than that.

MK
I like that it is not fully sketched or planned out—it is almost improvisational—and that you hope the viewer can get a sense of your process. I bring everything back to this, so I apologize, but it reminds me of skiing. You can ski the same run over and over, but no two runs are ever the same. It creates this state—the flow state or being in the zone. When you are creating the work, do you go to another place? Are you intensely focusing or is it more of a rational plotting out?

SS
It is both. It starts out with a line and a pale sense of what color I might want to use. The calligraphy is built from text, but is abstracted, so a word will begin on one side of the wall and end on the other. I use writings, bits of poetry, or song lyrics as a bridge for my hand to make an abstract gesture. It's also a more direct way for me to express myself emotionally. There is a freedom, but it's also necessary to step back and edit.

Growing up, I went to a high school for the arts and had a really traditional arts training where I had to learn how to

draw before I could paint. I had to know how to render life or understand light and perspective before I could even try to abstract something. They would always talk about varying the weight of the line, and maybe I misunderstood, but it stuck with me and extends to a lot of different ways that I work now. My teacher would torture us by making us do one single long gesture. It was about touch, from the lightest to the darkest, from very thin to very thick.

I think about it when I am working on a linear composition and balancing weight with a gesture along with the material that I place on it. It's a back and forth— there is a zone and a flow. I don't think I have ever felt that with anything else except maybe dancing with my eyes closed by myself when no one else is around. But there is manifested proof of the experience when I'm making something. Sometimes I get there and sometimes I don't.

MK
That zone comes from a place of deep technical understanding and then you can elevate your state of mind. Again, this reminds me of skiing, and hearing you talk about your experience, it really

becomes clear why movement is so apparent in your work and that focus on the fundamentals of the line.

SS

Finding the zone while skiing is similar to something I strive for when I'm working, but I don't always get there. I know it's not the same with every ski run, but with your level of skill, do you always reach that moment of flow and synchronicity or are there times where it's just completely off?

MK

Skiing is still very elusive for me. It's one of those things that is partly physiological, but so much of it is your state of mind. When you're feeling it, it just happens— everything from the line you pick to the runs you choose that day. You can get in the flow when you're on the right run, or on a powder day, you're out before everybody and you're in the right line. And on other days, you're just backwards.

What I find so interesting is that you can usually change one little thing, and all of a sudden, it changes, but it's finding that one thing that is tricky. Sometimes it's attitude, sometimes it's rolling your big toe

in at the beginning of the turn, sometimes it's technical, other times, it's about getting something out of your mind.

HZ

It's interesting to delineate between the different gestures in your work as well— between those that are pure abstraction and the ones that are textual references. I like the inclusion of the Jim Hodges lift ticket, for example, which reads, "GIVE MORE THAN YOU TAKE." There are things about the statement that reference Japanese culture—and I know that you're interested in Japanese calligraphy. What was the thought process that went into selecting that particular object and was your interest in that Buddhist notion or was it just about the sentiment?

SS

I was given some lift tickets because I wanted to incorporate things that were relevant from around here. I chose that one because of the color and what it said—I relate to that statement. Buddhism is definitely a philosophy that connects to a lot of different places, but for me, it was the overall sentiment. I

studied Japanese calligraphy when I was an undergraduate and I wrote graffiti as a teenager so that all has an influence on the gestures I make. It's all in there.

Shinique Smith was born in 1971, in Baltimore, Maryland, and lives and works in upstate New York. She studied at the Maryland Institute College of Art, Tufts University and the School of the Museum of Fine Arts, and the Maryland Institute College of Art. Smith has had numerous solo exhibitions at institutions including the Frist Center, Nashville, Tennessee; Center for the Arts at Virginia Tech, Blacksburg (both 2015); Museum of Fine Arts, Boston; Eli and Edythe Broad Art Museum, Michigan State University, East Lansing (both 2014); Los Angeles County Museum of Art (2013); Madison Museum of Contemporary Art, Wisconsin (2011); Museum of Contemporary Art, North Miami (2010); and the Studio Museum in Harlem, New York (2009); amongst many others. Her work has been featured in numerous major group exhibitions, including Women and Abstraction, Cornell Fine Arts Museum, Rollins College, Winter Park, Florida (2015); Between Critique and Absorption: Contemporary Art and Consumer Culture, Haggerty Museum of Art, Milwaukee, Wisconsin (2014); Painting Outside the Lines, Contemporary Art Museum, Houston, Texas; Etched in Collective History, Birmingham Art Museum, Alabama; and Spun: Adventures in Textiles, Denver Art Museum (all 2013). Smith has been the recipient of several prominent awards and fellowships including the Louis Comfort Tiffany Foundation Biennial Award (2013) and a Joan Mitchell Foundation Fellowship (2008).

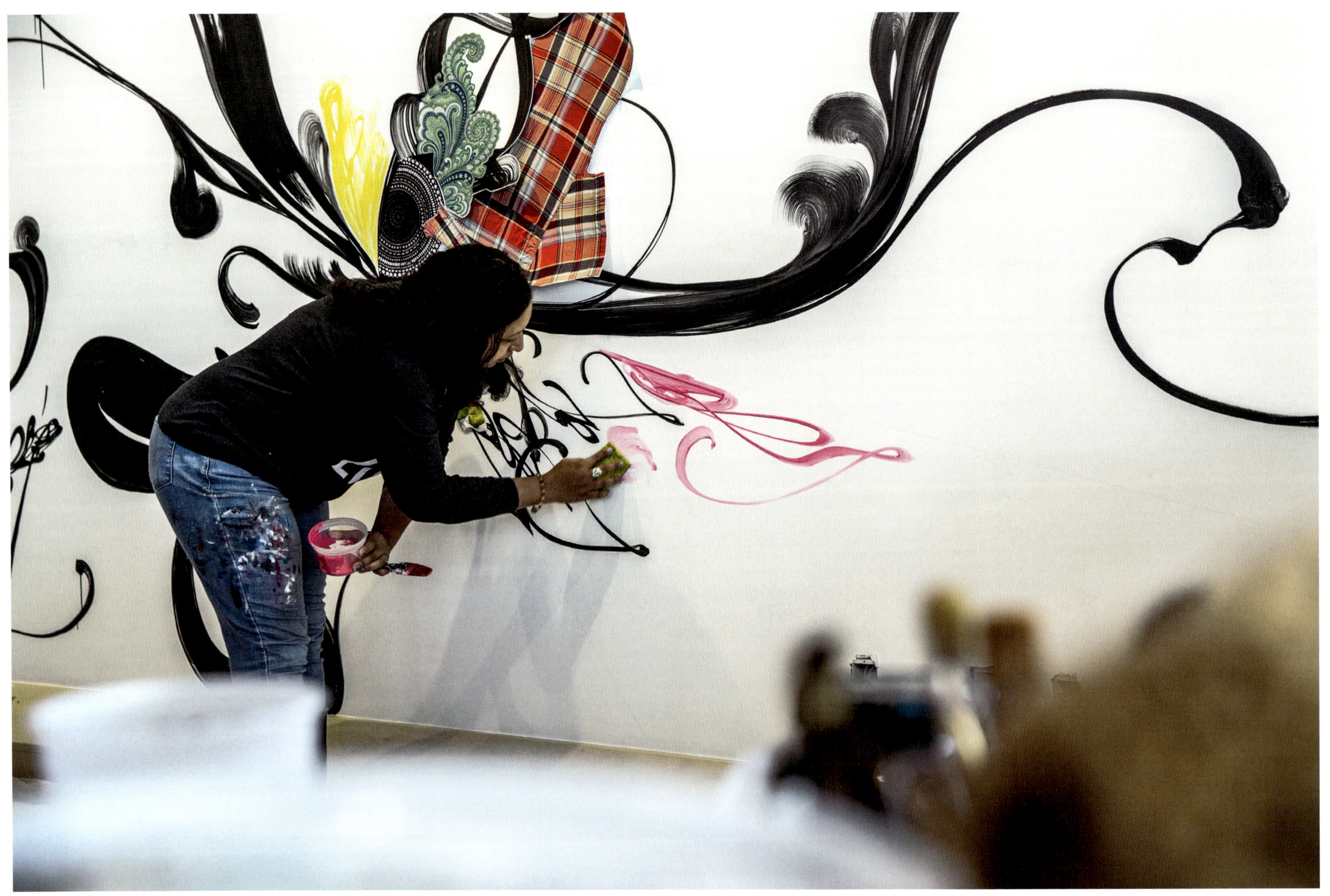

Shinique Smith
2015–16

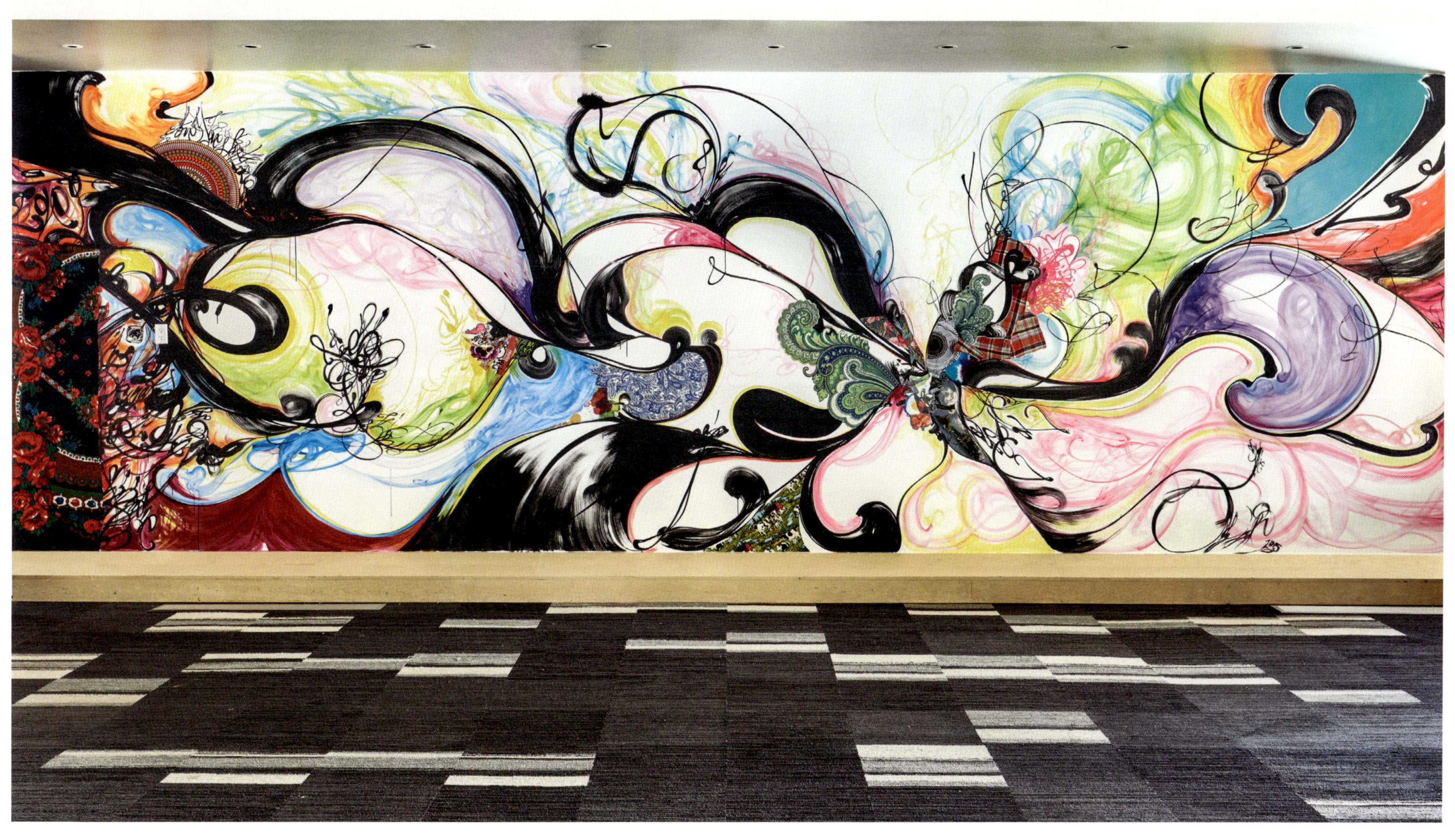

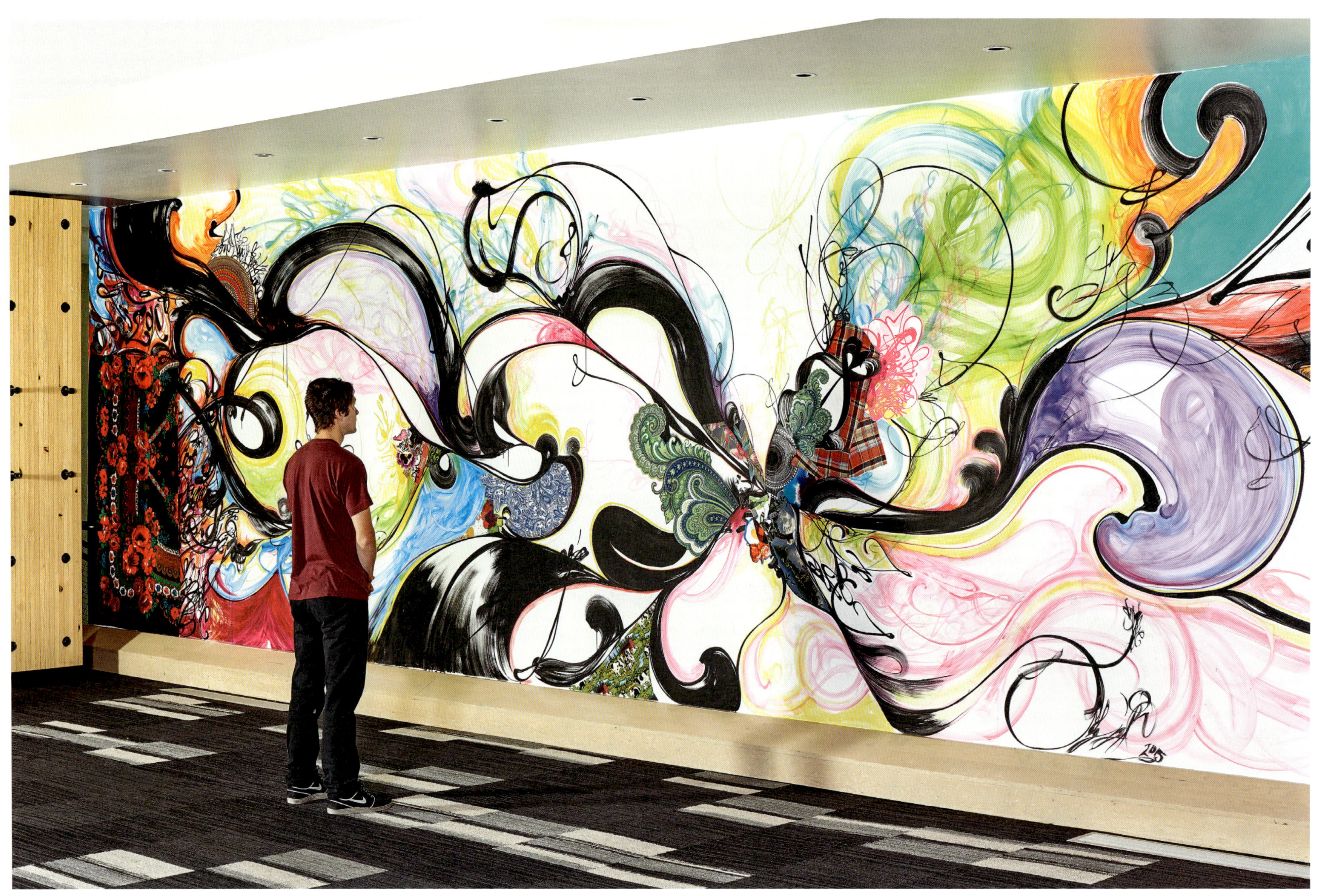

Shinique Smith
2015–16

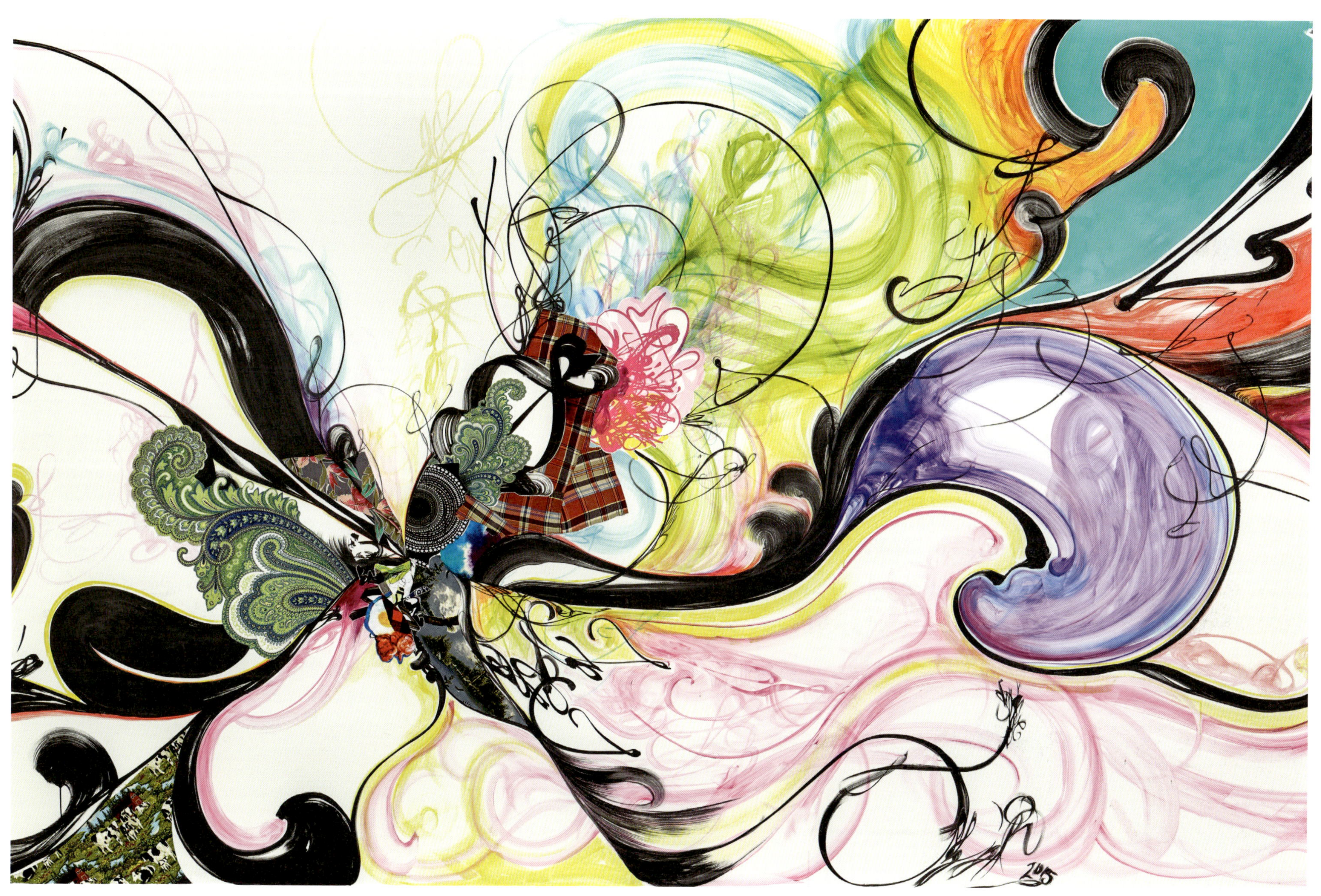

Art in
Unexpected Places II

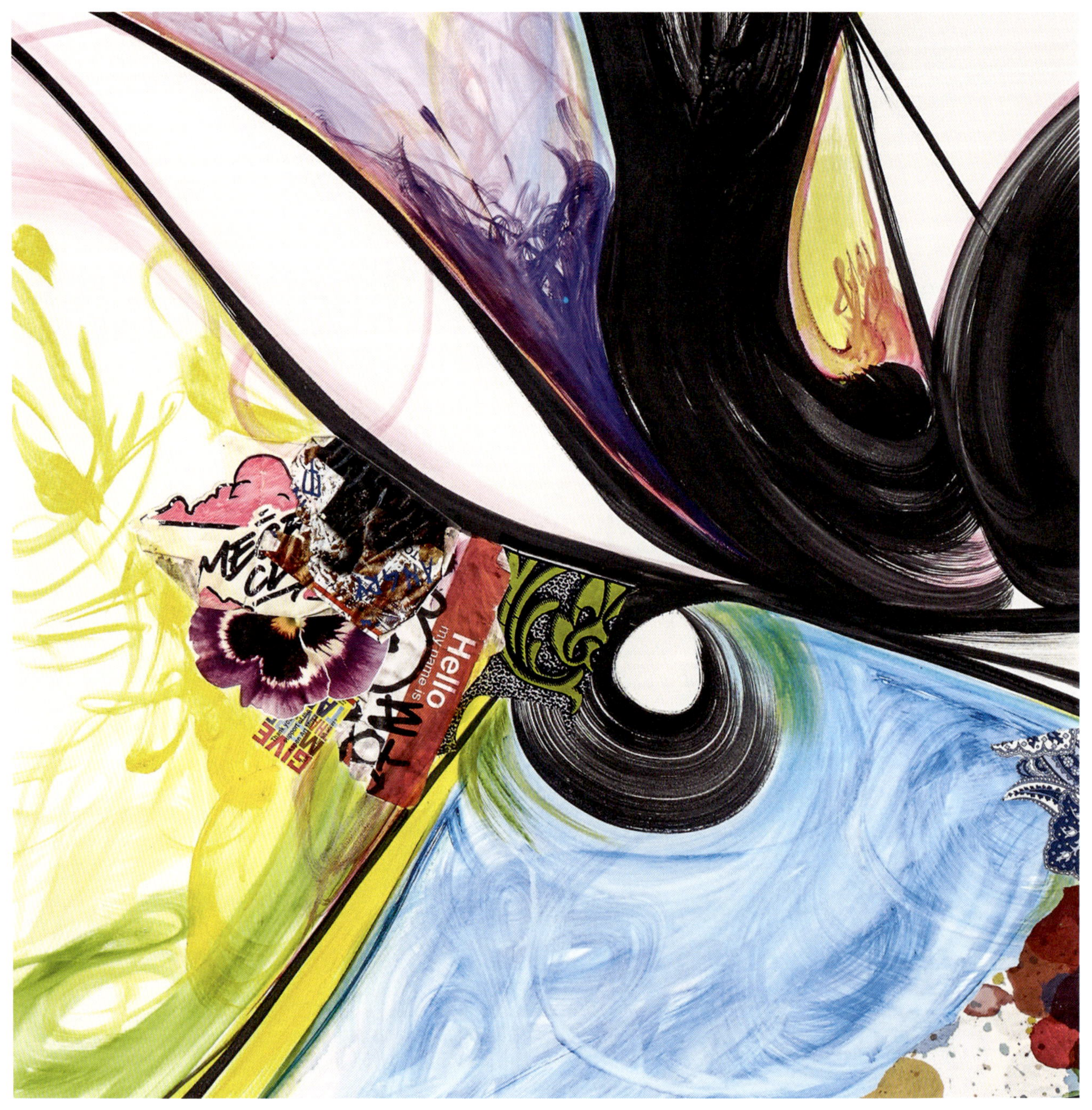

Installation views: Shinique Smith, _Resonant Tides_, 2015. Acrylic, fabric, and collage. Elk Camp restaurant. Courtesy the artist and David Castillo Gallery, Miami. Commissioned by Aspen Art Museum and Aspen Skiing Company

Shinique Smith
2015–16

The Aspen Art Museum and the Aspen Skiing
Company would like to thank the following
people and organizations:

Gretchen Bleiler
Blum & Poe
Mark Bradford
Dan Cameron
Christo and Jeanne-Claude
Anne Collier
Creative Time
David Zwirner Gallery
Agnes Denes
Dia Art Foundation
Elmgreen & Dragset
Teresita Fernández
Gagosian Gallery
Galerie Perrotin
Mark Grotjahn
Cai Guo-Qiang
Hauser & Wirth
Lehmann Maupin
Leslie Tonkonow Artworks + Projects
William Morrow
Dave Muller
Takashi Murakami
National September 11 Memorial & Museum
David Shrigley
Sikkema Jenkins & Co.
Shinique Smith
Stephen Friedman Gallery
James Turrell
Suzanne Vielmetter
Kara Walker
Walker Art Center

Acknowledgments

Dan Cameron

Dan Cameron founded Prospect New Orleans in 2006, and directed the organization and exhibition until 2011, a period when he was also Director of Visual Arts for New Orleans's Contemporary Arts Center. From 1995 to 2006, Cameron was Senior Curator at the New Museum, New York; and Chief Curator at Orange County Museum of Art from 2012 to 2015. As an independent curator, Cameron was Artistic Director for the 8th Istanbul Biennial in 2003 and Co-Curator of the 10th Taipei Biennial in 2006, and he was recently named Curator for the 13th Cuenca International Biennial, Ecuador, in 2016. Cameron is currently a guest curator for the Getty Foundation, where he is preparing an exhibition for 2017 on Latin American kinetic art of the fifties and sixties.

Paula Crown

After a successful career in investment banking at Salomon Brothers in New York, Paula Crown joined family-owned investment firm Henry Crown and Company in Chicago as principal in 1985. Most recently, Crown revived an early avocation as an artist and graduated in 2012 with an MFA in painting and drawing from the School of the Art Institute of Chicago. Recent solo exhibitions include *THE SUBLIME AND THE CENTER: DIMENSIONS OF LANDSCAPE*, Marlborough Gallery, New York (2015); Dallas Contemporary; EXPO CHICAGO; a site-specific installation in Miami's Design District, *TRANSPOSITION: Over Many Miles* (all 2014); and the Aspen Institute (2013). She has participated in group shows in New York, Chicago, and Aspen. In 2009, Crown was appointed to President Obama's Committee on the Arts and the Humanities. She is also a member of the board of trustees of the Museum of Modern Art, New York, and heads the Education Committee. In addition, she serves on the board of Clean Energy Trust, Duke University, Conservation International, and Lurie Children's Hospital, and is a member of the Aspen Institute Committee of the Arts.

Mike Kaplan

Mike Kaplan is President & CEO of Aspen Skiing Company, which includes oversight of the four mountains of Snowmass, Aspen Mountain, Aspen Highlands, and Buttermilk, as well as the hotel division, including the Little Nell and Limelight hotels. Kaplan started with the company in 1993 after earning an MBA at the University of Denver. After six years in management of the Ski & Snowboard Schools of Aspen/Snowmass, he was promoted to VP of ski operations in 1999, Chief Operating Officer in 2005, and to CEO in November of 2006. Kaplan learned the ski business under the tutelage of the Blake Family, Jean Mayer, and the rest of the crew in Taos, New Mexico, where he worked from 1986–1992.

William Morrow

William Morrow is a project-based independent curator and consultant. He was previously Associate Curator of Contemporary Art at the Denver Art Museum (DAM), where he curated noteworthy exhibitions such as *Araya Rasdjarmrearnsook: Recent Video Works* (2013), *Nick Cave: Sojourn* (2013), and *HEARD:DAM* (2013). Prior to the DAM, Morrow was the curator of the private collection of Laura Lee Brown and Steve Wilson and Founding Director of 21c Museum, Louisville, Kentucky. During his tenure with the Brown/Wilson Collection, the collection grew to over three thousand works with pieces by emerging international artists such as Lynette Yiadom-Boakye, Dinh Q. Lê, Zanele Muholi, Patricia Piccinini, Mickalene Thomas, Yinka Shonibare, and Kehinde Wiley. Noteworthy exhibitions at 21c Museum include *Cuba Now* (2011), *Creating Identity: Portraits Today* (2009), *Photo/Synthesis: James Baker Hal*l (2008).

Heidi Zuckerman

Heidi Zuckerman is the AAM's Nancy and Bob Magoon CEO and Director. Zuckerman's curatorial projects include major one-person exhibitions as well as numerous pivotal group shows. Previously, she served as the Phyllis Wattis MATRIX Curator and then the Chair of the Art Curatorial Department at the University of California, Berkeley Art Museum and Pacific Archive (1999–2005). Prior to this, she served as the Assistant Curator of 20th-Century Art at New York's Jewish Museum (1993–1998). Zuckerman's writing has appeared in numerous international exhibition catalogues and publications.

AAM exhibitions are made possible by the Marx Exhibition Fund. General exhibition support is provided by the Toby Devan Lewis Visiting Artist Fund.

Support for this publication is provided by the Toby Devan Lewis Publications Fund.

AAM education programs are made possible by the Questrom Education Fund. Exhibition lectures are presented as part of the Questrom Lecture Series and made possible by the Questrom Education Fund.

Lift ticket projects are commissioned by the Aspen Art Museum and the Aspen Skiing Company.

Create Your Own Lift Ticket is presented in collaboration with the Aspen Skiing Company. Translation is made possible by the Diane and Bruce Halle Foundation for Latin American Art.

Mark Grotjahn was organized by the AAM and funded in part by the AAM National Council with additional support provided by Linda and Bob Gersh and Barbara and Michael Gamson.

Sponsored by **NETJETS**®

Mark Grotjahn's sculpture installation was commissioned by the Aspen Art Museum in collaboration with the Aspen Skiing Company.

Dave Muller's *Aspen Skiing Company Music Survey Results and Generated Topography (The Hills are Alive…)* was commissioned by the Aspen Art Museum in collaboration with the Aspen Skiing Company. General support was provided by The Andy Warhol Foundation for the Visual Arts.

Mark Bradford was organized by the Aspen Art Museum, funded in part by the AAM National Council, with major underwriting support from Susan and Larry Marx and additional support provided by Melva Bucksbaum and Raymond Learsy, and June and Paul Schorr. General exhibition support was provided by The Andy Warhol Foundation for the Visual Arts.

Teresita Fernández's *Golden Panorama (Snowmass Mountain)* was commissioned by the Aspen Art Museum in collaboration with the Aspen Skiing Company, and funded in part by the AAM National Council. Additional support was provided by the Diane and Bruce Halle Foundation for Latin American Art.

Cai Guo-Qiang's *Black Lightning* was generously underwritten by Stefan Edlis and Gael Neeson.

Anne Collier was organized by the Museum of Contemporary Art Chicago.

This exhibition was overseen in Aspen by Heidi Zuckerman, Nancy and Bob Magoon CEO and Director. Additional exhibition support was provided by the AAM National Council.

Shinique Smith's *Resonant Tides* is commissioned by the Aspen Art Museum in collaboration with the Aspen Skiing Company.